top funds 2002

Building Your Mutual Fund Portfolio
for the 21st Century

top funds 2002

Nick Fallon Riley Moynes
Chris Moynes

ASHLAR HOUSE INC.

Riley Moynes, Nick Fallon and Chris Moynes are employees of Assante Capital Management Ltd. They are also shareholders in Assante Corporation Inc., parent company of both Assante Capital Management Ltd. and Assante Asset Management Ltd., which manages the Optima Strategy and Artisan Funds programs referred to in this book. In order to avoid any appearance of conflict of interest, neither family of funds was included as recommended funds or as Top Funds.

Prentice Hall Canada
A Pearson Company
Toronto

Canadian Cataloguing in Publication Data

Top funds (Scarborough, Toronto, Ont.)
Top funds : building your mutual fund portfolio

Annual.
2000–
ISSN 1490-845X
ISBN 0-13-062270-2 (2002 ed.)

1. Mutual funds—Canada. I. Title.

HG5154.5.M68 2000- 332.63'27 C99-901264-9

ISBN 0-13-062270-2

Editorial Director, Trade Division: Andrea Crozier
Acquisitions Editor: Andrea Crozier
Managing Editor: Tracy Bordian
Copy Editor and Proofreader: Jodi Lewchuck
Art Direction: Mary Opper
Cover Design: Michael Stokely
Cover Image Photograph: Lorella Zanetti
Production Manager: Kathrine Pummell
Page Layout: Monica Kompter

1 2 3 4 5 TRANS 05 04 03 02 01

Printed and bound in Canada.

ATTENTION: CORPORATIONS
Books are available at quantity discounts with bulk purchase for educational, business, or sales promotional use. For information, please email or write to: Pearson PTR Canada, Special Sales, PTR Division, 26 Prince Andrew Place, Don Mills, Ontario, M3C 2T8. Email ss.corp@pearsoned.com. Please supply: title of book, ISBN, quantity, how the book will be used, date needed.

Prentice Hall Canada

A Pearson Company

Contents

Introduction

Mutual funds are without doubt the fastest growing and most popular type of investment available to investors today. New funds are appearing on the scene on a daily basis and Canadians can now invest in parts of the world and sectors of the economy that were inaccessible to retail investors a few short years ago.

This rising popularity has spawned a number of good books on the subject of mutual funds. There are several reasons why we feel that you need this book.

The first is that there are well over 4,000 mutual funds available to Canadians. Think about it. 4,000! Imagine the confusion if there were 4,000 different types of cars that you could buy. Our role as investment professionals is to reduce that overwhelming array of choices into a more manageable group of 100 or so recommended funds.

The second is that investors are bombarded with advertising that focuses almost solely on one-, three-, five-, and ten-year performance statistics. Most Canadians make their decisions to purchase mutual funds based on these performance numbers. In our view, this is a risky approach to take. Our performance measurement system goes deeper. We look at consistency, manager style, volatility, management fees, as well as other qualitative information. Our recommendations are truly Top Funds!

We are big believers in the portfolio approach to investment. A mutual fund is not a stand-alone investment; it should be part of a package or portfolio of different types of funds that is crafted to meet your investment goals. That's why each Top Fund has an accompanying complementary Top Fund, as well as a similar Top Fund. This will allow you to create a better performing and less risky portfolio. After all, it's not just the funds you own that is important; it's how you put them all together.

Our research isn't just number crunching. We've talked to many fund managers and company executives about their funds. And, of course, we've factored in our personal experiences with Canadian investors. The mix of both qualitative and quantitative research is what makes *Top Funds 2002* so unique. We hope that this combination will provide our readers with information that is easy to understand and, most importantly, a useful guide to the world of mutual fund investing.

Acknowledgments

Many individuals and organizations have contributed their time and support to this project. We'd like to thank the Investment Funds Institute of Canada for use of their data, as well as Garnet Anderson of Assante Corporation for his past and continuing help in crunching the numbers and providing needed advice.

Sincere thanks also to Andrea Crozier of Pearson PTR Canada, and Loring Ward Investment Counsel.

We'd particularly like to thank Rob Bell, Allan Lauder, and Al Votary of Morningstar Canada. They were asked to provide the Top Fund performance data on short notice, and they didn't let us down.

Lastly, we'd like to thank and acknowledge our wives—Lou, Yvonne and Pam—for their patience and support.

1

Investing in the 21st Century

The Canadian mutual fund industry has been one of the fastest growing industries in Canada over the last 16 years. According to the Investment Funds Institute of Canada, since 1986:

- The number of unitholder accounts has jumped from 1.7 million to over 52 million.
- Assets under management have grown from $22 billion to over $406 billion.
- The number of funds has risen from 155 to well over 4,000.
- The number of fund managers has increased from 58 to over 1,500.

Explaining the Growth

What can account for such extraordinary industry growth? There are several factors that have had a major impact:

Low Interest Rates

Since 1988, the prime rate has fallen from nearly 14% to 5.25%, lowering the yield on traditional investments to painfully unattractive levels. GIC investors have been forced, often against their will, to seek alternatives.

top funds close up

Registered Education Savings Plans

The changes that the Canadian government made to the RESP program in 1998 make these plans very appealing for parents and relatives hoping to save for a young one's education. The Canadian Education Savings Grant program will contribute 20% on the first $2,000 of contributions made to an RESP per beneficiary, for a maximum yearly grant of $400. The maximum lifetime grant per beneficiary is $7,200 and the $2,000 yearly "room" can be carried forward. Any gains or income accumulated over the years are tax sheltered until they are withdrawn. The very low tax rates that students typically have usually means that any taxes payable are insignificant. If the beneficiary doesn't attend an eligible postsecondary institution, then the grants must be repaid, but the accumulated growth in the plan doesn't have to be repaid. Subject to certain restrictions, the growth portion plus all contributions can be rolled into the contributor's RRSP, if there is sufficient room. We have two simple rules. Rule 1: If the government offers you money, take it. Rule 2: Refer to Rule 1. We think these changes are tremendous. See your financial advisor for all the details.

Demographics

The portion of the Canadian population age 45 or over has risen steadily over the last 10 years and will continue to do so. This population shift has coincided with the remarkable growth in mutual fund assets. Typically, once an individual reaches his or her peak earning years at age 45 or older, mortgages and loans are paid off and the focus shifts to saving money for retirement.

The aging of the Canadian population has been well documented and publicized in books such as *Boom, Bust & Echo 2000* by David Foot. This aging segment of the population has another 20 years of earning and savings power and, as a result, the mutual fund industry will likely continue to grow strongly at least over this period of time. The significant impact of baby boomers on the mutual fund industry is discussed in more detail later in this chapter.

Retirement Planning

The Canada Pension Plan (CPP) is running an increasingly large deficit and has reached the point where its payments to retirees have surpassed contributions by workers. Without changes to either benefits or contributions, this trend will continue. Motivated by growing concerns those expected benefits might not be made available, Canadians have begun to save for their own retirement, primarily through the use of RRSPs because of the tax-free growth of assets as long as these stay within the plan.

Since most people see saving for retirement as a long-term proposition, Canadians are increasingly becoming long-term investors. With interest rates so low, stocks have grown in popularity, especially since they have outperformed interest-bearing investments over longer time frames.

Mutual funds offer investors a diversified portfolio of stocks—both domestic and international—along with professional money management; these are benefits most people probably could not afford otherwise.

Pension Shifts

Over the past 10 years, savings have moved increasingly from defined benefit pensions to defined contribution plans. This shift has provided people with the freedom to choose among various investment alternatives. At the same time, companies concerned with potentially large pension liabilities have encouraged this transfer of risk whereby the responsibility is on employees to generate sufficient returns to ensure their future well being. Again, mutual funds have benefited from this shift in savings.

Education

The pressures and changes outlined in the preceding pages have motivated Canadians to learn about investment alternatives. Mutual fund company advertising, newspaper attention to mutual funds—their returns, their management, and factors impacting returns—and books such as *Top Funds* have assisted in providing the information and knowledge that people seem so hungry to obtain.

As well, several banks, faced with erosion of their deposit bases, have become significant players in the field and have helped increase public awareness about mutual funds. In 1986, banks and trust companies held only about 16% of the mutual fund assets in Canada; by May of 1999, they controlled over 31% of industry assets.

These developments have helped the mutual fund industry grow very rapidly over the last 10 years, and are expected to ensure continued strong growth over the next 20 years or so. A CIBC Wood Gundy research paper, "The Canadian Mutual Fund Industry: The Rising Tide," published in January 1997 projected mutual fund asset growth at about $650 billion within 10 years. On June 30, 2000, total assets under management by members of the Investment Funds Institute of Canada were $406 billion.

So, welcome to the era of "managed money"—an era that promises to offer you more investment choices than ever. And that's where we come in. Because it's our job to assist you in selecting the mutual fund or funds that best suit your needs.

Fund Phenomenon

Actual and Projected Growth of the Canadian Mutual Fund Industry

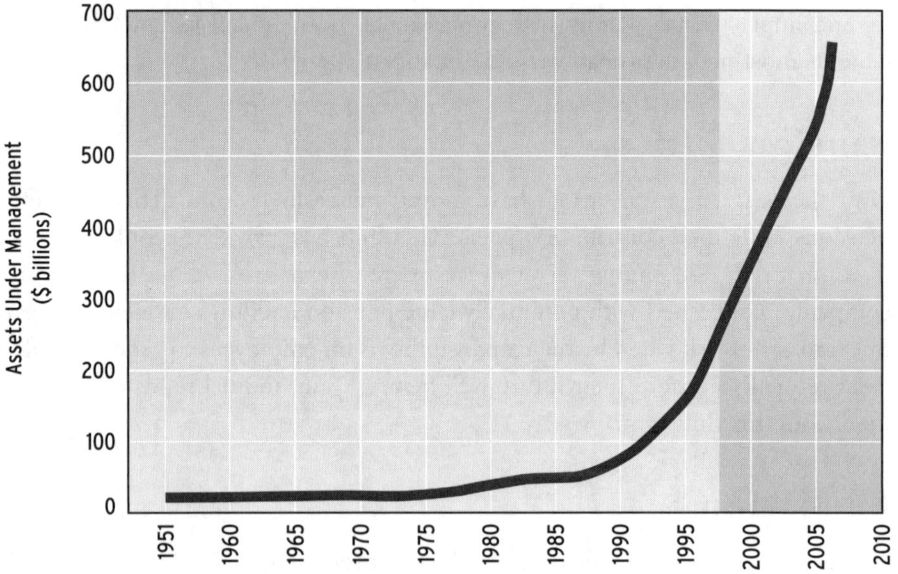

Why Mutual Funds?

As you know, a mutual fund is a "pool" of money into which thousands of people contribute. This pool of money is overseen by professional money managers in accordance with a specific fund's investment objectives. Managers typically concentrate on one or more asset classes such as Treasury bills (T-bills), safe and secure government or corporate bonds, and shares of generally proven Canadian and international corporations. They keep a watchful eye on the economy; on political, demographic, and economic trends; and on international events in order to determine where and how the pool of money can be invested to produce the most solid, long-term growth. The benefits of investing in mutual funds continue to hold true today and can be summarized as follows:

Professional Money Management

Most people haven't got the time to oversee their financial affairs effectively. Moreover, they're not trained to be expert money managers. But with an investment in mutual funds, they benefit from the experience and skills of some of the world's best money experts.

One of the most successful mutual funds ever, the Templeton Growth Fund managed by Sir John Templeton and his team, provides a good example. If you had invested $10,000 in this fund when it began in 1954, you would have seen your investment grow to be worth $5.5 million by April 30, 2000. That's an average annual compounded growth rate of over 15%!

Diversification

Most people aren't wealthy enough to be able to diversify properly on their own by buying stocks of various companies in a number of countries. Due to the size of the mutual fund "pool," often totalling millions or billions of dollars, investors can purchase a share of a vast array of securities, bonds, and other investments. As a fund investor, this diversification allows you to achieve the security that comes from "not putting all your eggs in one basket."

"Hands Off" Investment

As mentioned earlier, most people don't have the time, the inclination, or the expertise to do the research necessary to make wise investment decisions. By investing in a mutual fund, all the big decisions are looked after by professional money experts for whom managing money is a full-time job.

research news

Not So "Great Expectations"

Two different studies have come up with remarkably similar forecasts for U.S. equity markets. Thomas Phillips created an analytical model that successfully explains the long-term return of U.S. equities, as well as the phenomenal returns investors experienced in the '80s. Unfortunately, the same model is predicting future returns of only 6.5% from the S&P 500. In a similar vein, Gary Brinson, one of the pioneers in asset allocation research, looked at real economic growth, inflation expectations, and dividend yields to come up with a 7% return forecast. Investors with visions of 20% annual returns dancing in their heads would have dismissed these conclusions last year as too pessimistic. This year we suspect that many can only dream of a 6.5% to 7% return on their U.S. equity portfolios.

Thomas K. Phillips, "Why Do Valuation Ratios Forecast Long-Run Equity Returns?" *The Journal of Portfolio Management* (Spring 1999).

"Investment Management in the 21st Century," (presentation at the Association for Investment Management and Research Annual Conference, May 1998).

> research
> **news**
>
> **Emerging Markets Update**
>
> Investors have always had a love/hate relationship with emerging markets. The stomach-churning volatility is painful, but the spectacular returns do help ease the pain. At least that was the theory; a recent study questions the high returns part of the equation. The authors contend that, contrary to popular belief, emerging markets don't offer statistically higher returns than developed markets. In fact, emerging markets have underperformed both the S&P 500 and Nasdaq since 1975.
>
> Why bother? Well, investors shouldn't ignore the diversification attributes of emerging markets. The above research noted that adding the higher-risk emerging market assets to a 100% U.S. equity portfolio actually created a less risky portfolio. Conclusion? Buy emerging markets mutual funds for risk reduction purposes only, and you won't be disappointed.
>
> Christopher B. Barry, John W. Peavy III, and Mauricio Rodriquez, "Performance Characteristics of Emerging Capital Markets," *Financial Analysts' Journal* 54, no. 1 (January/February 1998).

Many Choices

Regardless of your circumstances, there are mutual funds that can meet your needs. Some people want income now; others, who will require income later on, opt for growth instead. Some investors are aggressive while others are much more conservative. Some people select equity funds, others prefer real estate funds, and others still like mortgage funds—or a mixture of a few types. Some investors wish to hold specialty funds like gold; others like holdings in specific foreign regions like Japan or Europe. With so many funds available to choose from, there is truly a fund to meet just about every need.

Objectivity

When it is your own money, there can be worry and anxiety associated with the endless decisions needed to manage a diversified portfolio. Is this stock overpriced and should I sell it? Should I build up cash reserves? The decisions are seemingly endless and, for many, emotionally draining. By having professionals take over, you can have an objective expert make these decisions and take the emotional burden off your shoulders.

How Will Mutual Fund Investors Fare in the 2000s?

We forecast that the first decade of the 2000s will be very successful for the entire mutual fund industry, for specific mutual fund and other wealth management companies, and for individual mutual fund investors. Here's why.

There are two major factors in this rosy forecast: the predictability of people and the phenomenon knows as the "baby boomers." The combination of these factors has given rise to the term *boomer economics* or *boomernomics*.

Let's start with the baby boomers. The baby boom occurred in post–World War II Canada, the U.S., Australia and, later, in Europe and Japan. But it was most pronounced in North America. From about 1945 to about 1965, North American women gave birth to more babies per person on average than at any other time in history before or since. At the peak, around 1960, the average Canadian family had 4 children and the average American family had 3.7 children. In Canada, that worked out to over 400,000 new births every year.

What happened? Most importantly, the war came to an end. It was a time of peace, prosperity, and happiness. Young soldiers returned home from overseas by the thousands to a country of safety, filled with wonderful potential. They wanted to start families. In addition, Canada adopted a liberal immigration policy after the war, allowing larger numbers of people into the country. Since most of them were in their mid-20s, they added to the boom both as immigrants and as new parents. By the time the baby boom period was over in the mid-'60s, Canada's population had exploded by nearly 10 million people.

It was a similar story in the U.S. where the population grew by a staggering 76 million. Combined with the figures in Canada, we have about 85 million people in North America going through the same phases of their lives, doing the same things at generally the same time (that's where the predictability comes in, and we'll say more about it later). The combination of post-war euphoria and a liberal immigration policy created a demographic cohort or generation over four times the size of the previous generation, so everything the boomers do in a predictable manner has a far greater impact on the economy than the actions of their predecessors (see the birth index on page 8). Today, the boomers represent over one-third of the overall population of North America, and everything they do has a huge impact on the economy and will continue to do so in the future.

So what are the boomers presently doing that's so predictable? Before we dive into that question, let's revisit what they've done in the past and what impact those actions have had on society and the economy.

In the '50s, '60s, and '70s, boomer babies entered a school system woefully ill equipped to deal with them. A school building blitz was necessary to house them, advertisements for the teaching positions needed to instruct them filled page after page in the *Globe and Mail*, and school systems across the country entered an unprecedented period of expansion.

Immigration-Adjusted Birth Index

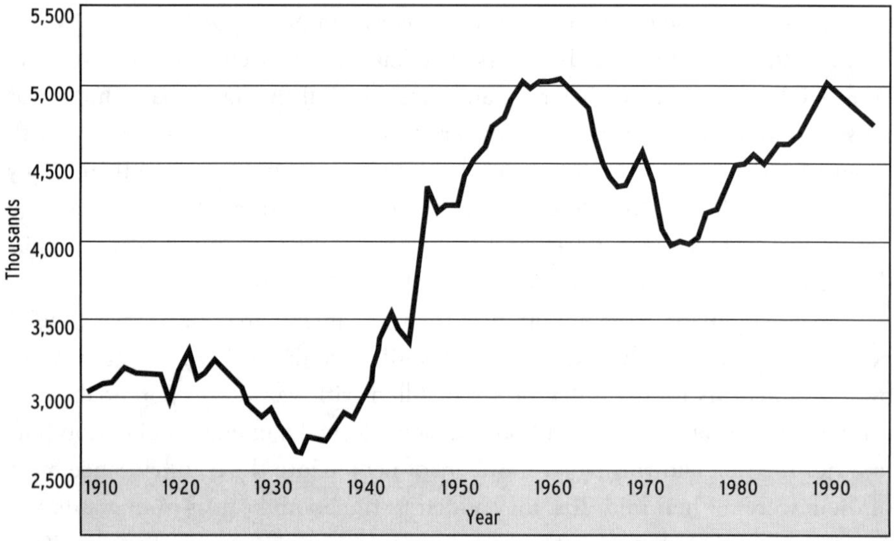

SOURCE: Reprinted with the permission of Simon & Schuster from **The Roaring 2000s** by Harry Dent. Copyright © 1998 by Harry Dent.

Much of the political upheaval of the '60s and '70s can be attributed to the boomers struggling to shape their identity and to find purpose and meaning in their lives. In the '70s and '80s, 85 million boomers wanted to own homes in which to raise their families. Debt levels skyrocketed as hundreds of millions of dollars were borrowed in the form of mortgages and car loans; the effect on interest rates was dramatic, as huge demand sought out a limited supply. Inflation reached 14% in the '80s, mortgage rates were as high as 19% and 20%, and, in 1981, Canada Savings Bonds paid 19%! The return to "family values" that we heard so much about in the '80s and '90s wasn't a new concept—it was simply a reflection of a huge number of people focusing on raising families and trying to do it right.

In retrospect, had we viewed these developments through the boomer "filter," they might have made more sense to us than they did at the time.

So What of the Future?

Going forward, how can we use our knowledge of the predictability of human generations, and this one in particular, to forecast general economic trends over the next decade?

Average Annual Family Spending by Age

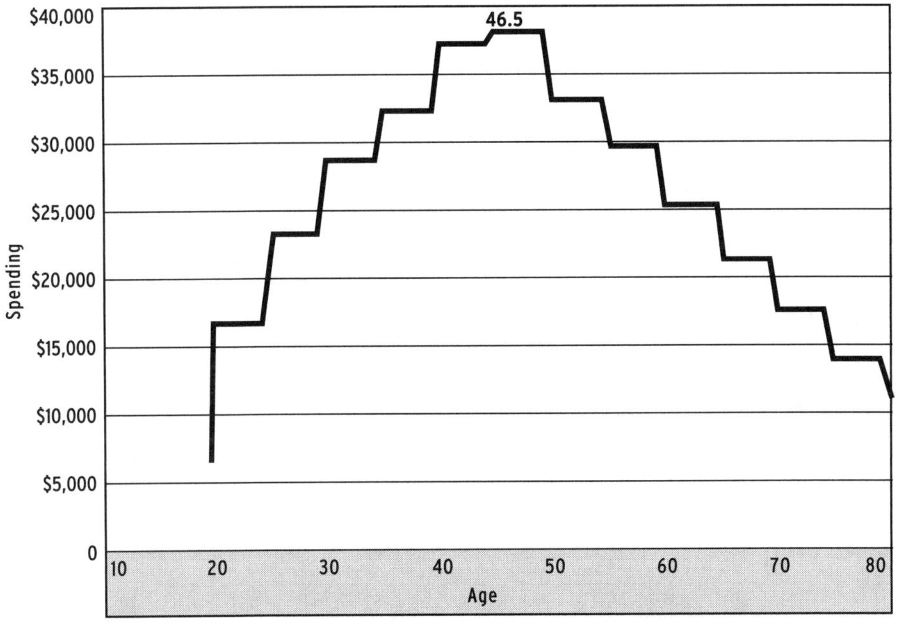

SOURCE: Reprinted with the permission of Simon & Schuster from **The Roaring 2000s** by Harry Dent. Copyright © 1998 by Harry Dent.

Let's look first at spending and saving. In Harry Dent's books *The Great Boom Ahead* (1993), *The Roaring 2000s* (1998), and *The Roaring 2000s Investor* (1999), he demonstrates the predictable pattern of spending and saving that individuals go through. As the spending chart above demonstrates, we begin a pattern of increased spending at about age 19 (as we move out of our parents' house to go to school or get a job and need to finance our first apartment, buy our own food, etc.). That spending level continues to rise until our spending peaks between the age of 45 and 50 and then begins to decline. Dent's research shows that peak spending takes place at an average age of 46.5 years. At the same time, our savings patterns are clear. We start to get serious about saving at about age 35, go through a drop between age 45 and 50 while funding our children's post-secondary education costs, and then focus on saving for retirement from about age 45 to 65. (See the family savings chart on page 10.)

In general, it's fair to say that our peak earning years are from age 45 to about age 60. Not coincidentally, our peak spending and saving years are also those between age 45 and about age 60.

Average Family Savings
5-Year Age Groups

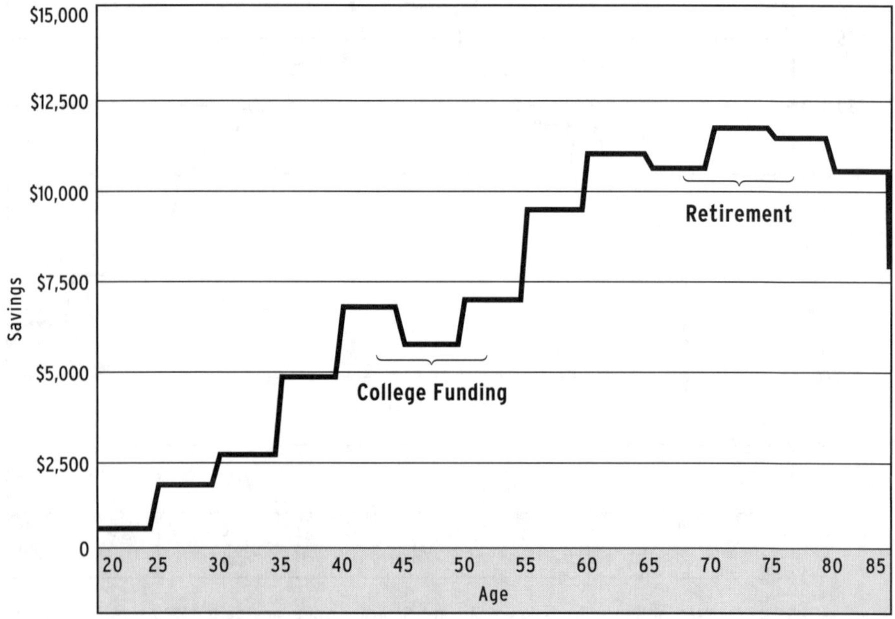

SOURCE: Reprinted with the permission of Simon & Schuster from **The Roaring 2000s** by Harry Dent. Copyright © 1998 by Harry Dent.

Dent's research has demonstrated a remarkably close relationship between spending patterns and stock market growth over the years. If we examine the spending chart on page 11, we'll note that it integrates several key ideas. First, it represents the birth pattern chart displayed earlier in this chapter, but it "pushes" the chart forward 46.5 years in an attempt to forecast when peak spending by the boomers will take place. You can see that the year of peak spending is forecast to be around 2008 (peak births in 1961 plus 46.5 years = 2007–2008). Notice too that increased boomer spending started in about 1981 (1961 plus about 19 to 20 years), that it continues to be strong, and that it will be strong for much of the first decade of the 2000s.

Second, the chart shows the quite close relationship between boomer spending and stock market performance as represented by the Dow Jones Industrial Average (DJIA). Note that the Dow has been in a growth mode (with bumps and grinds and corrections along the way) since 1982, largely the result

The Spending Wave

Births Lagged for Peak in Family Spending

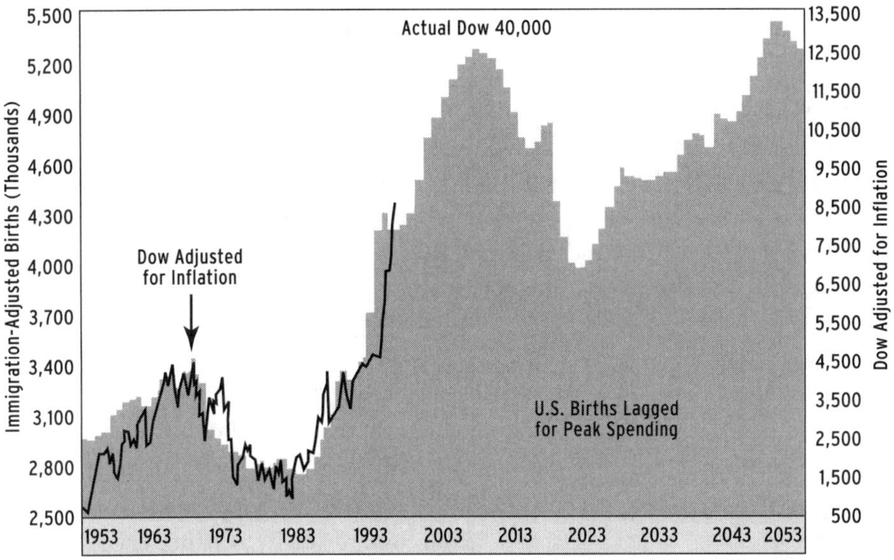

SOURCE: Reprinted with the permission of Simon & Schuster from **The Roaring 2000s** by Harry Dent. Copyright © 1998 by Harry Dent.

of boomer spending, and is projected to be in a growth mode for much of the decade.

Third, Dent forecasts the Dow at about 40,000 near the end of the decade! This probably sounds ridiculous as we read today that the Dow is around 10,000 at the time of writing. But the Dow has grown by about 14% per year since 1982 and if it continues to do so, it will double twice over the next decade. (The Rule of 72 tells us that at 14%, the value will double in five years, taking the Dow to about 20,000, and double again in the next five years, taking it to about 40,000 by the end of the decade). It's not impossible that similar growth could take place in the Canadian market as represented by the TSE 300 Index.

If much of the underpinning of Dent's forecasts is based on consumer spending at unprecedented levels, the other side of the equation—consumer savings—appears to reinforce this sunny view. Over the next decade, boomers will—according to savings patterns linked to age—save unprecedented amounts of money for their retirement. With government surpluses the norm, low inflation anticipated, and interest rates low, it's reasonable to assume that much of the money being invested for retirement will find its way into equities rather than into the more traditional Canadian investments (largely interest-bearing investments such as Canada Savings Bonds, T-bills, and savings accounts).

In fact, a research study published by the Toronto Stock Exchange in May of 2000 showed that 49% of Canadian adults own stocks, either directly or through mutual funds. That's up from 37% in a similar survey in 1996, and up from 13% in a 1983 survey. Significantly, interest rates have fallen from their highs in the early 1980s and investors have reduced their investments in fixed income vehicles simultaneously.

Strong Economic Sectors

Dent and other leaders in the field, including David Foot (author of *Boom, Bust & Echo 2000*) and Bill Sterling (author of *Boomernomics* with Stephen Waite, 1998) believe that certain areas of the economy are likely to experience "super-growth."

> surfing
> **the web**
>
> From funds to stocks, personal finance to insurance, this site has a lot to offer. It's the new address for the old Fund Counsel site. It contains breaking investment news and forums where investors can chat directly with other investors about what's going on. As most sites do, it has a section dedicated to market updates and portfolio tracking. There are some great articles and insights in the impressive mutual fund section.
>
> **www.investment.com**

Technology is the first field singled out by these experts as being poised for exceptional growth. Included under the technology heading are several components, including Internet access and content, e-commerce, hardware and software solutions, digital video discs (DVDs), high definition television (HDTV), and satellite systems. The prediction of a boom in this field has not only come to fruition, but the technology sector has already experienced a market correction. Many investors were caught off guard when tech stocks took a dive in late 2000 and early 2001, but they can rest assured that the market will cycle and technology will find itself in favour once again. Despite the impression you've probably received from recent media hype, companies that lead in the areas outlined above are likely to be strong long-term investments.

A second market sector expected to enjoy strong growth over the decade is *communications*. Under this heading we include the provision of telecommunications services and equipment, high-speed Internet access, cellular and wireless services, and cable telephone services. In addition, as we see a global communications boom, the demand for increased bandwidth will be strong, and providers are likely to do well.

A third anticipated growth area is *health care*. As North Americans age and live longer, there will be growing demand for pharmaceuticals and lifestyle drugs, innovative medical devices, and technology, biotechnology, and health care services.

A fourth growth area will likely be *financial services*. As boomers enter their peak earning and saving years, the demand for professional advice and counsel will likely increase. This trend will represent good news for brokerage firms, investment counsel firms, banks, insurance companies, and mutual fund companies. Look for global consolidation of products and distribution as smaller companies are removed from the playing field by huge international juggernauts such as the British holding company AMVESCAP. They own AIM Mutual Funds, which recently purchased Trimark Mutual Funds. Reasonably large by Canadian standards with about CDN$24 billion in assets, Trimark pales in size with AMVESCAP, which manages U.S.$565 billion worldwide.

Finally, don't overlook the *consumer products* sector. With consumer spending forecast to increase through much of the decade, look for strength from retailers with global brand names (such as Coca-Cola) and specialty retailers who carve out small lucrative niches. Expect growth in the recreation and entertainment areas as well as leisure and travel—aging boomers have larger amounts available for discretionary spending.

Many mutual fund investors will do well during the first decade of the 2000s, but some may not. Given the prospects for unprecedented growth, why won't everyone do well? We think there may be several reasons.

First, although the numbers appear to be declining, many people will continue to invest their money primarily in low-return, interest-bearing instruments such as GICs, T-bills, or Canada Savings Bonds.

Second, even if people invest in equities, they may not be aware of, and therefore miss, the anticipated supergrowth in the areas identified above.

Third, even if we invest with reasonable strength in equities and in the "right" sectors, we may fall prey to our emotions from time to time and make wrong decisions. Why? Because we are driven by *fear* during times when our investments are underperforming our expectations and *greed* when we see others in "hot" funds while ours are "cold." We sell low, buy high, and then during a correction for our recently purchased funds, we panic and again sell low. Trusted financial advisors truly earn their money when they manage client emotions through difficult markets, helping investors to avoid making the wrong decisions (see the section entitled "Common Investor Mistakes" later in the chapter for a more in-depth discussion of this topic).

As always, those investors likely to do best will be diversified by asset category (stocks, bonds, cash, real estate, etc.), geography, management style, and security selection. We anticipate growth in the key areas outlined above, and recommend a reasonable weighting in these areas. We also repeat that, ultimately, what counts is adhering to a long-term plan: recognize that you should focus not on *timing* the market (it's impossible to do consistently anyway) but *time in* the market! The next decade will be a wonderful time for investors, but one has to be there consistently to take full advantage of the incredible opportunities that will present themselves.

2001 Midyear Review

While looking at the year ahead in January of 2001, consensus held that while the year on the whole would be positive, the first six months would be ugly. And so they have been, using nearly any benchmark you may choose. As you can see from the graph ("2001 World Market Returns") on page 15, overall market returns have been, on average, –9.5% over the last six months.

In fact, the last year in its entirety has been a struggle; overall market returns have been, on average, –21% over the 12 months ending June 30, 2001 (see "12-Month Equity Market Returns," page 15).

When assessing the climate in world markets, however, it is always important to put things in perspective by comparing overall results with the results achieved by the average Canadian investor. An easy way to do this is to look at the Assante All-Fund Index, a benchmark that reflects the returns of all the mutual funds in Canada (see "GICs or Mutual Funds?" page 16).

You'll notice that over the midterm, average mutual fund investor returns as measured by the All-Fund Index have been flat. Over the last five years, however, average mutual fund investor returns, again measured by the All-Fund Index, are +5.4% per year. The difference in the short-term results compared with the long-term results is an important detail to keep in mind.

2001 World Market Returns

In $U.S., through to June 30, 2001

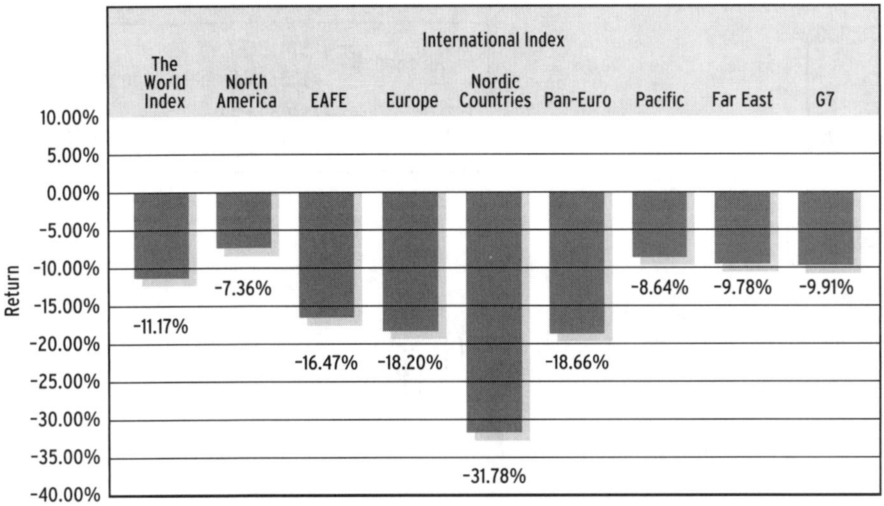

SOURCE: Assante Advisory Services
DATA SOURCE: MSCI

12-Month Equity Market Returns

June 30, 2000 to June 30, 2001

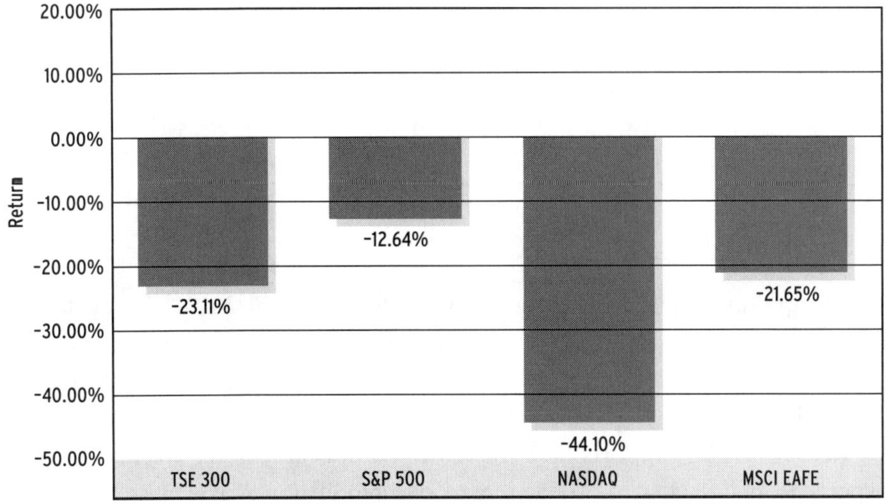

SOURCE: Assante Advisory Services

GICs or Mutual Funds?

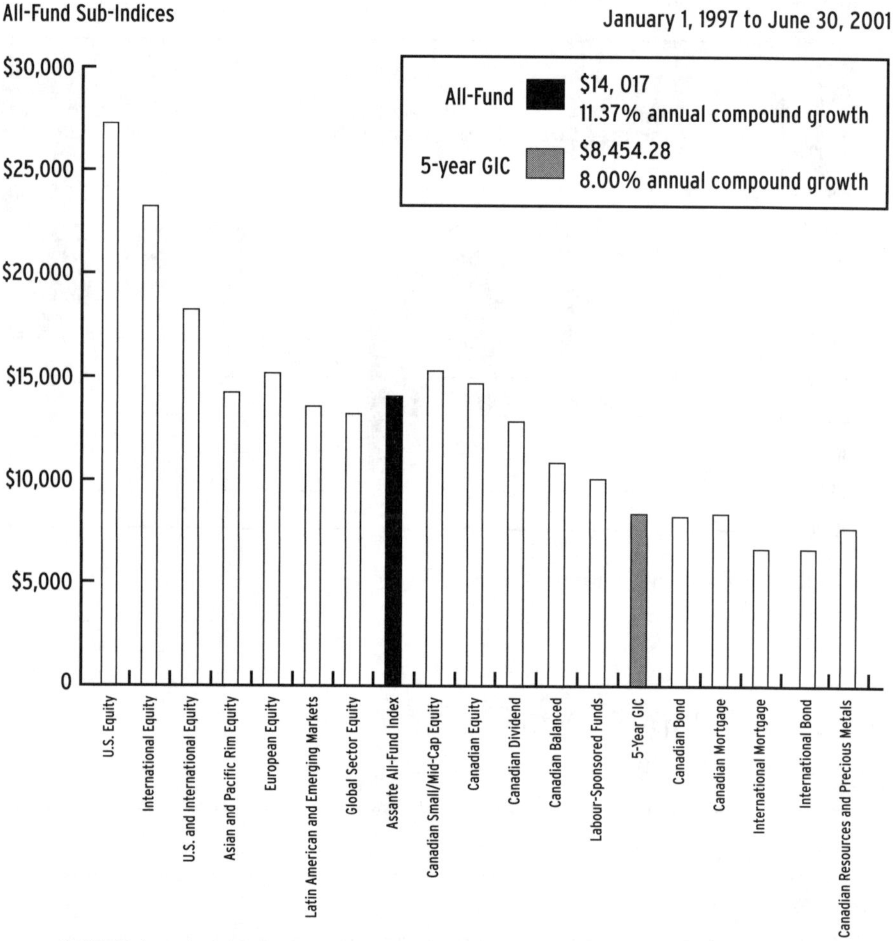

SOURCE: Assante Advisory Services

What's Ahead

The general assumption in the financial world is that the Bank of Canada and the U.S. Federal Reserve will lower interest rates and these rate reductions will trickle through the system, making a positive impact for the latter part of this year and into 2002.

Recent earnings reports have tended to be upbeat as well, prompting most experts to believe that the recent market turmoil was as rough as things are going to get and the second half of the year will likely bring much better stock market results. We agree and remain firm in our belief that the economy and stock market work cyclically, and that we have been at a low in the cycle for the three years since July 1998 when many portfolios suffered their biggest ever quarterly declines (ranging from 5% to 10%). As we have seen 5 or 6 times in our 18-plus years of experience, things will indeed turn around eventually, allowing us to enjoy once again those periods when increases of 8%, 9%, and even 10% in one quarter are not uncommon, as was the case in 1996 and 1997.

Of course, a well-balanced portfolio will continue to protect investors through the kind of market downturns we have seen over the past six months to a year, and allow above-average growth through the kind of upturns we have seen over the longer term of five years and more. To reiterate the point we made earlier, what matters most is the time you spend in the market: carefully chosen, strategic investments held over the long term will weather all market conditions.

The Investment Policy Statement

Until recently, there has been a huge gap in the way the average investor and the more sophisticated investor (individuals or pension funds) determine the overall structure of their portfolio. Our experience tells us that the average investor has generally taken an eclectic, ad hoc approach to portfolio development with an emphasis on including last month's or last year's winners. The result is that there is no overall master plan against which to determine whether changes to the portfolio are appropriate. In the absence of such a plan, decisions to make changes are often driven by the twin emotions of fear and greed, fired by heavy reliance on daily price as a guide.

Now, however, we are beginning to see increased usage of a variety of portfolio management services, several of which use the Investment Policy Statement as an integral part of the investment and reporting process. This approach is consistent with the one employed by individual million-dollar accounts and successful pension funds. We see it as a positive development, and one that is likely to become increasingly used in the years ahead.

What's the Purpose of an Investment Policy Statement (IPS)?

In essence, an IPS is a business plan detailing one's personal financial affairs. It's not intended to be written in stone, but rather to change as circumstances change. It provides a direction and a framework within which investment decisions can be made more rationally than might otherwise be the case. Without such a plan, your investment strategy might well be at odds with your requirements, and this can lead to short-term tactics that introduce greater risk into the portfolio.

Components of the IPS

There are typically several sections to the IPS document, including the following:

- Investment profile
- Portfolio constraints
- Recommended portfolio asset allocation
- Expected return and risk factors

Investment Profile

The investment profile is constructed from a number of important building blocks, including one's investment goals and the related time frame in which these goals must be achieved. Another important component of the profile is the level of investment risk appropriate to an individual's situation.

Obviously a younger person with an extended time horizon and a goal of capital accumulation presents a different profile than someone who may be older and anxious to receive lifetime income from their investments. In the former situation, with no immediate cash or income needs, there would be less concern about riding through a market decline than in the latter situation, where the need to draw

surfing
the web

This is one of the 700 about.com Web networks, and the site is, well, about investing in Canada. With great information—from banking to venture capital and everything in between—bookstores and video shops round out this comprehensive site. It also includes tips on how to get the most out of your RRSP bucks and how to receive a monthly newsletter.

www.investingcanada.about.com

income even when the portfolio posts negative returns can seriously deplete assets.

Other priorities may include preserving capital, protection from inflation, maximizing a legacy, saving for a large purchase, or as is often the case, a blend of these requirements. These priorities must all be identified before a proposal can realistically be made to allocate investment dollars. This information is often achieved at least in part through the use of a questionnaire intended to cast light on these matters. We think the profiles developed by Garmaise Investment Technologies and used in Mackenzie's STAR and Private Trust programs are among the best available.

Portfolio Constraints

Portfolio optimization—from both an investment and a tax perspective—is more easily achieved if the IPS takes into account all of an investor's assets, even though they may not be included in the money to be invested immediately. When outside assets are not included, the big picture can't be seen. This may lead to an overall strategy that could be too conservative or too aggressive, thus placing a constraint on portfolio performance.

Most people give relatively little thought to the amount of foreign content in their portfolio. Our experience is that Canadians generally err on the side of too little foreign exposure. Canada constitutes only about 3% of world markets and yet we often see overwhelming Canadian content in a portfolio. On the other hand, without a target international weighting, you can go too far the other way and take on more risk than you are aware of or may be comfortable with. For these reasons, we think it's a good idea to set a target for foreign content holdings in the 50% range. An IPS quantifies the level, so you can constantly monitor it and adjust it if necessary.

Recommended Portfolio Asset Allocation

Using all of the information outlined earlier, we can now come to a thoughtful and research-based recommendation about the right asset mix of stocks, bonds, cash, and real estate in Canada, the U.S., and around the world.

Most IPSs will target a percentage of the portfolio to be allocated to each of the above types of stock and locations. Subsequent reporting discloses quarterly weightings so that a client can compare the actual weightings with the target weightings, and most asset management services actually rebalance the weightings automatically should they stray from the targets by a significant amount.

Expected Return and Risk Factors

Some, though not all, IPSs go so far as to project an expected return above and beyond that achieved by T-bills, based on historical data. For example, one IPS states that the expected return for a moderately invested portfolio would be in the range of 3.5% to 4.0% above T-bills. Thus, if T-bills returned 6.0% over a period of five years let's say, this portfolio could be expected to provide a return of the percentage provided for T-bills plus 3.5% to 4.0%, or about 9.5% to 10.0% per year on average.

This IPS goes on to analyze downside potential as well, again linked to the historical performance of T-bills. It notes that clients should be fully informed about the risks or downside potential of their portfolios. It also states that the client's recommended portfolio has a 32% chance of underperforming T-bills over a one-year holding period and a 15% chance of underperforming over a five-year holding period.

In our experience, very few clients have ever been exposed to that level of detail and disclosure. However, in an industry increasingly under pressure to inform clients in more depth, we believe that such an approach is not only helpful, but will become mandatory in the future.

Indexing or Active Management? The Debate Heats Up

What Is Active Management?

Active management involves analysis of a range of financial criteria such as price/earnings ratio, price/sales ratio, and price/book value ratio in an attempt to identify stocks that are likely to do well over time. Managers of an actively managed fund will decide which stocks to buy and sell based on this specialized research, as well as on interviews they often conduct with the management of the companies in which they may be considering an investment. Many mutual fund companies invest heavily in their research capability in the belief that by doing their homework, they'll be able to deliver returns to investors that beat the benchmark used by the fund to measure their success. Fidelity Investments, for example, is renowned worldwide for investments using its research capability. As economic conditions change, managers may adjust the mix of holdings within the fund in order to meet the fund's objectives.

What Is Indexing or Passive Management?

Index or passive management uses computer programs to build portfolios that mirror a market index such as the Toronto Stock Exchange (TSE) 300 or the Standard & Poor's (S&P) 500 in the U.S. An index manager will attempt to achieve this goal of mirroring or mimicking a market index by holding all or a representative sample of the stocks in the target index. Unlike an active money manager, a passive manager will not generally invest in individual stocks or market sectors in an effort to try to surpass the index.

What Are the Pros and Cons of Each Type of Management?

In an effort to do justice to both approaches, let's look at each under the headings of cost, performance, and risk.

Cost

There is little doubt that, overall, index investors face lower management fees than their active fund counterparts. Management expense ratios (MERs) are often less than 1%, compared with something in the range of 2.5% or so for actively managed funds. Look carefully, because some index funds have MERs every bit as high as actively managed funds. Someone must pay for all of that research, so if price is your overriding consideration, indexing may be best for you. For many people, though, it's not just price, it's value for money spent, so they would consider other criteria including performance and risk.

Index products *may* have lower portfolio turnover (that is, less buying and selling of stocks) and therefore lower transaction costs, especially if their index is somewhat limited (for example, the Dow Jones Industrial Average comprises only 30 stocks). If an index product mimics the S&P 500, for instance, there may be greater turnover and higher cost. It's probably true to say that, overall, index managers would have lower turnover than an actively managed fund, but it's not *automatically* true because many active managers (as distinct from index managers) are "buy-and-hold" advocates, experiencing relatively low turnover and therefore lower attendant costs.

Another cost argument advanced by proponents of indexing is that, unlike actively managed funds, index funds are nearly always fully invested. That is to say, about 99 of the cents in every dollar in an index fund are invested in the index stocks. By comparison, depending on the fund and the manager's outlook, an actively managed fund may have a cash position ranging from 5% to 20% for redemptions and as a war chest (available for buying opportunities). Indexers would say that investors are, in this case, paying about 2.5% to manage up to 20% of their assets, which are in T-bills or cash, and assert that that's expensive. Active management proponents counter this statement by arguing that having a reasonable cash holding available allows the experienced manager the opportunity to make timely purchases that may be reflected in overall fund performance substantially above the index's.

Performance

If 1999 were used as a case study, indexing certainly would have been the winner. In that year, the TSE 300 Composite Index returned 31.7%. By comparison, the average Canadian equity manager returned 24.1%, a full 7.6% below the Index. According to SEI, a global investment and consulting firm that measures how fund managers perform against their index benchmarks, the fact that many Canadian stock portfolios were underweighted in Nortel and BCE in 1999 could account for much of the 7.6% shortfall in performance *vis-à-vis* the TSE 300 that year. The two companies combined represented over 27% of the total market capitalization of the TSE 300.

But don't forget what happened only a few years ago when purchasing the TSE 300 index meant buying the likes of Bre-X and YBM Magnex. Being forced to buy these shares by buying the index not only indicates that in-depth examinations of companies in the index are not made, but that it is often a case of "buy poor quality high."

Using the index approach means that, by definition, it's impossible to beat the market index because when fees are deducted, you'll always underperform. In theory at least, by judicious selection, an active fund manager can produce a much higher return. On the other hand, research shows that in the U.S. only about 30% of active managers outperform the market in a given year; in Canada about 40% to 50% outperform. For those prepared to do their homework or who have a trusted financial advisor to rely on, it seems reasonable to be able to identify this core of highly competent managers who can provide higher returns net of their management fees.

Risk

Some indexers argue that an index fund is a one-stop decision, precluding them from having to worry about which stocks or funds to buy and enabling them to create instant portfolio diversification (and therefore lower risk) efficiently and cheaply. Active management types make the very same argument in defence of their style.

Index investors believe they can often achieve higher and less volatile returns than those who invest in actively managed funds. Active management proponents use exactly the same words to support their approach.

Indexers say that since such a large percentage of active fund managers fail to beat the benchmark annually, they are assuming lower risk by indexing. Active management supporters acknowledge the fact that while many managers fail to beat the benchmark, a substantial percentage do (as stated previously, 30% in the U.S. and closer to 40% to 50% in Canada). They argue that with the help of professional assistance, they can identify these managers and take advantage of their expertise.

top funds

close up

Real Estate for Diversification

Unfortunately, the information we are about to relay will probably seem a bit like closing the barn door after the horse has bolted. However, the study we cited in this very spot in last year's edition of *Top Funds* still remains an excellent example of the benefits of diversification, so we're repeating the message in this updated volume. Two U.S. investment analysts, Todd Carter and Keith Pauley of LaSalle Investment Management, have concluded that over the past six years, real estate investment trusts (REITs) have had the highest negative correlation with technology stocks. Simply put, REITs are a great diversifier. This study was completed before the technology meltdown of the past 18 months and, sadly, seems to have been ignored by the investing public.

Canadian investors have a choice of 14 mutual funds that specialize in either Canadian or international real estate. During the past 12 months, as the average science and technology mutual fund was falling by 39.9%, the average real estate fund gained 11.5%. None of the 14 funds have had a negative rate of return over the past 2 years.

For 5% to 10% of a diversified portfolio, real estate deserves a good look.

So What's an Investor to Do?

Why not use the principle of diversification here too? We recommend a range of asset categories in our portfolio. We recommend international diversification. We also recommend more than one management style. You never know which asset category, which area of the world, or which management style will excel in a given year. So you should cover your bases. You can do the same here and have some portions of your portfolio actively managed and some portions managed using the passive or index approach.

A New-Look Prospectus

We're used to telling clients (with tongue firmly in cheek) that if they're having trouble getting to sleep at night, they need only pick up and read a mutual fund prospectus. They'll be asleep within seconds! In fact, we even quip that they are supplied in paperback rather than hardcover because if you drop a hardcover prospectus as you quickly drift off, you'll break your nose.

And while prospectuses are never likely to be exciting reading, they are becoming more reader-friendly. That's because on February 1, 2000, National Investment 81-101 took effect and is being phased in gradually as fund companies file annual prospectus renewals and launch new funds.

Plain language and a standard format will likely assist in improving the new publications. Also, for each fund, all of the key information an investor needs to make a better-informed decision will be contained on just one or two pages. While the changes do not go far enough to satisfy all the critics—some feel there should be disclosure of even more details of the fund's operation—most investors, we think, will agree that the changes are very positive. Here are some of the improvements you'll find:

1. **A list of the fund's top 10 holdings within 30 days of prospectus date.** This information, while helpful if current, can quickly become dated, stale, or simply wrong. Look elsewhere, like at Morningstar.com or globeinvestor.com for information that's updated monthly.
2. **A bar chart showing year-by-year returns over a period of up to 10 calendar years.** We like this feature, particularly because it shows consistency of performance over calendar years, and avoids the misleading effect of a stellar year of performance that's possible when showing average annual compound rates of return. Some have been critical of the fact that there aren't category averages shown to put these results into context.
3. **A line graph of the fund's performance against an appropriate market index** over either the last 10 years or since inception, using a hypothetical $10,000 investment. The graph also gives cumulative amounts,

showing how much more or less money the fund made than the index.

4. **A comparison of annual and compound annual returns of the funds** compared with an appropriate market index for periods of one, three, five, and ten years, depending on the age of the fund. Returns are based on time periods ending December 31, so the later in the year the prospectus is filed, the less current the annual returns will be. Again, you can update the data by visiting sites that track funds monthly.
5. **Distributions and net asset value (NAV).** This table shows income, capital gains, or returns of capital over the last five years or since inception. This information can be helpful for those who want regular income or taxable investors who wish to calculate or defer capital gains.
6. **Ratios and other data.** This table shows net assets of the fund, management expenses (MER), and portfolio turnover over the past five years or since inception. The rate of turnover may give a sense of management style (that is, buy and hold or a more aggressive approach). Higher turnover can raise fund costs and cause capital gains distributions to be paid sooner rather than later.
7. **An example of the effect of fund expenses.** A table shows the cost of expenses (MER) in dollar terms, assuming a $1,000 investment in a fund

top funds

close up

Dollar Cost Averaging

We like dollar cost averaging, a process that involves investing a specific amount consistently on a periodic basis. Most investment professionals advise it, the media preach it, and Canadians do it. Indeed, there is even a new Canadian mutual fund based on dollar cost averaging. The Dundee Dollar Cost Averaging Fund will take your investment and put it into a money market account. Over the next year, a weekly transfer is made from that account into a diversified stock portfolio. At the end of the year, the investor is fully invested in the market.

The irony is that there is no research that supports this practice. Indeed, all the studies we've seen roundly criticize it. The body of research, which goes back 20 years, has resulted in the same conclusions: Dollar cost averaging is an inefficient practice, there is little risk reduction, and investment returns are reduced. Why? Well, in a nutshell, because markets go up. Over time, investors are better off being invested *right now.*

A working paper by Dr. Moyshe Milevsky, a York University finance professor, and Steven E. Posner is the latest study to repudiate the practice.

Why do we *still* like dollar cost averaging? Despite the academic evidence, it still remains one of the best ways for investors to cope psychologically with bad markets. If dollar cost averaging keeps them in the markets, then it's certainly worth leaving a few dollars on the table.

and an average annual return of 5%. This 5% return assumption seems somewhat low, especially for equity funds. As well, expenses will be higher than shown because of the impact of GST, which is not included in the example.

8. **Impact of deferred sales charges (DSC).** A chart shows the dollar amount of deferred sales charges payable on a $1,000 investment over holding periods of one, three, five, and ten years. Most fund DSCs decline to zero after about seven years; however, if a fund charges a redemption fee after five years but before ten years (which most do), you'll have to figure out the amount yourself.

We think this new prospectus format is a huge improvement, and that it'll be very helpful in giving more practical, meaningful information than was previously presented to investors.

Common Investor Mistakes

Novice investors are not the only ones who make poor investments decisions from time to time. Even seasoned investors can trip up occasionally and find themselves futilely chasing a hot stock or attempting to time an upswing in the market. So whether you're new to funds or an industry veteran, the better your understanding of the common traps that ensnare investors, the better your chances of avoiding them and sticking to the road leading to long-term stability and success.

Here is a look at the errors we see investors make most frequently:

Having Unrealistic Expectations

"Our next-door neighbours are making 20% a year with their investments. Why aren't we?"

Comments of this kind have been heard all over Canada in the last couple of years. People today are upset with returns of 15% a year, and the media has compounded the issue by making lots of unfounded statements about the kinds of profits investors can expect to make.

Recently, investors have been harbouring some extremely unrealistic expectations for their investments. These expectations have their root in the market boom of the late '90s, when investments were returning unprecedented profits.

The average return of the Dow Jones Industrial Average was 17.88% for the 10-year period to December 31, 2001 and 18.21% for the 5-year period to that same 2000 year-end date. Those returns were well above historical averages, but many investors expected the market frenzy to continue.

To put this exceptional period of growth into context, let's look at long-term results for the Dow Jones and S&P 500. You'll notice that the huge scores of the previous decade are the exception in a collection of more modest numbers:

Dow Jones Industrial Average Historical Returns

Time Period (Years)	Start Date (through to December 31, 2000)	Average Return
70	12/31/30	10.88%
50	12/31/50	12.36%
25	12/31/75	15.03%
10	12/31/90	17.88%
5	12/31/95	18.21%
1	12/31/99	-4.66%

DATA SOURCE: AIM Funds

Dow results assume reinvestment of dividends. An investment cannot be made directly into an index.

S&P 500 Historical Returns

Time Period	Average Return
1950s	19.34%
1960s	7.82%
1970s	5.88%
1980s	17.54%
1990s	18.19%

DATA SOURCE: AIM Funds

S&P 500 results assume reinvestment of dividends. An investment cannot be made directly into an index.

Investors also need to understand that returns must be viewed with a little perspective and common sense. Rates of return relate directly to the types of securities held within specific funds and your individual choice of funds will vary according to your own particular needs and financial goals. Consequently, how much your neighbours' investments are returning, or what the media is saying you can expect to earn, should be of little consequence when evaluating the success of your own portfolio.

Giving in to Short-Term Results

When markets are on the decline, it's extremely easy to forget the times when they've been strong. The TSE 300 Index, for example, has registered almost twice as many up years as it has down years. In fact, since 1920, the TSE 300 has posted positive annual returns for 53 years. In addition, investors in the TSE have enjoyed double-digit returns in 35 out of 80 years, and returns greater than 20% in 22 out of 80 years since 1920.

Of course, there have also been periods of decline. The TSE's 27 down years averaged a –12.21% return (keep in mind, however, that the 53 up years averaged a +17.19% return).

Our point? Over time, markets have dipped, but they've also shown a remarkably consistent upward trend. So whenever you tune into market movements, try not to focus on the short-term; remember what history has shown and stay focused on the long-term goals you've discussed with your financial advisor.

Chasing the Hot Sector

One of the key rules in modern warfare is to keep your forces spread out so that one well-placed strike cannot wipe out your ranks entirely.

The same theory holds true when it comes to investing. Unfortunately, there are a number of investors who believe that this piece of information doesn't or shouldn't apply to them. Not coincidentally, these are the same people who have suffered significant capital depreciation lately as their heavy concentration of tech holdings took a beating early in 2001. As the technology sector was heating up in the late '90s, many investors became restless when their funds invested in other sectors were returning comparatively meagre numbers. Scores of these investors decided to chase the hot sector; they pulled their money out of other areas and sunk it all into technology. Any profits they made likely went through the floor along with the tech sector itself early in the year.

The scenario we've just described here becomes even clearer if you take a look at the table at the top of page 29.

Sector Returns in 1999 and 2000

Economy Sector	Average Return in 1999	Average Return in 2000
Technology	+116.40%	-16.22%
Real Estate	-4.62%	+26.37%
Bonds	-0.82%	+11.63%
Utilities	+14.53%	+8.57%
Health Care	+10.35%	+43.67%
Financials	-4.39%	+26.74%

DATA SOURCE: AIM Funds

A smart investor sees the spread of numbers above and realizes that it is important to have a piece in *all* sectors of the economy. By spreading your investment dollars around you reduce the risk of being devastated if one sector goes sour, while still being able to pursue high returns in a sector that is performing well.

Listening to the So-called Experts

The average investor, intimidated by the notion of trying to determine which individual firms represent the greatest opportunity for investment, generally feels much more comfortable leaving such a task in the hands of the experts. In the financial world, the professionals in charge of making sense of market climate and trends are called analysts.

An analyst is an employee of a bank, brokerage, financial advisor, or an actual mutual fund, who studies the companies that present investment potential and then makes appropriate buy and sell recommendations. Analysts are sometimes more specifically referred to as financial analysts or securities analysts, and they often specialize in a single sector of the market or in a certain industry.

Based on definition, you would probably feel very confident leaving market predictions in the hands of these knowledgeable people. If they're giving recommendations to institutions and financial industry experts, they must understand market behaviour better than anyone else. Right?

The simple answer to that question is "No." Case in point: the *Wall Street Journal* took the 2000 year-end price of several high flying stocks and compared that price to the 12- to 18-month target highs predicted by analysts at the outset of the year. The results of the comparison look like this:

Year 2000 Share Price Predictions vs. Actual Year-End Close

Company Name	Analyst Prediction per Share	Actual Closing Price on December 18, 2000
Lucent	$120.00	$17.81
Priceline	$150.00	$1.81
PSINet	$86.00	$1.81
Redhat	$115.00	$8.63
Yahoo!	$300.00*	$33.00

*split adjust

DATA SOURCE: *Wall Street Journal*

What is the moral of this story? Well, it's obvious from the table above that even the "experts," the people who study trends for a living, can't actually predict where individual stocks and the market itself are going. So how, you may be asking, does an investor cope with an unpredictable market that resists being mastered, even by the analysts? The answer lies in diversification. By making sure your investments are well balanced by asset class, geography, and management style, you can relax in the knowledge that you have a portfolio suited to ride out any market trend—predictable or not—over the long term.

Trying to Time the Market

Consider the following quote by value-style investment guru Warren Buffet:

> The most common cause of low prices is pessimism....We want to do business in such an environment, not because we like pessimism but because we like the prices it produces. It's optimism that is the enemy of the rational buyer.

Buffet's comment makes the job he does so well—searching out and investing in undervalued stocks—sound easy. For the average investor, however, timing the market to capitalize on opportunities during a decline is extremely difficult because it requires two near-perfect actions: getting in at the right time *and* getting out at the right time. This precarious endeavour ensures that you most likely won't be in the market when you really need to be, on those days when it turns red-hot. Conversely, people who are *already* invested reap the benefits of being right where they should when the market goes on a tear.

To illustrate our point, we've pulled some numbers that clearly highlight the potential danger you face if you are shifting your money in and out of the market. Think about this: There were 2,528 trading days from 1980 to 1994. If you had been invested in an S&P Index for all of those 2,528 days, your average annual return would have been a staggering 17.5%. However, if you had missed the 10 best trading days in those 14 years, your average annual return would have been dramatically reduced to 12.6%. And if you had missed the 40 best days, your average annual return would have plunged to only 3.9%!

These numbers, (compiled by Ibbotson Associates), show that if you had been trying time the market by switching in and out of investments as they rode market waves, you most certainly would have missed many of those hot trading days. Even missing just a few of those crucial days would have chipped away considerably at your overall return.

And speaking of waves, here's a surfing analogy to keep in mind when it comes to investing: You need to be in the ocean in order to catch the waves that will deliver you to the beach resort you've chosen for your retirement (or to whatever financial goal you've set for yourself). If you're not actually *in* the ocean, you'll obviously miss whatever currents develop to propel you to your final destination!

research

news

Viva Las Vegas

The authors of this particular study decided to look at the issue of market timing and the problems inherent in actually measuring the performance of market timers. We've always been skeptical of those who claim the ability to forecast the appropriate time to get in and out of various asset classes. Using a "roulette wheel" approach (i.e., random switching), these researchers concluded that it was indeed difficult to outperform a buy-and-hold strategy. An interesting part of their analysis, however, revealed that this difficulty varies considerably over time. For example, during the period from 1995 to 1999, a buy-and-hold strategy for large-cap U.S. stocks would have outperformed 99.8% of the switching combinations available to the market timer. In other words, a successful market timer during this period would have been either very smart or very lucky! However, in 1994, the same buy-and-hold strategy would have beaten only 40.9% of the random monthly switching choices available. Consequently, a successful market timer during this period would not have been all that hard to find.

Richard J. Bauer Jr. and Julie R. Dahlquist, "Market Timing and Roulette Wheels," *Financial Analysts' Journal* 57, no. 1 (January/February 2001).

Letting Emotions Rule

There is no question about it: Investing is an emotional experience. It's a proven fact that ongoing market cycles create predictable investor emotional cycles. As the figure below outlines, upward market trends create a sense of optimism, flat markets incite a feeling of denial, and sharp declines can trigger fear and depression. Once markets normalize, the emotional cycle begins again and the investor feels a renewed sense of hope.

Knowledge, however, is a powerful thing. By simply knowing that we all go through a predictable range of emotions each time the market cycles, we have the capacity to take a much more rational approach to market volatility. Take another look at the investor emotion cycle below; this time we'll show you where the periods of greatest financial opportunity and risk lie.

Optimism drives every investment, so as the market begins to rise, hope encourages you to act. As your investment begins to grow through the market's upturn, your expectations become reality and excitement and euphoria take over. At this point, when your confidence it as its peak, you experience the time

Typical Investor Emotion Cycle

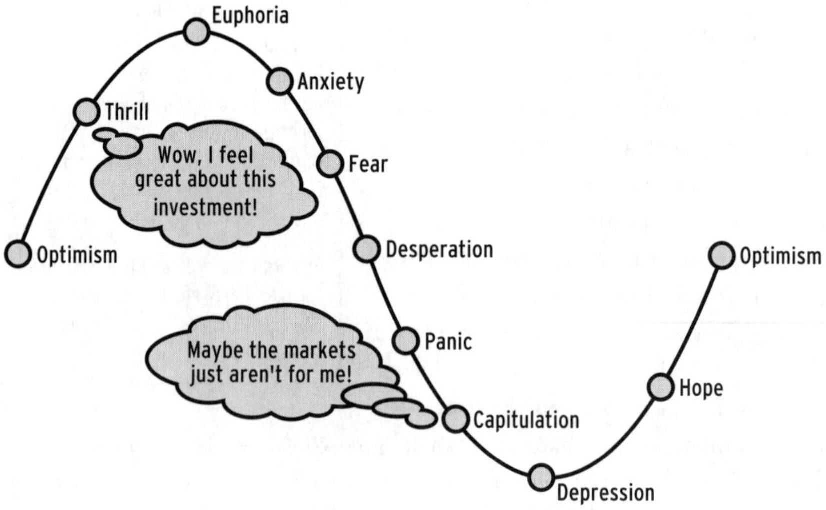

SOURCE: Westcore Funds/Denver Investment Advisor LLC, 1998

of greatest financial risk; feeling no fear, you may make decisions based on the assumption that the market will stay buoyant indefinitely.

What goes up must come down, however, and the market is no exception. As it starts to level off, your euphoria turns into anxiety. Denial about the inevitable downturn comes next, as does fear about your investments. If the market falls off sharply, you quite likely will feel panic and despondency as you question your place in the investment world. At this low emotional ebb lies your greatest financial opportunity; by reviewing your investment objectives at this time and remembering that you're invested for the long term, you're less likely to make any rash decisions that could have a negative impact on your returns down the road.

A thorough understanding of the range of emotions investing can create allows you to anticipate and navigate what will be difficult periods for you in the market cycle. You will also likely want to have a financial strategy in place ahead of time; you can refer to it when heightened confidence tempts you to be frivolous and when despondency prompts you to be hasty. A financial advisor can help you devise such a strategy.

Investment Opportunity Cycle

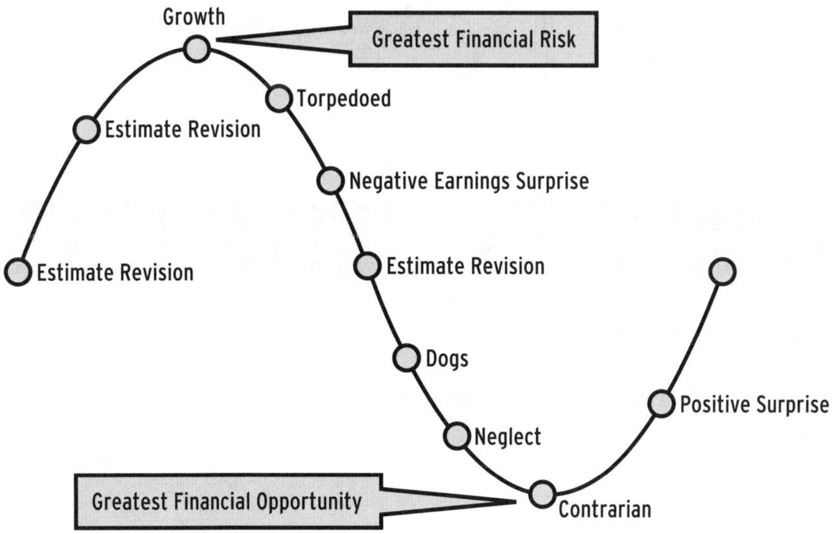

SOURCE: Westcore Funds/Denver Investment Advisor LLC, 1998

Letting Fear Dictate Investment Decisions

Here's an example that illustrates how unchecked investor emotions can provoke questionable investment decisions.

The recession of 1973–74 saw the S&P 500 drop from its high of 120.24 on January 11, 1973 to a low of 62.28 on October 3, 1974, a decline of over 48%. Outlined below is how three hypothetical investors reacted to the market low during that recession:

- **Investor #1** knew that as the market declined, the purchasing power of his investment dollars increased. He viewed the decline as an excellent opportunity to bargain shop and invested $10,000 in the market on December 31, 1974.
- **Investor #2** saw the same decline and hesitated. She watched others pull out of the market, listened to the media hyping the market downturn, and was very confused about what to do. She ended up waiting an entire year until prices began to recover, and invested $10,000 in the market on December 31, 1975.
- **Investor #3** was completely whipsawed and had absolutely no idea how to handle the recession. To make matters worse, he decided that making any decision was better than making no decision at all and in a panic, he put the $10,000 into a T-bill on December 31, 1974.

So how did each of our investors fare? We've charted below the growth of a hypothetical investment in the S&P 500 according to the decisions our investors made, as described above.

Growth of $10,000 in the S&P 500

Example	Investment Decision	Final Figure as of December 31, 2000
Investor #1	Invested at market low on December 31, 1974	$485,893
Investor #2	Invested on December 31, 1975 as the market was rising	$357,077
Investor #3	Invested in a T-bill on December 31, 1974	$65,047

DATA SOURCE: AIM Funds

What an astronomic difference in dollar figures! The results here prove that uninformed decisions made in the throes of market gyrations can have disastrous consequences. Investor #1 stayed cool, ignored the hype, stuck to basic investing principles, and came out leaps and bounds ahead of the rest of the field.

Investors facing more current market fluctuations can also fall prey to the same mistakes we outlined above. In this next example, we will follow the actions of investors contending with two market events that had a huge impact on the financial world a couple of years ago: the Asian Flu and the Y2K scare.

Investor A invests $100,000 on July 1, 1998 as follows: one-third in the TSE 300 Total Return Index (TRI); one-third in the S&P 500 TRI; and one-third in the Scotia McLeod Bond Universe Index. He leaves his money fully invested through to December 31, 2000.

Investor B, on the other hand, starts with the same $100,000 portfolio, but moves to T-bills on October 1, 1998, fearing the market correction due to currency problems in Asian countries. Once the markets stabilize on January 1, 1999, Investor B moves back into her original portfolio. She lets her money run to September 30, 1999. On October 1, 1999, she returns her money into T-bills, fearing a market decline at the turn of the millennium. On March 1, 2000, the markets stabilize once again and wanting to make up lost ground, Investor B reinvests her portfolio as follows: one-third in Nasdaq; one-third in the TSE 300 TRI; and one-third in the Scotia McLeod Bond Universe Index. Her money stays in this portfolio until December 31, 2000.

Here are the results for each of our Investors:

Market and Emotion Cycles

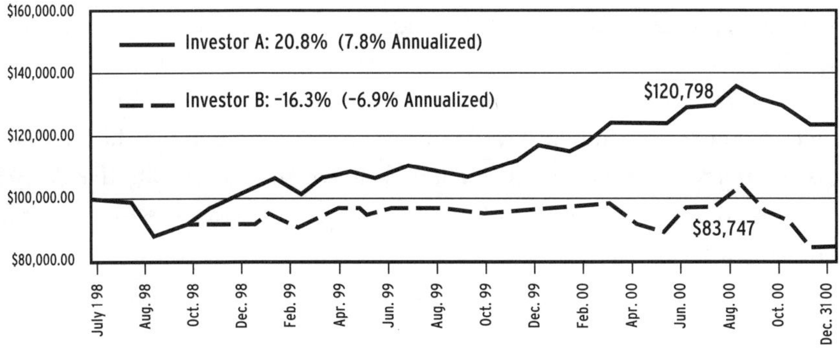

($100,000 Invested in the Market: July 1, 1998-December 31, 2000)

Source: Assante Advisory Services

At the end of two-and-a-half years, Investor A has earned $120,798 while Investor B has only made $83,747. Put another way, Investor A has earned a return of 20.8% (7.8% annualized) while Investor B has earned –16.3% (–6.9% annualized).

Once again we see how level-headed decisions made with confidence in a diversified portfolio produce a dramatically different result than decisions that stem from anxiety during specific periods in the market cycle.

Succumbing to Market Obsession

It has been recently stated that 40% of financial advisors believe it is much more difficult to retain clients today than it was five years ago. One of the reasons for this observation can be traced to the fact that the majority of clients have become less realistic with their expectations of investment performance, believing that even profits of 15% a year are too low. Clients are also much more anxious about quarter-to-quarter returns and some industry observers will even go so far as to say that clients are beginning to obsess about the effect of daily stock market fluctuations.

Furthermore, many market investors mistakenly believe that if they can just pick up the rules—figure out, for instance, that stocks go up in the spring and down in the fall—they'll be home free. Thousands of financial magazines and Web sites survive by feeding the fallacy of finding a simple investing formula. But think about it for a moment: when was the last time that reading a magazine articles or poring over a financial Web site saved you from the most recent market correction? What all investors need to realize is that there is no complete, accurate, valid model of the global financial system. No one holds the magic key to overnight investing success.

Through countless examples in this section, we've pointed out the traps the average investor (and the more experienced one) can fall into at any given time. In each case the solution is the same: Construct a properly diversified portfolio that allows you to stay fully invested with minimal worries about the inevitable swings the market will experience. There is so much more to life than instant quotes, research reports, and company conference calls. Invest wisely and then get on with your life!

A Final Word: Funds Do Better

Tempted to abandon mutual funds for the seemingly more "secure" pastures of GICs? Think again. Over the past 23 years, through about four full market cycles, mutual funds have outperformed GICs. From those 23 years, today's investor can glean a few important lessons.

The first is that mutual funds deliver excellent value. They not only do better than GICs, they have outperformed the TSE stock index, including dividends, and they have clobbered inflation. And not just over some lucky period when things were going well, but over a long time, through periods of inflation, deflation, war, recessions, referendums, 20% interest rates, and boom times.

Another lesson is that a balanced portfolio is the best blend of risk and return. A portfolio composed of all types of funds, geographic regions, and management styles succeeds in capturing returns with reduced risk. Magic? No, it's just plain and simple math; while one type of fund, region, or style zigs, another zags and the balanced investor enjoys a smoother ride.

A final lesson is this: don't even try to time the market. Instead of moving in and out of investment options, hang on to your funds and put the market to work for you. Even during times of severe recession, a balanced plan that allows you to remain fully invested is your best long-term option. Investors tend to lose sight of the big picture in tough times. But what that big picture shows is clear: Funds do better!

2

How to Build a Top Funds Portfolio

We believe that the research presented in the "100 Top Funds of 2002" list in Chapter 4 can be valuable to individual investors, but only if it is applied. Knowledge is not power; *applied* knowledge is power.

So let's get started on building your Top Funds portfolio.

The Importance of Asset Allocation

What is the most critical factor in successful mutual fund investing? Like many people, you may believe that it all depends on picking the "right" fund—the one with the best numbers. But as most fund managers know, consistently high returns do not depend on putting money into specific securities; rather, they depend on putting money into the right *types* of securities. The same rule applies to mutual fund investing: Put your money into the right fund categories, and chances are you'll be further ahead in the long run.

The categories of funds you choose and the weighting of each category relative to the portfolio as a whole is known as asset allocation. And research has shown that it accounts for between 85% and 92% of the difference in total returns in a broadly diversified portfolio. (By contrast, the same research puts the contribution of security selection—that is, choice of specific investments—at only about 2%!)

Clearly, the overriding decision in the development of any investment portfolio is the mix of assets within it. Traditionally, however, individual investors have given the least consideration to this most important decision.

Conversely, the selection of individual components (securities) is of relatively little importance. Yet investors usually spend the most time and energy in making this least significant decision.

research

news

What Every Bond Investor Should Know

The authors of a research study looked at U.S. bond markets from 1857 to 1997, as well as U.S. stock markets from 1871 to 1997, and have made some interesting observations. They determined that, contrary to popular belief, bonds can outperform stocks over fairly long time periods—up to 10 years in some cases. However, from 1926 onward, stocks have outperformed bonds by almost 5% a year.

Inflationary expectations seem to be the prime determinant of bond prices; unfortunately, investors look at the recent past when forecasting inflation. Bond yields are very high today because, despite low and stable current inflation rates, investors remember the high rates of the 1980s and early 1990s, and current prices reflect these long memories.

The authors also concluded that a portfolio composed of 20% stocks and 80% bonds carries about the same risk as a portfolio that contains 100% bonds. In other words, stocks have a place in almost everyone's investment portfolio. Leaving them out isn't any safer and the returns are lower.

Charles P. Jones, CFA and Jack W. Wilson, "What Every Bond Investor Should Know," *Journal of Private Portfolio Management* 1, no. 3 (1998).

What Asset Categories Should Be Included?

A well-balanced portfolio should include the following mixture:

Fixed income investments, such as

- Cash or cash equivalents (Canada Savings Bonds, term deposits, Treasury bills) for liquidity in an emergency or an opportunity situation;
- Canadian bonds for stability and high income;
- International bonds for protection against Canadian interest rate risk.

Equity (stock) investments, such as

- Canadian equities, for participation in our growth via a number of worldclass Canadian success stories;
- International equities, for hedging the "Canada risk" and for the broadest possible range of investment choices;
- Real estate, for inflation protection with tax benefits and income;
- Precious metals, including gold, for protection from inflation and crises;
- Oil and gas, for inflation protection with tax benefits and income.

What's the Right Balance for Me?

There is no "perfect" asset mix that's right for every investor. It will vary from person to person, depending on factors such as time horizon, investment objectives, and risk tolerance.

Here are some super-simplified guidelines that will help you approximate the mix that's right for you:

1. Start with your age.

   The total percentage of your portfolio held in fixed income investments (that is, cash and cash equivalents, as well as government and corporate bonds) should approximately match your age. So if you have a $100,000 portfolio and you are 40 years old, about $40,000 should be held in fixed income. This is a very rough rule of thumb, but without a questionnaire or interview with an advisor, this is the best way for you to determine a fixed income allocation on your own.

2. Assess your risk tolerance.

   Imagine a scale ranging from 1 to 10. A "1" represents the most pathologically cautious, nervous type of investor—the sort of person who keeps money under the mattress anticipating the banks' collapse. A "10" is (or would like to be) a professional gambler.

   Which number are you? In our experience, nearly everyone has an intuitive sense of where they fall on the scale.

3. Adjust your fixed income percentage.

   Here we combine the previous two factors: age and risk tolerance.

   If your risk tolerance is in the middle of the scale at "5," then make no adjustment to the fixed income component of your portfolio based on your age.

   For every number higher than 5, reduce the fixed income component by 5%. For example, if you are 40 years old and rate yourself a "7" on the risk tolerance scale, reduce your fixed income component by 10%—in this case, from 40% to 30%.

   For every number lower than 5, add 5% to the fixed income component. For example, if you are 40 years old and rate yourself a "2" on the risk tolerance scale, increase your fixed income component by 15%—in this case, from 40% to 55%.

Notice that the effect of these guidelines is to increase the conservative component of your portfolio as you become less aggressive.

Modifying the "Age Rule"

Percentage variation to the Fixed Income/Equity split										
Investment Split \ Risk Tolerance (1-10)	1	2	3	4	5	6	7	8	9	10
Fixed Income	+20	+15	+10	+5	age	-5	-10	-15	-20	-25
Equity	-20	-15	-10	-5	only	+5	+10	+15	+20	+25

What About the Other Asset Weightings?

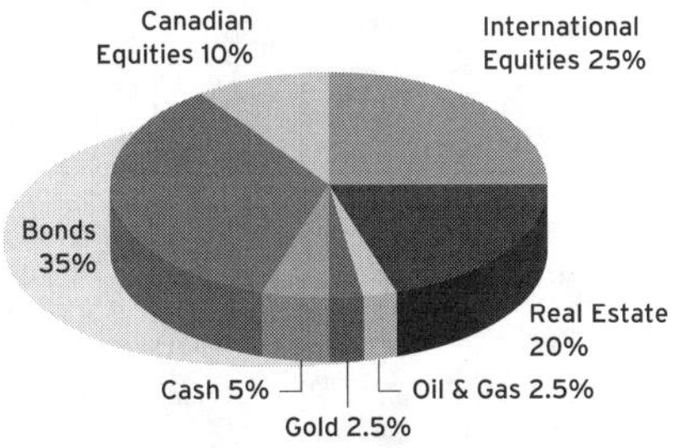

Again, other asset weightings will vary from person to person. But let's continue with the example of our 40-year-old investor who ranks a "5" on the risk tolerance scale.

For this individual, a reasonable balance might look like the adjacent pie chart.

How do we know that this balance will work? Well, history is on our side, as you'll see. Just study the table on page 42, which outlines the portfolio that's been developed for our 40-year-old investor. It shows that a balanced portfolio has offered a number of major advantages over the investment period.

The bottom line for the balanced portfolio is that it can provide above-average returns with reduced risk and offer preferred tax treatment at the same time. (See pages 226–227 for more on tax-efficient mutual fund investing.) Our experience is that investors who can obtain all three of these advantages are very happy indeed.

Clearly, there's a lot to be said for developing the right balance among asset categories.

The Importance of Diversification

A Nobel Prize was awarded for research related to investments. The prize-winning conclusion: It's better not to put all your eggs in one basket! Sounds simple, and it is. But what does it mean for individuals and why is it so important?

We've already discussed the concept of a balanced portfolio—where that balance is achieved by weighting your holdings across various asset categories. There are other ways to diversify, some of which were discussed earlier in the book.

Returns by Asset Type

Year	Cash	Bonds	Canadian Equities	International Equities	Real Estate	Oil & Gas	Gold	Balanced Portfolio
Asset Allocation	5%	35%	10%	25%	20%	2.5%	2.5%	100%
1978	9	4	30	21	12	16	8	13
1979	12	-3	45	14	13	82	91	14
1980	13	7	30	33	23	46	43	21
1981	18	4	0	-5	26	-29	-38	5
1982	14	35	6	21	1	-14	39	20
1983	9	12	36	25	7	19	-2	16
1984	11	15	-2	16	12	-9	-20	11
1985	10	21	25	40	10	11	33	23
1986	9	15	9	29	13	-2	29	17
1987	8	4	6	5	14	18	17	7
1988	9	10	11	10	17	-8	-28	10
1989	12	13	21	21	20	25	5	17
1990	13	8	-15	-12	1	-10	1	0
1991	9	22	12	22	0	-9	-12	14
1992	7	10	-1	6	-6	23	2	5
1993	6	18	33	22	-7	68	83	18
1994	6	-4	0	10	-3	-12	-3	0
1995	8	21	15	26	2	13	-17	16
1996	5	12	28	19	3	51	22	14
1997	3	10	15	30	11	-9	-34	14
1998	5	9	-2	30	-6	-41	-4	8
1999	5	-6	32	0	16	13	11	4
2000	6	13	7	-17	12	22	-1	5
Average	8	12	12	31	11	13	11	13
Variation high to low	15	53	71	159	42	184	147	34
# of years of positive rates	31	26	23	52	24	16	17	29
# of years of negative rates	-	5	8	10	7	15	14	2

Courtesy of Assante Advisory Services

SOURCES:

Cash	91-day T-Bill
Bonds	SCM Long-Term Bond
Cdn. Equities	TSE 300 Return Index
Int'l Equities	S&P Total Return (Cdn.$), MSCI EAFE (Cdn.$)
Real Estate	Russell Canadian Property Index
Oil & Gas	CRB Energy Index (Cdn.$)
Gold	Price of Gold-London (Cdn.$)

Diversification Type	Examples
Geography	Canada, U.S., Pacific Rim, Latin America
Investment Style	value, growth
Investment Objective	growth, income
Management Team	Fidelity, Mackenzie, Templeton, Trimark

Portfolio Risk

Portfolio Risk Decreases as the Number of Asset Classes Increases

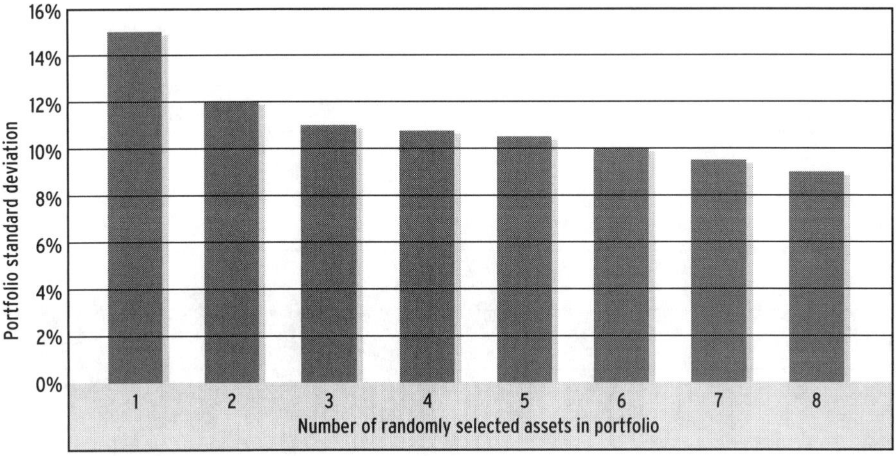

SOURCE: Ibbotson Sales Builder™ Presentations, © 2001 Ibbotson Associates, Inc. All rights reserved. Used with permission.

As your portfolio becomes appropriately balanced, it becomes more diversified, and there are major advantages to this diversification.

The chart above shows how diversifying across asset categories helps to reduce risk. Notice that with one asset category in a portfolio (that is, all your eggs in one basket), the risk (measured by standard deviation) is about 15%. With each additional asset category the risk declines, so with representation in eight asset categories (and there really aren't many more), it's cut almost in half to 9%.

Similarly, when dealing with stocks only, unsystematic risk is substantially reduced by going from owning one stock to owning 128 (although research shows that after 50 stocks

top funds

close up

Can You Be Overdiversified?

Our rule on diversification is this: Don't buy two items that do the same thing. That is, you don't need three small-cap Canadian equity value funds. They're just too similar. If you're going to buy three Canadian equity funds, you should get three with legitimately different styles. We would argue that such a strategy could lower the risk to your portfolio through diversification. In his introduction to *Bogle on Mutual Funds*, Paul Samuelson shows that returns of underdiversified managers are lower. And Morningstar has proven that such managers do have higher risk. Those two arguments prove it's overduplication that's the enemy, not overdiversification.

How Many Stocks to Hold

Portfolio Risk Decreases as the Number of Stocks Increases

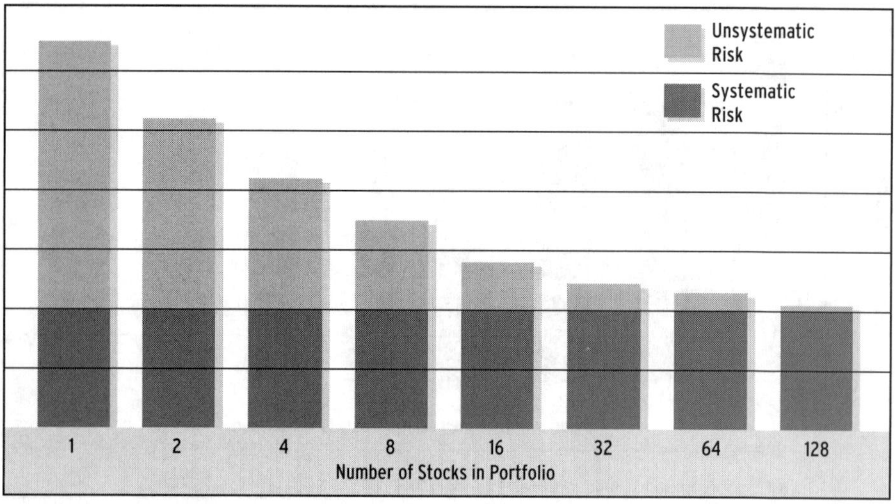

SOURCE: Ibbotson Sales Builder™ Presentations, © 2001 Ibbotson Associates, Inc.

are in a portfolio, subsequent additions reduce risk only minimally), as shown in the chart above.

Essentially, diversification is a conservative strategy that acknowledges that you not always be right in your selection of securities, geographic location, or manager. By not overweighting your position in any one of these areas, the negative impact of being wrong is reduced. Once you acknowledge that you will not be right all the time, you are able to adjust your thinking to achieve more consistent (if less spectacular) growth and avoid big, and potentially devastating, losses.

Portfolios and Mutual Fund Classifications

You blink twice and the number of mutual funds available to Canadians balloons to over 4,000. Along with the proliferation of funds, the number of classifications has expanded in order to accommodate the wider spectrum of fund types. While finding your funds in the newspaper has become more of a challenge, the narrower classifications do facilitate more meaningful comparisons between funds and against benchmarks. Standardization has been introduced as the industry has determined fixed classifications to be used by fund companies, fund dealers, and media sources. Also being determined is the investment holding criteria that funds have to meet in order to qualify for inclusion in a particular classification.

Most retail portfolio management systems accomplish their diversification objectives by using broad asset classifications. This is not bad idea, as it does the job and is easier for investors to understand. But as an investor accumulates a larger portfolio and covers the basic classifications, it is possible to seek out asset classes that are more focused or are managed in different styles, allowing an investor to further tailor a portfolio to a desired risk level. The additional classes

Allocation of Funds

Portfolio Classifications	The Basics for Portfolios Less Than $100,000	Fine Tuning for Portfolios Greater Than $100,000
Money Market	Canadian Money Market	U.S. and International Money Markets
Short-Term Bond	Canadian Short-Term Bond	
Canadian Fixed Income	Canadian Long/Midterm Bond	Canadian Mortgage
Global Fixed Income	International Bonds	
Canadian Equity	Canadian Large-Cap/Diversified Blend	Canadian Large-Cap/Diversified Value Canadian Large-Cap/Diversified Growth Canadian Small/Mid-Cap Canadian Dividend Canadian Sector Canadian Resources & Precious Metals
U.S. Equity	U.S. Large-Cap/Diversified	U.S. Small-Cap
International Equity	International	Global Global Sector European North American Latin American & Emerging Markets Asia & Pacific Rim
Balanced	Canadian Tactical Balanced Canadian Strategic Balanced Global Balanced Asset Allocation Services	

tend to be somewhat riskier on a stand-alone basis, but they add some further diversification to an established portfolio. Remember to cover the basics first before you scamper off into the more specialized classes.

Investors can also take their investment decisions to an even more basic level by selecting funds or "funds of funds" where a company manages the rebalancing and allocation among various funds.

A Fund Family Approach to Investing

Good fund families contain all or most of these characteristics:

- Broad choice of consistent funds;
- Reasonable expenses;
- Easy availability (e.g., not only available to civil servants in P.E.I.);
- Good administration/service/communication;
- Deep stable of talented analysts on staff or on contract;
- Sufficient resources to hire the best people, promote funds, and stop the company from being acquired (when your fund company is bought, the new owners often bring in their own team, even if it's not as good).

Top Five Canadian Fund Families (September 30, 2001)

Fund Family	Strengths	Weaknesses
Investors Group/ Mackenzie	Conservative approach (IG)/ STAR Program and "Ivy" funds (Mackenzie)	Bond funds (IG)/"Industrial" funds (Mackenzie)
Royal Mutual Funds	Bond, dividend, and resource funds	BIG funds, difficulty beating the market
AIM/Trimark	International Equity funds	Canadian Equity funds
Fidelity Investments	International Equity funds, Global Sector funds	U.S. Equity funds
TD Asset Management Inc.	Sector funds	N/A (see "Top Funds Fund Company of the Year," page 214)

Caution Dysfunctional Families

Avoid fund families with

- Few strong, consistent funds;
- High likelihood of a takeover;
- High, unjustified MERs;
- Inability to hire or keep good managers;
- Organization not conducive to talent (poor pay, structure, prestige).

Let's explore the merit of the fund family approach to investing. Try to pick a great family (or a couple of them if you've got a lot of dough), that's strong all around: great stock funds in Canada and abroad, and great bond and specialty funds. Since few fund families actually possess all of these attributes, the top six fund families in Canada are listed in the table on page 46, based on assets as of September 30, 2001 and the best/worst characteristics of each. Decide which are best suited to you by leaning toward those that are strong in areas you favour.

Number of Funds and Types of Funds

How Many Funds Are There?

According to the Investment Funds Institute of Canada (IFIC) as of May 2000, there were 1,434 funds available; IFIC claims to represent about 98% of the assets in Canadian mutual funds. This figure seemed curiously low to us, so we decided to attempt to count the actual number of funds ourselves. We used the *Globe and Mail* Report on Business for Saturday, June 24, 2000 and here's what we discovered.

We examined the nearly four full pages that listed a vast array of mutual funds. We found listings for 1,971 traditional mutual funds and asset management services, including Mackenzie STAR portfolios, Artisan portfolios, and Keystone portfolios. It's true that these portfolios include several individual funds used to create the portfolios, so some "double counting" occurs.

We also found 1,099 segregated funds developed by or in partnership with insurance companies. Several mutual fund companies, including AIC, C.I., Mackenzie, Trimark, and Templeton, have created segregated versions of their "regular" funds. As well, several insurance companies have hired mutual fund managers to create segregated versions of "regular" funds. London Life, for example, has hired Mackenzie, Sceptre, and AGF to manage segregated versions of their regular funds; Maritime Life has hired AGF, Fidelity, and Global Strategy to do the same. Thus, there is overlap here too, although there were still over 1,000 distinct segregated funds.

research
news

Why You'll Get Burned Chasing "Hot" Funds

Every year we update our study that looks at how Canadians fared when they invested in mutual funds based solely on recent performance. While this approach certainly runs counter to what professional advisors recommend, we know from experience that it's exactly how many do-it-yourselfers invest.

We looked at the first-quartile performers in the Canadian diversified equity fund category each year from 1986 to 2000. Then we reviewed their performance the following year to see how investors who purchased them would have fared.

Once again, our results confirm the folly of this investment "strategy." Less than 29% of the hot funds repeated their first-quartile performance the next year. In fact, 31% were fourth- or bottom-quartile performers.

Last year was an abysmal year for "hot" fund investors. As of June 30, 2001, only one fund, Hirsch Performance, was a repeat top-quartile performer. Of the 64 first-quartile performers in the 12 months leading up to June 30, 2000, an astounding 61 were fourth-quartile performers a year later. Only 2 of the 64 had positive returns!

The message is clear: Invest in the latest, hottest fund at your peril!

In addition to the numbers cited above, there were 24 labour-sponsored venture capital funds. These mutual funds qualify for special income tax consideration.

There were also (in addition to those listed above) 120 money market funds, 14 segregated money market funds, 127 pooled funds (designed for pension plans, group RRSPs, or large individual investors) and 116 "others" (including closed end, variable annuity, and limited partnerships).

In total, then, there were about 3,470 investments generally referred to as mutual funds listed, each showing the latest net asset value (NAV), dollar change, and weekly data, including weekly high price, low price, and percentage change.

According to IFIC, in June 1999 there were only two RRSP-eligible "clone" funds (both Mackenzie) with assets of about $420 million. In May 2000, IFIC alone counted 133 clone funds with assets of $19.1 billion. That's a huge increase, both in numbers and assets. This increase can be attributed largely to the fact that Canadians discovered a way to increase foreign content in their RRSPs well beyond the antiquated and arbitrary limits of 25% in 2000 and 30% in 2001 set by the government, and yet still be "onside" with the Canada Customs and Revenue Agency (formerly Revenue Canada).

But the reality goes beyond these figures. In one survey, we counted 202 RRSP-eligible clone funds of the 1,971 referred to above and another 23 within the 1,099 segregated funds previously referred to. Thus, there seem to be about 225 RRSP-eligible clone funds out there, not the 133 noted by IFIC.

We completed another analysis related to the number of U.S. dollar funds available. These are funds that invest in U.S. dollars rather than Canadian dollars. Although we hadn't determined the number of U.S. dollar funds available in previous years, we were astounded to discover that there are about 201 (of the 1,971 regular funds) now offered by most of the major fund companies. As well, 21 of the 120 money market accounts are available in U.S. dollars.

The range of investment opportunities under the general heading of mutual funds continues to grow almost exponentially, it seems. And while in general terms we would argue that more choice is better than less choice, the challenges that come into play in attempting to monitor and evaluate this vast range of options both quantitatively and qualitatively grow as well. It seems incomprehensible to us that effective tracking and analyzing can be done on anything less than a full-time basis with the assistance of sophisticated tracking software. The advantages of working with a trusted financial advisor seem self-evident.

Segregated Funds

Segregated funds have often been called the life insurance industry's "best kept secret." Well, that secret is now out in the open as numerous mutual fund companies working directly with insurance companies are launching segregated fund product lines.

Essentially, a segregated fund combines the features of an investment fund with the elements of an insurance contract. As a result, you end up with an open-ended investment fund that is combined with death benefits, maturity dates, and guarantees, as in many other insurance contracts. The term *segregated* refers to the requirement that assets in these funds must be kept distinct and separate from the other assets of the issuing insurance company.

> **surfing the web**
>
> Here is a great place to read up on complex financial planning issues without feeling that they are difficult to understand. The site covers issues such as RRSP versus Mortgage Paydown, and the Psychology of Investment Management—all the things you need to know about but can't easily find anywhere else. As one of the about.com Web networks, the creators really have been able to get people thinking with this site.
>
> **www.financialplanca.about.com**

Segregated funds provide a number of advantages that have led to skyrocketing sales in past years. First, these products usually afford a guaranteed return of anywhere between 75% and 100% of your initial investment, on the earlier date of maturity (typically 10 years) or your death. The percentage death benefit guarantee often varies by age, so this detail should be examined in the specific contracts.

Lately, a number of companies have been allowing investors to reset their maturity guarantee several times a year. This means you are able to apply a new term on the guaranteed return of your investment amount, ensuring you can update the return of a principal guarantee on an ongoing basis. This feature has been particularly attractive to conservative investors or those who are concerned with the high valuations of today's markets.

Second, segregated funds can provide an important element of creditor protection under certain circumstances. This protection is due to the fact that under provincial insurance laws, insurance monies may be protected from creditors if certain conditions exist. For example, one condition asserts that the named beneficiary must be the spouse, parent, child, or grandchild of the annuitant (or, in Quebec, the contract holder). Notably, the creditor proofing may be nullified if the investor is found, during the creditor proofing process, to be insolvent at the time that the money is deposited into the plan. Additionally, there have been cases where family dependants have been able to access such monies. Hence, if credit protection is a factor in your decision to purchase a segregated fund, you should consult directly with your financial and legal advisors about your personal circumstances.

Third, if you name a beneficiary other than your estate, your investment will bypass the probate process, thereby saving fees. Probate fees vary radically by province and must be investigated on an individual basis.

Are all of these benefits supplied at no cost? Of course not. There is a charge for the maturity and death benefit elements on top of the normal management expense ratio (MER) charges for the investment element of the fund. For example, in the case of Trimark's family of segregated funds, the maturity and death benefits guarantee adds approximately 0.20% to the cost of fixed income funds, 0.45% to the cost of balanced funds, and 0.80% to the cost of equity funds. Others are similarly priced. So you are paying a hefty extra fee for these benefits.

A major criticism of segregated funds is that a 10-year guarantee adds little real value, given that, with the exception of the Great Depression of the 1930s, equities in Canada and in the U.S. have never lost money over a 10-year period, as measured by the major stock market benchmark indices. In fact, a recent study of over 500 mutual funds in all categories in Canada with at least 10 years of performance history indicates that only nine funds actually ended up losing money. For many individuals, buying term insurance combined with mutual funds may actually be a much cheaper approach. Finally, the potential benefits of credit proofing and avoidance of probate fees are individual-specific. Depending on your occupation, age, and the province in which you live, these factors may or may not be of benefit to you.

To add more fuel to the topic, both Trimark and Templeton announced that they would stop selling segregated versions of their mutual funds effective July 31, 2000. The reason was related to regulations that took effect January 1, 2001. These rules placed hefty new capital requirements on the insurance companies with whom Templeton and Trimark were in partnership. The fund companies would need to back up the guarantees provided as part of the contract. The new requirements made it much more expensive to offer the guarantees.

Trimark and Templeton were the number two and number three players in the field. C.I. has the biggest market share in segregated funds at about $1.5 billion. C.I., Mackenzie, and AIC continue to sell segregated versions of their funds.

A New Twist: Defined Portfolios

Although defined portfolios (also called unit trusts) have been in existence in the U.S. for about 25 years, they are quite new in Canada.

A defined portfolio is a fixed portfolio of professionally selected securities with a specific maturity, usually five years. Investors purchase units, which represent undivided ownership in the entire portfolio, like a mutual fund. However, unlike traditional mutual funds, which buy and sell securities on an ongoing basis, the stocks in a defined portfolio are fixed on the date of deposit, and (except in extremely unusual circumstances) no changes are made to the composition of the portfolio for the length of the portfolio's existence. At the end of the term, the portfolio is dissolved, assets are paid out to investors, and new portfolios are created.

Defined portfolios combine some of the advantages of individual stocks and mutual funds, as shown in the chart below.

Advantages	Individual Stocks	Defined Portfolios	Mutual Funds
Fully invested	Yes	Yes	No
Known portfolio	Yes	Yes	No
Daily liquidity	Yes	Yes	Yes
Diversification	No	Yes	Yes
Convenience	No	Yes	Yes
Low minimum	No	Yes	Yes
Professional selection	No	Yes	Yes
Reinvestment	No	Yes	Yes

Other features of defined portfolios include the following:

- **Tax advantages.** Because of the buy-and-hold philosophy and virtually no trading, these portfolios may be more tax efficient than typical mutual funds.
- **Low expenses.** Traditionally, the portfolios have offered MERs in the range of 1.95% compared with around 2.6% for traditional mutual funds.
- **Daily liquidity.** Like mutual funds, units are priced daily and may be redeemed on any business day at net asset (market) value.
- **Professional portfolio selection and supervision.** Also like mutual funds, defined portfolios have experienced, knowledgeable professionals who research and select stocks appropriate to each different defined portfolio.
- **Full investment.** Unlike mutual funds, which may have a substantial cash position at a particular time depending on circumstances or the manager's outlook, defined portfolios have limited cash positions so more of your money may be at work in the market.
- **Greater concentration.** Under normal circumstances with mutual funds, it would be unusual for a single holding to constitute more than 10% of the fund's assets. In a defined portfolio, while all of the 20 or 25 stocks selected

begin with equal weighting, it's possible through outstanding performance that an individual stock could come to assume a substantial percentage weighting in the portfolio over the five-year period.

In Canada, First Trust Portfolios is the largest provider of defined portfolios. According to their data, they currently manage $350 million. Defined portfolios tend to pursue themes or invest in specific market sectors, such as pharmaceuticals, technology, or e-business—although First Trust also has a broadly based portfolio called Canada's Leading Companies Trust for the Year 2001 as well as one entitled The Lehman Brothers 10 Uncommon Values Trust for 2001.

These portfolios are developed annually and are offered for approximately 12 months before being closed not only to new investors, but also to any additional contributions from existing investors.

You probably wouldn't want to build a portfolio using defined portfolios exclusively, but they can nicely complement your existing investments if you want to concentrate on some specific areas or themes. You're likely to hear more about them in the future.

Counting the Cost

There are two basic types of costs involved in the purchase of a mutual fund: sales charges and management fees. Both can have an impact on your bottom-line returns. Some miscellaneous charges may also apply. In this section we'll provide an overview of these costs and offer some tips that may be helpful as you make important investment decisions.

The Obvious Costs: Sales Charges

Front-End Loads

If you opt for a front-load fund, an agreed-upon percentage of your total investment will be deducted. So if you pay 4% on a $10,000 purchase, the actual amount invested will be $10,000 – 4% = $9,600.

While it used to be normal to pay loads of up to 9%, the situation is quite different today. It's now extremely unusual to pay more than 5% on even a small investment; on large amounts, a lower rate can usually be negotiated between you and your broker or advisor. Of course, when you purchase a front-load fund, there is no percentage charge when you sell.

Large investors (for example, those with $250,000 or more) can sometimes negotiate no front-end commissions at all. The advisor and the firm are compensated with modestly higher trailers or service fees from most fund companies when they negotiate this option.

One exception to negotiable front-end loads is in the discount brokerage community, although here the loads are already quite low. For example, one discount broker advertises a rate of 2.5% on mutual fund investments under $5,000, 2% on orders from $5,000 to $25,000, and 1% on orders larger than $25,000. Other discount brokers are in the same range.

One important note regarding front-load funds is that every dollar taken off your investment will have a negative impact on growth over time; the higher the load, the greater that impact will be (assuming all other things, including rate of return and operating and management costs, are identical).

Back-End Loads

Sometimes referred to as deferred sales charges (DSCs), this option offers an advantage over front-load funds because all of your money goes to work for you—nothing is deducted. This type of fund was introduced in 1987 and has become very popular over the intervening years.

Here's how it works. If you redeem these units before a certain period (usually about seven years), you pay a fee based on the value of your investment. This percentage declines over time, as shown in the following example:

Back-End Load Charges

Year	Loads (Percentage)
1	4.5
2	4.0
3	3.5
4	3.0
5	2.5
6	2.0
7	1.0
–	0.0

Several companies charge the redemption fee on the original amount invested; a few, however, charge on the market value of funds when you cash them in. In most cases (specifically where you redeem the fund units for more than what you paid), the former approach is preferable for the investor.

The following table shows how several of the larger fund companies currently handle their redemption charges:

Redemption Charges

Redemption Policy	Acquisition Cost	Redemption Value
AIC	X	X *
AGF	X	
Canadian International		X
Dynamic	X	X
Fidelity	X	X **
Global Strategy	X	
Guardian	X	
Investors		X
Mackenzie		X
Spectrum/United	X	
Templeton	X	
Trimark	X	

* Pre-July 1, 1998 based on acquisition cost; after July 1, 1998 based on redemption rules.

** Pre-April 2, 1999 based on redemption costs; after April 2, 1999 based on acquisition costs.

Due to the popularity of back-end load funds, many funds that used to charge only a front-end load can now be purchased either way. Trimark, for example, set up a select group of DSC funds to mirror their successful front-load funds, such as the Trimark Fund (Trimark Select Growth) and the Trimark Canadian Fund (Trimark Select Canadian Growth Fund). Similarly, Guardian has both "classic" (front-load with lower expenses) and "mutual fund" (back-end with higher expenses) versions of their fund offerings.

While it appears at first glance that the back-load approach is the way to go, there are two additional factors that should be considered before making a final decision:

- **Management fees.** Some fund companies charge higher management expenses if funds are purchased on a back-load basis than if they are purchased on a front-load basis, often tacking on an extra 0.25% to 0.5%. Trimark is a striking example. Their back-load funds cost as much as 0.7% more annually to own. So investors should probably choose the front-load option at Trimark.
- **Net return.** These costs fall directly to the bottom line, meaning that the difference in net return can be significant. When compounded over several years, this factor can make a big difference in the value of the fund.

Despite these additional conditions, people still tend to resist upfront costs. Indeed, our research shows that people are opting overwhelmingly for back-load funds, as about 75% of load-fund sales are of the back-load variety.

No-Load Funds

Until very recently, no-load funds were available predominantly from banks and trust companies, as well as a few management companies (most notably Altamira) that sold directly to the public. When dealing with these companies, you are usually speaking with a salaried employee rather than an independent financial advisor. Not surprisingly, these employees are able to provide information only about the funds offered by their company.

But there is growing evidence of ongoing change in the mutual fund industry. Only a few years ago, it was not unusual to pay a front load of up to 9% on a fund you purchased. Then came the back-end load funds, and the practice of paying a front load became much less widespread. Recent statistics suggest that about 75% of mutual fund sales are purchased on a back-end load and about 25% are processed on a front-load or no-load basis. There has been a similar trend towards no-load funds, though it comes in fits and starts. With nothing deducted on purchase and no redemption charges, this approach obviously has benefits for the investor. It is becoming increasingly popular in the U.S., and there are a number of fund companies in Canada that have introduced no-load options.

In this situation, brokers, mutual fund salespeople, or financial advisors receive little or no upfront commission from the fund company; instead, they receive a slightly higher-than-normal ongoing service or trailer fee. Typically available only to larger clients at this time, but likely to spread, this development will probably make life more difficult for newcomers to the business, since upfront commissions are likely to be significantly reduced. However, for those who have an established clientele, the increased trailer or service fees could generate substantially more ongoing income. So it looks like we're soon going to see a situation that investors are really going to love: a much wider range of funds available on a no-load basis and ongoing financial advice at little or no direct cost.

What You Don't See: Management Expenses

The second and more poorly understood cost involved in the ownership of mutual funds is management fees. A survey of mutual fund fees conducted by Scudder Funds of Canada in late May of 1997 found that 45% of Canadians who purchased mutual funds during the past year believed their mutual fund did not charge management fees at all, while 8% were unsure.

Well, just like any business, mutual fund companies—including those with no-load funds—charge these fees. Fees are the means by which the fund managers are reimbursed for their time, expertise, and (one hopes) the attractive returns they generate for their unitholders. Management fees also pay for costs incurred in establishing, maintaining, and promoting the fund, as well as for service fees paid to advisors and their firms.

Management fees generally range between 1% and 2.5% of the total assets under management. In some cases, this percentage will decline as the assets held by the fund increase. But most often the fees are determined by the type of assets held and, presumably, the work required to manage them—usually 2% to 2.5% for equity-based funds, and about 1% for cash management funds. Management fees are typically charged directly to the fund, which means investors do not receive a statement of the amount. But make no mistake—they do have an impact on the fund's return. For example, if a fund charges a 2% management fee and earns a 20% return in a given year, the investor's net return is 18%.

While some critics feel these fees are too high, there are a growing number of funds offering lower management fees. Scudder Funds of Canada, which started in October 1995 and offers a family of no-

> surfing
> **the web**
>
> If you want to take an Investment 101 course, this site is easy to understand and easy to use. The financial calculators are a perfect example of the user-friendly features. Explaining everything from stocks to bonds, brokers to investment clubs, this site is great for an avid learner who craves to learn from the bottom up. Another great about.com invention.
>
> **www.beginnersinvest.about.com**

load funds, is a prime example. Further, many investors are looking for more than returns. First, they want guidance in selecting the right funds from the bewildering choices available when building a portfolio. Also, in today's complex world of ever-changing economic and financial trends as well as tax and pension legislation, they want their funds integrated into a coherent financial plan. And when implemented, they want their plan accompanied by ongoing education, advice, and service. Given these needs and the superlative returns of the past decade, the case against higher fees diminishes. Interestingly, it is the no-load funds—which typically do not involve advisors—that are much more expensive relative to their U.S. counterparts. Fees, however, do matter. Investors have to pick the right funds and, if applicable, the right advisor to ensure that they are getting value. Also, we believe that as the industry continues to grow and mature, we will see a trend towards lower fees.

Investors should pay more attention to the management expense ratio (MER) than to management fees. This figure is expressed as a percentage of the fund's total assets, and it represents the total of all management fees (those referred to above) as well as other expenses charged to the fund. Typically, these include legal, accounting, custodial, and safekeeping costs, as well as the costs of producing prospectuses and other reports. All else being equal, the higher the management expense ratio, the more money being spent by the manager and the lower the return to the investor, so be sure to examine these factors when considering any fund purchase.

Trading Costs

One of the biggest hidden costs in any mutual fund is the commission cost or brokerage fee paid to trade the underlying stocks and bonds. Because these costs are buried in the price of the securities, they are not visible to the investor. Funds that move in and out of stocks and bonds on a frequent basis will have higher trading costs and, hence, will have to perform that much better to deliver returns to investors.

Those Little "Extras"

There are a few other charges that may apply to the fund you are considering. These include the following:

- **Set-up fee.** This is a one-time fee often charged by no-load companies. It's usually in the range of $40 to $50.

- **Close-out or transfer fee.** You may be charged a modest fee for closing out your account with a particular fund company. Many fund companies charge about $25 to $50 on the termination or transfer out of a tax plan for an RRSP or an RRIF. Growing numbers of financial institutions are also charging this fee.
- **Trustee fee for RRSPs, RRIFs, or RESPs (Registered Education Savings Plans).** For these types of accounts, an annual trustee fee may be charged, usually about $25 to $50. Some fund companies have eliminated their RRSP and RRIF fees altogether, so remember to enquire before you invest.
- **Systematic withdrawal fee.** A systematic withdrawal plan (SWP) allows investors to receive regular income from their fund. A few companies charge an annual fee for this service, while others charge a fee for each withdrawal.
- **NSF cheque charge.** If you set up a regular investment program and invest monthly by preauthorized cheque, you may have to pay a service charge. If the identified bank account has insufficient funds to make the systematic investment, expect to pay a fee of about $15.
- **Switching fee.** Nearly all companies allow switching from one fund to another within the same family. Often the prospectus will allow for a negotiable charge of between 0% and 2%. You should not usually expect to pay for occasional switches.

  However, in order to control costs for the typical investor, many mutual fund companies are now charging a small fee for trades above a minimum level in a bid to ensure that market timers and sector players pay for their own excessive trading.
- **GST.** Don't forget that the act of managing money on the investor's behalf is a service and is therefore subject to GST.

Building Your Personalized Portfolio

Now we get down to the business of building a portfolio that is customized to your needs and goals. We're going to provide you with 24 specific portfolios here: 12 are RRSP, and 12 are non-RRSP or non-registered. We have distinguished six types of portfolios:

1. Very conservative
2. Very to moderately conservative
3. Middle-of-the-road (moderately conservative)
4. Moderate to high growth
5. High growth
6. Aggressive

These portfolios have been developed in consultation with experts in the field of modern portfolio theory and strategic asset allocation. We hope you'll find them helpful as you put together your own personalized portfolio.

Remember two key things as you read on. First, these are examples intended as a guide; for your personal needs, you should seek assistance from an experienced, professional financial advisor. It's too big and important a decision to be making without some experienced professional help. Second, this asset mix decision is the most important decision you'll make. It will account for about 90% of the returns of your portfolio. So take time here, get assistance, and do it right.

Earlier, we identified two key factors that you can use in deciding the right allocation between the two major asset categories of fixed income and equities: your age and risk tolerance, identified on a scale from 1 to 10.

A more sophisticated method of determining the asset mix that's right for you is to complete one or more of the client profile questionnaires that have been produced in the last few years by various fund companies and brokerage houses. The one we like best was developed by Garmaise Investment Technologies in support of Mackenzie's STAR Strategic Asset Allocation Program. By completing the STAR Investor Profile, investors will learn the appropriate asset mix for them based on their response to about 15 questions. While the appropriate asset mix will be identified within STAR's 17 portfolio offerings, the data can also be used to put your own portfolio together, based on our guidelines for the creation of 24 personalized portfolios.

On the next page are six model RRSP/RRIF portfolios. Note that they all contain 30% foreign content and no real estate.

For our six model non-registered accounts shown on the next page, we are guided by long-term research studies indicating that in very conservative portfolios, the ideal overall mix of Canadian to foreign content is about 55% Canadian and 45% foreign. This appears to be the ideal "trade-off" between

Registered Accounts (RRSP/RRIF)

Asset Category	Type of Portfolio					
	Very Conservative	Very to Moderately Conservative	Middle of the Road	Moderate to High Growth	High Growth	Aggressive
Short Term	20%	25%	19%	0%	0%	0%
Canadian Fixed Income	32%	28%	24%	27%	24%	0%
Global Fixed Income	30%	29%	17%	15%	0%	0%
Canadian Equity	18%	22%	27%	42%	46%	70%
U.S. Equity	0%	0%	0%	9%	10%	10%
International Equity	0%	1%	13%	6%	20%	20%
Real Estate	0%	0%	0%	0%	0%	0%
Total	**100%**	**100%**	**100%**	**100%**	**100%**	**100%**
Foreign Content	30%	30%	30%	30%	30%	30%

Diversification Reduces Risk and Improves Return 1984–1996

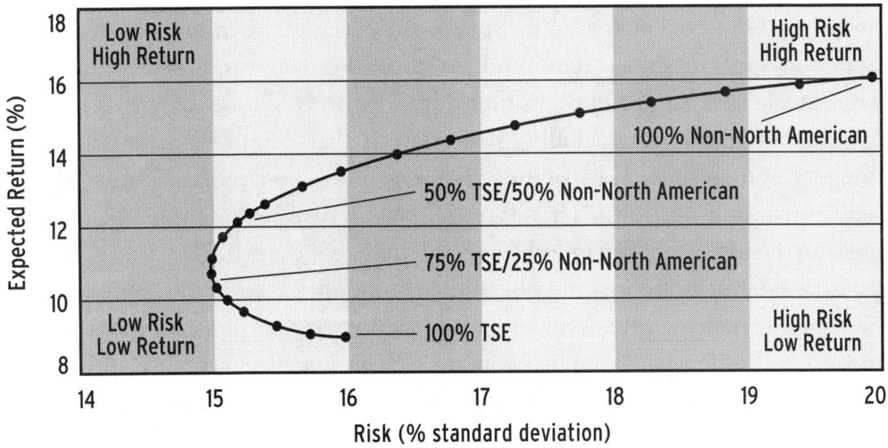

SOURCE: Assante Advisory Services

risk and reward. More growth-oriented portfolios incorporate more foreign content and, correspondingly, more short-term volatility.

The following table on page 62 shows six non-RRSP/RRIF portfolios with no real estate weighting:

Non-Registered Accounts (Non-RRSP/RRIF)

Asset Category	Type of Portfolio					
	Very Conservative	Very to Moderately Conservative	Middle of the Road	Moderate to High Growth	High Growth	Aggressive
Short Term	25%	20%	16%	4%	1%	0%
Canadian Fixed Income	21%	17%	16%	17%	9%	0%
Global Fixed Income	24%	19%	16%	13%	8%	0%
Canadian Equity	11%	9%	10%	11%	10%	7%
U.S. Equity	14%	21%	25%	33%	41%	51%
International Equity	5%	14%	17%	22%	31%	42%
Real Estate	0%	0%	0%	0%	0%	0%
Total	**100%**	**100%**	**100%**	**100%**	**100%**	**100%**
Foreign Content	43%	54%	58%	68%	80%	93%

The practical limitation to including real estate in the ideal portfolio is that there are so few real estate funds currently available in Canada. Having said that, we know that research suggests the inclusion of real estate in a well-balanced portfolio. One reason for doing so is its correlation with stocks and bonds. Generally speaking, real estate tends to do well during times of high inflation, while stocks and bonds tend to suffer during periods of inflation.

Another reason for including real estate is that it represents another asset category and as such it distributes your eggs into another basket and helps to reduce risk in a portfolio. Therefore, on page 63 we include the 12 portfolios presented earlier, this time modified to include real estate.

Real estate can be included by adding some of the few real estate funds in Canada—Dynamic, Investors, and Royal LePage are all players in this field—real estate limited partnerships, commercial property, or rental property. Real estate is the world's largest asset category and there should be consideration given to including it in a well-diversified portfolio. This is an advisable action even though the choice of real estate funds is currently quite limited, many real estate limited partnerships have struggled, and commercial or rental real estate has not always been liquid or ideal.

See page 63 for are our six model RRSP/RRIF portfolios, with real estate included.

Using these portfolio models, you can now select some of the Top Funds you wish to use to build your own personalized portfolio. Again though, we urge you to see this information as a guideline and to enlist the help of a full-time profes-

Registered Accounts (RRSP/RRIF) (Including Real Estate)

Asset Category	Type of Portfolio					
	Very Conservative	Very to Moderately Conservative	Middle of the Road	Moderate to High Growth	High Growth	Aggressive
Short Term	25%	19%	20%	4%	0%	0%
Canadian Fixed Income	30%	30%	21%	28%	2%	0%
Global Fixed Income	20%	12%	9%	2%	2%	0%
Canadian Equity	17%	21%	29%	38%	57%	70%
U.S. Equity	4%	8%	10%	14%	14%	15%
International Equity	1%	5%	6%	9%	9%	10%
Real Estate	5%	5%	5%	5%	5%	5%
Total	**100%**	**100%**	**100%**	**100%**	**100%**	**100%**
Foreign Content	30%	30%	30%	30%	30%	30%

sional advisor to assist you in making the best decisions. Remember, this asset mix decision is the most important investment decision you will make, so it's vital to get it right, and then to monitor and rebalance it when necessary to keep on track!

Finally, here are our six model non-RRSP/RRIF portfolios, with real estate included:

Non-Registered Accounts (Non-RRSP/RRIF) (Including Real Estate)

Asset Category	Type of Portfolio					
	Very Conservative	Very to Moderately Conservative	Middle of the Road	Moderate to High Growth	High Growth	Aggressive
Short Term	24%	19%	13%	6%	0%	0%
Canadian Fixed Income	21%	14%	10%	9%	3%	0%
Global Fixed Income	21%	21%	16%	11%	7%	0%
Canadian Equity	10%	7%	9%	4%	1%	1%
U.S. Equity	14%	21%	28%	36%	48%	55%
International Equity	6%	12%	15%	22%	26%	39%
Real Estate	4%	6%	9%	12%	15%	5%
Total	**100%**	**100%**	**100%**	**100%**	**100%**	**100%**
Foreign Content	50%	63%	70%	83%	96%	99%

Mutual Fund Checkup

Is your fund portfolio a mess? Many are. Many investors acquire funds like groceries; they buy whatever strikes their fancy at a particular moment. They end up with too many funds, too much paperwork, and no real plan. Here are some questions to consider to identify whether you're making some of the more common mistakes:

> research **news**
>
> **How Many Funds to Own**
>
> Most academic studies have put the number of individual stocks necessary for sufficient diversification at 25 to 40. Because the average growth fund in the U.S. holds 78 securities, it is generally believed that there are no further diversification benefits to holding more than one mutual fund.
>
> While the traditional use of standard deviation as a risk measure supports this view, using the "dispersion in terminal period wealth" as a risk measure reveals that holding *as few as four growth funds* will reduce the dispersion in wealth for 5- to 19-year holding periods by half, and will reduce the downside risk.
>
> These conclusions are particularly important for investors who are investing for fixed horizon goals (e.g., retirement, capital purchases). Even if we were to double the number of funds listed here, the conclusion suggests that the outside number of funds to hold is about eight for purposes of diversification.
>
> Edward S. O'Neal, "How Many Mutual Funds Constitute a Diversified Mutual Fund Portfolio?" *Financial Analysts' Journal* (March/April 1997).

Is Your Asset Allocation Off Balance?

Asset allocation is by far the most important determinant of how your investments perform over time, so don't ignore it. Some investors hope that great funds in a random mix will help them prosper. But even owning great funds (in the wrong asset categories) can sink you. Achieving a balanced portfolio is critical to reducing risk and making more money. Use the simple Age Rule guide on page 40 or an asset allocation questionnaire like Mackenzie's STAR to determine your optimal asset allocation. Re-jig within the same families you already own to achieve a more appropriate mix if necessary.

Are You Using Too Much Leverage?

One financial planning firm in Ontario advocates a ton of leverage for most client accounts. That approach has worked well as funds have risen and interest rates have fallen. The tax deductibility of investment borrowing adds to the appeal of the leveraging strategy (see The Leveraging Strategy section on page 224 for more details). But going forward, excessive leverage can be dangerous. Use the one-third rule (even if you're aggressive): Be certain to borrow no more than one-third of the value of your total investment portfolio. And don't allow debt payments from your own income (not income on the funds) to exceed one-third of your total income.

Do You Own Too Many Funds?

While there's no magic number of funds investors should own, here's a sensible guideline that can help you keep your records simple and your wallet fat: Never own two funds that do the same thing. Just because you're uncomfortable with a big chunk going into, say, one broad Asian fund doesn't mean that you should buy four to mitigate risk. Better to buy a Japanese fund—historically they have actually shown a negative correlation to Asian funds, and this correlation is a real risk-reducer. More than a dozen funds creates a mess for most people. We try to keep positions to no less than $10,000 per fund.

Are You Tax-Backwards?

Too many investors hold GICs outside their RRSP, and they get the full tax whack. Then those same investors hold equities inside their RRSP, considering them a long-term investment that's naturally suited to the retirement account. It's better to reverse this situation, holding equities (which are tax advantaged by nature) in an open account where the tax benefits can be realized. Then hold the bonds or GICs inside the RRSP where they'll grow tax-free until retirement.

Portfolio Management Programs

Asset Allocation Funds and Services

With the continuing growth in technology and increasing public awareness of portfolio management theory and practice, the diversification concept underlying balanced funds has evolved into a sophisticated range of asset allocation funds and services now available to Canadian investors.

There are two dramatically different types of asset allocation funds or services available. Although they share the same function—asset allocation—they are worlds apart philosophically, so you should know the difference between them and what it is you are buying.

The first philosophy is *tactical* asset allocation. Using this market timing approach, the manager attempts to move into the right asset group at the right time based on forecasts of superior short-term market performance. These funds differ from balanced funds in that their approach is frequently more quantitative and they tend to trade more frequently. Typically they have the right to invest 100% in cash, bonds, or equities. As such, their returns can be much more volatile than the average balanced fund, but when they are successful, they can also achieve much higher returns.

Tactical asset allocation is implemented either directly in a fund through purchases of appropriate securities or by switching between members of a fund family. AGF, for example, has its Canadian and American tactical funds, which buy and sell stocks, bonds, and cash within the fund, as well as its Canadian Asset Allocation Service, which implements its strategies using three of their Canadian funds.

The second approach is *strategic* asset allocation. Unlike the tactical philosophy, which tries to time the market—making one market call for all investors—strategic asset allocation defines an optimal portfolio for investors based on their individual risk tolerance, age, return needs, and the like. In fact, clients must complete a detailed questionnaire to properly identify their needs.

The optimal portfolio is based on quantitative models of long-term returns, volatility, and patterns of movement among the asset classes, and the manager strives to achieve the highest possible return for a given level of risk. Hence, a range of portfolios is identified, from very conservative to very aggressive, and a client is directed to the portfolio that best suits his or her needs.

The section on portfolio management programs later in this chapter will explore in depth these exciting new investment alternatives.

One of the main problems with building a Top Funds portfolio is having both the inclination and the time to do it. Creating an appropriate asset allocation and choosing the appropriate funds can be a difficult task. Ongoing monitoring of the managers, rebalancing the portfolios when capital markets conditions change, and accurately determining your own personal risk/return relationship can be almost impossible to accomplish without professional help. Many Canadians use an investment advisor or financial planning professional. For an increasing number of Canadians, however, the solution now also includes the new kid on the investment block. Known variously as wrap accounts, asset allocation services, fee-based investing, or portfolio management programs, these services or programs are becoming a popular alternative to the traditional approach to mutual fund investing.

These programs have some features in common: They have replaced transaction-oriented commission structures with annual fees; they use asset allocation methodologies that replace ad hoc investment picking with research-based processes; they create custom portfolios that more closely meet client needs; and some programs also rebalance the portfolios automatically, as well as provide tax optimization. More about these later.

However, there are also many differences. Investors can choose from programs offered by banks, mutual fund companies, or stockbrokers. While some use in-house, proprietary products, others use public funds. A few use both in-house and public funds. Investment minimums range from $500 to $500,000 and the degree of customization extends from only one portfolio choice with Dynamic Fund of Funds, through 16 for Mackenzie's STAR program, to "the sky's the limit" for most high-end programs. Fees also vary widely. Some programs levy a fee that covers everything. Others charge a fee on top of the underlying fund management expense ratios, while a few don't charge a separate fee at all.

There are many different approaches available to Canadian investors, and new programs are being announced almost every day. Many of the programs cater to the high net worth investor, usually defined as someone with $500,000 in investments. Luckily, the advent of lower-cost computer software and more efficient investment methods have allowed the introduction of programs that cater to the average Canadian mutual fund investor. We'll focus on these programs—those that have minimum investment thresholds of $100,000 or less. We've also broken them down into two broad categories—those that take the packaged approach and those that apply the custom portfolio (see the tables on pages 71–73 and 76–77).

Getting Your Feet Wet: The Packaged Approach

Henry Ford once said, "People can have the Model T in any colour, so long as it's black." In the same vein, the packaged approach to asset allocation says that people can have their choice of asset allocation, so long as they fit into one of five (or six or seven) investor profiles. With the packaged approach, the minimum investment amount is usually low, but the degree of customization is also quite low. The available choices start with the "fund of funds" approach, which, as the name implies, is a mutual fund that invests in other mutual funds. At the next level, individual mutual funds are packaged into a portfolio, usually at a higher cost than the "fund of funds" programs.

Profiling Your Risk Tolerance

Most programs offer a selection of portfolios that the investor can choose from. Many also use a questionnaire or investor profile to determine the investor's risk-versus-return profile and to recommend an appropriate portfolio. A well-designed questionnaire can be a very useful tool, and we recommend it. The risk profile of an investor is difficult to determine accurately without one. The following programs use a questionnaire:

- Altamira Managed RSP Portfolio
- CIBC Choice Funds
- First Canadian MatchMaker
- Great West Life Discovery
- Loring Ward Artisan
- Mackenzie STAR/MRS Keystone
- Scotia Autopilot
- Spectrum United Portfolio
- Talvest/Maritime Life Synchrony

> surfing
> **the web**
>
> The *FundLibrary* is an excellent resource Web site for investors. It provides updates on mutual fund industry news and it has a comprehensive database on mutual fund prices and rates of return, as well as an online store where investors can purchase over 40 books on mutual funds and investing. The Learning Centre section offers investors 500 links to other sites. There is also something for neophyte investors called "Mutual Funds 101," a comprehensive introduction to the topic. If Canadian mutual fund investors could access only one investment Web site, this would be our choice.
>
> **www.fundlibrary.com**

The Synchrony questionnaire asks only four questions. In fact, an investor requiring income from the portfolio is steered towards an appropriate portfolio after answering only one question. In contrast, STAR and Keystone both use a detailed 15-question investor profile, which is based on the asset allocation research of program manager Gordon Garmaise. The CIBC Choice Funds questionnaire, SAM or Strategic Asset Manager, is interactive and is available to investors on CIBC's Web site. Similarly, the Spectrum United questionnaire is on its Web site.

Rebalancing Your Portfolio

The role of the portfolio management program manager shouldn't end once the investor agrees to the initial asset allocation recommendation. The initial asset allocation will change as markets ebb and flow. For example, let's look at a simple portfolio that consists of 50% bonds and 50% stocks. If the stock market goes up 20% and the bond markets fall by 20% over the course of the year, that initial 50–50 asset allocation would change to 60% stocks and 40% bonds. This is a more aggressive portfolio than the original mix, and a prudent investor would sell some stocks and buy bonds to bring the mix back to normal. This action is known as *rebalancing*. It helps reduce portfolio volatility and provides the additional benefit of selling high and buying low, a much desired but seldom achieved investment strategy. (See also the Rebalancing Your Portfolio section on pages 222–223.)

Many programs offer portfolio rebalancing as part of their services. The frequency of rebalancing and the degree of asset mix variation that triggers the rebalancing process vary from program to program. For example, the CIBC Choice Funds program monitors investor holdings on a regular basis, and makes adjustments when necessary. Great West reviews the Discovery portfolio profiles on an annual basis, and may make changes when necessary. This is not individual account rebalancing *per se*, but rather a change in asset allocation targets based on revised capital markets expectations. Mackenzie STAR and Keystone reallocate client portfolios automatically, while Scotia Autopilot investors receive quarterly rebalancing. First Canadian MatchMaker portfolios are periodically monitored, and rebalancing occurs, if necessary, every six months. Loring Ward Artisan rebalances daily by allocating fund cash flows to maintain the appropriate portfolio weightings.

Choosing Your Portfolio Management Program (Part 1)

Most of the portfolio management programs available to Canadian investors are based on the strategic asset allocation research and modern portfolio theory that we discussed earlier in the section on Building Your Personalized Portfolio, starting on page 59. There are, however, many variations in how the research is applied. The table on the following pages looks at what's available.

The Next Level: Custom Portfolios

Our review up to now has looked at what are really semicustom programs. Each program offers portfolios that are created for a particular risk/return profile. Investors are slotted into the appropriate category, with no discussion about unique needs, unusual tax situations, or other circumstances that might have a significant impact on the best investment approach to take. For custom portfolios, we must go to the next level.

Like their junior counterparts, these portfolio management programs vary greatly, and it's difficult to make apples-to-apples comparisons. Fortunately, that's our job and we'll help sort out what's available to Canadian investors. We'll also point out what we feel are things to keep an eye out for.

The Packaged Approach

Program Name	Minimum	# of Portfolios	Costs	Rebalancing?	Investment Type	Web Site
Altamira Managed RSP Portfolios	$10,000	7	$50 (note: In addition to MERs of individual funds in each portfolio)	Yes	Altamira mutual funds	www.altamira.com
CIBC Active Portfolio Rebalancing Services (A-PRS)	$500	14	MERs of individual funds in each portfolio	Yes	CIBC mutual funds TAL Global Asset Management	www.cibc.com
CIBC Portfolio Rebalancing Services (PRS)	$500 per fund	14	MERs of individual funds in each portfolio	Yes	CIBC mutual funds TAL Global Asset Management	www.cibc.com
CIBC Choice Funds	$25,000	10	1.50% on 1st $49,999 1.25% on next $50,000 1.00% on next $50,000 0.75% on assets over $149,000 (note: In addition to MERs of individual funds in each portfolio)	Yes	Third party mutual funds CIBC mutual funds TAL Global Asset Management Gordon Pape	www.cibc.com
Dundee Fund of Funds	$1,000	1	2.40%	No	Dynamic mutual funds	www.dundeefunds.com
First Canadian Matchmaker	$1,000	14	MERs of individual funds in each portfolio	Yes	First Canadian mutual funds	www.bmo.com
Great West Life Discovery	$300	5	2.94% to 2.46%	No	Great West Life seg. funds	www.gwl.ca

The Packaged Approach (continued)

Program Name	Minimum	# of Portfolios	Costs	Rebalancing?	Investment Type	Web Site
Loring Ward Artisan	$2,000	15	MERs of individual funds in each portfolio plus management fee 0.25%	Yes	Third party mutual funds	www.loringward.com
Mackenzie STAR	$2,500	17	0.10% of total assets ($100 maximum) (note: In addition to MERs of individual funds in each portfolio)	Yes	Mackenzie mutual funds	www.mackenziefinancial.com
MRS Keystone	$2,500	10	0.10% of total assets ($100 maximum) (note: In addition to MERs of individual funds in each portfolio)	Yes	Third party mutual funds	www.mackenziefinancial.com
Opus 2 Direct	$10,000	15	MER 1.85%	No	Third party mutual funds Opus 2 William M. Mercer	www.opus2direct.com
Primerica Concert Allocation Series	$500	9	MERs of individual funds in each portfolio	No	AGF Group of Funds Salomon Smith Barney	www.primerica.com
Scotia Co-Pilot	$5,000	5	$25 per account (note: In addition to MERs of individual funds in each portfolio)	Yes	Scotia mutual funds	www.scotiabank.ca

The Packaged Approach (continued)

Program Name	Minimum	# of Portfolios	Costs	Rebalancing?	Investment Type	Web Site
The Scotia Leaders Program	$10,000	2	MERs of individual funds in each portfolio plus asset allocation fee 1% on $10,000 to $50,000 0.75% on $50,001 to $100,000 0.50% on $100,001 plus	Yes	Chand Carmichael & Co. Ltd.	www.scotiabank.ca
Spectrum United Portfolio	$500	6	1.65% to 2.25%	No	Spectrum United mutual funds	www.spectrumunited.ca
Talvest/Maritime Life Synchrony	$500	5	2.85% to 3.10%	No	Maritime Life and Talvest mutual and seg. funds	www.maritimelife.ca
TD Fund Smart Managed Portfolios	$2,000 RSP $5,000 non-RSP	N/A	MERs of individual funds in each portfolio	Yes, after 60 days' notice	Third party mutual funds TD Asset Management William M. Mercer	www.tdbank.ca
TD Green Line Managed Portfolios	$2,000 RSP $5,000 non-RSP	6	MERs of individual funds in each portfolio	Yes, after 60 days' notice	TD Green Line mutual funds William M. Mercer	www.tdbank.ca
TD Green Line Managed Index Portfolios	$2,000 RSP $5,000 non-RSP	N/A	MERs of individual funds in each portfolio	Yes, after 60 days' notice	TD Green Line Index funds William M. Mercer	www.tdbank.ca

> surfing
> **the web**
>
> Here is another great site, and we aren't just saying that because we're teamed up with them! Here you'll find Canada's most comprehensive mutual fund analysis, research, and sales software. This site is updated monthly with the ratings that you see here in the book. It is quick and easy to understand, and you can track your portfolio daily. It also includes some interesting commentary from noted figures in the industry on an ongoing basis. If you are so inclined, links include Morningstar USA, Japan, and Australia.
>
> **www.morningstar.ca**

Pooled Funds or Mutual Funds?

Many programs use *pooled* funds instead of mutual funds as their investment vehicle. It really doesn't make a difference. Both approaches "pool" individual investor contributions into a big lump of cash that can be managed more efficiently. The securities regulations that relate to pooled funds are less onerous, and therefore are usually a little cheaper for an investment manager to operate. Pooled funds also usually charge their fees directly to the investor, while most mutual funds charge their fees to the fund itself. This reduces the reported rate of return of the investor by the amount of the fees. Pooled funds are also "pure." Unlike a regular mutual fund that usually has some cash on board, as well as some foreign content for RRSP purposes, pooled funds aren't intended to be stand-alone investments. A Canadian equity pool will be made up of 100% Canadian equities—nothing else.

Segregated Funds or Pooled Funds?

Don't get confused! Segregated investments in this case refer to whether your individual investments are held separately in your name by your broker, or whether they are held in pooled (or mutual fund) form. They have nothing to do with the life insurance investment products.

Some professionals argue that having segregated investments allows maximum customization for the investor. Theoretically, each individual investment is purchased for that client and that client alone. In fact, in most instances, a good investment for one client is a good investment for another. Costs are an issue. Bulk purchases—whether stocks or toilet paper—are cheaper than buying individual units. Transaction costs, including brokerage fees and commissions, should be lower for pooled investments than for segregated accounts.

Efficient portfolio diversification can be affected by pooled purchases. Smaller portfolios may require only a few hundred dollars of each security if the diversification process is thorough enough. Purchasing a small amount of stocks on, for example, the Singapore Stock Exchange would be prohibitively expensive. Most portfolio managers wouldn't bother and a less than perfectly diversified portfolio would result.

The reality is that most programs that promote their segregated approach to money management still use pools for their international investing. The majority of programs with investment minimums of $100,000 or less use pools exclusively. However, the segregated portfolio approach does allow for a greater degree of customization. If you own a particular stock and you don't want to sell it—whether for tax or sentimental reasons—then many segregated programs can accommodate you. Pools are usually less flexible.

Investment Policy Statement (IPS)

We think an IPS is important. Most portfolio management programs at this level provide an IPS and usually rely on a combination of questionnaires and advisor input for their creation. Some investment policy statements are produced manually by the advisor, others are generated automatically by the program software, and a few are created by specialists employed by the program manager. Each approach has its advantages. The key is ensuring that the resultant document truly reflects the investor's unique circumstances.

Tax Optimization

Higher net worth investors are more likely to have investments outside of their RRSPs and RRIFs. For them, the whole issue of after-tax returns takes on a lot more importance. The asset allocation process should take your personal tax rate into account, as well as the different tax rates for dividends, capital gains, and interest rates. Most of the programs do address this issue and make portfolio recommendations accordingly. A few take the "family of accounts" approach, which acknowledges that most Canadians treat their household accounts as one portfolio. If each family member has a different tax rate and if there are RRSPs, RESPs, trusts, or holding company accounts, then the tax issues become a lot more complicated, and the asset allocation requires more thought.

Choosing Your Portfolio Management Program (Part 2)

The following table shows what's available:

The Next Step: Custom Portfolios

Name	Minimum	Fees	Investment Policy Statement?	Automatic Rebalancing?	Questionnaire?	Asset Classes	Web Site
AGF Harmony	$70,000	2.25% advisory fee MER 0.25% to 0.80% max	No	Yes	Yes	5 asset classes 10 managers 7 pools	www.agf.com
AGF Private Investment Management	$500,000	1.25% on 1st million 1% on next $2 million 0.75% on next $2 million 0.50% on remaining balance plus custody fee of 0.11%	Yes	No	Yes	1 manager	www.agf.com
C.I. Insight	$75,000	2.20% on 1st $250,000 2.00% on $250,000 to $500,000 accts 1.85% on $500,001 to $1 million 1.70 $1 million+ plus MER 0.25% to 1.2% max	Yes	No, but recommended when variance is 5%	Yes	6 asset classes 13 managers 15 pools	www.cifunds.com
CIBC Trust Index Portfolio Services (IPS)	$100,000	0.90% to 1.25% (depends on asset mix), plus MERs	No	Yes, daily	Yes	6 asset classes 8 funds	www.cibc.com
CIBC Trust Personal Portfolio	$100,000	0.80% to 2.25% (depends on asset mix), plus MERs	No	No	Yes	5 asset classes 1 manager	www.cibc.com

The Next Step: Custom Portfolios (continued)

Name	Minimum	Fees	Investment Policy Statement?	Automatic Rebalancing?	Questionnaire?	Asset Classes	Web Site
Dynamic Mutual Funds Viscount Wealth Management Program	$100,000	2.50% advisory fee on $100,000, plus MER	Yes	No	Yes	8 asset classes 5 pools	www.dundee funds.com
Loring Ward Optima Strategy	$100,000	2.40% to 3.15% (depends on asset mix) Fee reduction after $250,000	Yes	Yes, quarterly	Yes	8 asset classes 11 managers	www.loring ward.com
Merrill Lynch Horizons	$100,000	1.50% to 3.0% on 1st $500,000 (depends on asset mix)	Yes	No	Yes	4 asset classes 13 managers 26 strategies	www.canada. ml.com
Nesbitt Burns Quadrant	$50,000	2.00% to 2.50% (depends on asset mix)	Yes	Yes	Yes	6 asset classes 23 managers	www.nesbitt burns.com
RBC Sovereign	$50,000	2.50% advisory fee plus MER, max of 1.23%	Yes	No	Yes	7 asset classes 18 styles 19 managers	www.rbcds.com
Scotia McLeod Pinnacle Program	$50,000	2.50% on 1st $250,000 2.25% up to $500,000 2% on $500,001 to $1 million 1.5% on $1 million+ plus MER 0.5% max	Yes	No	Yes	5 asset classes 11 managers 12 funds	www.scotia capital.com

Our View

We like asset allocation programs. We are firm believers in diversification and in investment processes that result from academic research and analyses. However, as our review indicates clearly, each portfolio management program available to Canadian investors is different: different fees, different approaches, different investments. Our advice to you is to ask a lot of questions and to find out exactly what you're getting and for what actual cost. Due diligence is a must.

Good luck!

3

The Top Funds Selection Method

In Search of "Real" Performance

Take a look at any mutual fund advertisement and chances are you'll find a lot of impressive numbers that attest to the fund's performance over the past six months, a year, three years, or five years—all of which makes the fund look like a pretty attractive investment. But take a look at the fine print down near the bottom of the ad, which usually reads something like this: "The performance data represents past performance and is not necessarily indicative of future returns..."

So what gives? Well, the disclaimer comes to you courtesy of your provincial securities regulator, who recognizes that performance figures can be deceiving.

Consider, for example, a fund that advertises an average annual rate of return of 65% over one year, and 25% over three years. Sounds good, doesn't it? But these figures could reflect a disturbingly roller-coaster performance record—say, a 30% loss followed by a 50% gain, followed by a 65% gain. In this scenario, you would have done fine if you had held the fund for the entire three-year period. But what if you'd panicked and sold after the first-year loss? Or if you'd sold after two years for an average gain of 2.5%?

The fact is that just about any fund can make itself look good if it chooses the right measurement period.

So are the securities regulators right? Is past performance an unreliable indicator of future performance? Well, most investors think that past performance is important. And so do we—but only if the performance is measured properly. The problem is that it's almost impossible to find that kind of performance data in conventional sources.

What Newspaper Listings Will (and Won't) Tell You

If you're one of the many people who spend hours comparing mutual funds in the monthly or quarterly surveys published by the *Globe and Mail Report on Business* or the *National Post*, then we needn't tell you how seductive past performance figures can be. Past performance is, after all, the only tangible, comparative thing investors have to go on. It's also the easiest yardstick for comparison, making it seem very easy to find the best mutual fund in the paper. Trouble is, you've then got a handle on what was the best fund over that particular period—whether that's six months or ten years. You are by no means assured of having identified what fund is "best" for investors now.

The other problem that comes from looking at past performance figures is that we often compare them over the "wrong" time periods. Our research into the use of standard time periods shows that this factor has a remarkable effect in blurring the line between good and bad funds. In some cases, we've found that reliance on these periods can be worse than useless—it can be hazardous to your wealth!

The Fatal Flaw: End-Date Bias

The rates of return for one, three, five, and ten years typically listed in the newspaper are all tied to a single ending day. To illustrate (albeit somewhat unrealistically) the weakness of this approach, let's imagine that a fund doubled in value on the day just prior to September 30, 2001—the ending date for all the data in this edition of *Top Funds*. Now, that incredible one-day return will exaggerate (upward) historic returns. It would suddenly look as though the fund had done much better over three, five, and ten years—all because of the heavy weighting unconsciously given to the most recent performance.

In fact, this example is not as far-fetched as it sounds. In mid-1998 some funds were posting one-year returns of 50% to 80%. Their historical performance appeared (as in the case above) to suggest that these funds had done well over the long term. The result of the postings was that the funds attracted a lot of investors, many of whom were unaware of the cyclical market forces that are inevitably poised to cool down those super-hot funds in a big hurry.

The Solution: Multi-Period Composites

To determine the Top Funds featured in this book, we've developed a simple mathematical model that eliminates end-date bias, and allows us to evaluate the past performance of funds in a fairer and much more informative way.

We call this approach the Multi-Period Composite (MPC), and it is not unlike the scoring system used to place athletes in multisports events such as the decathlon. Let's explore this analogy a little further.

In the decathlon, we don't add up the number of seconds that an athlete spends running the 100-metre and 400-metre events, and compare that sum with the sums of the other athletes. We treat the events separately. Why? Simply because a one-second difference in the 100-metre run is vastly more significant than a comparable difference in the 400-metre run.

Consequently, decathletes are awarded scores that reflect relative performance within each of their respective events. The overall winner is the individual whose average "place" is the highest.

Think of each year as a decathlon event and different mutual funds as decathletes, and you have the essence of the MPC approach. Not only does the MPC treat time periods as independent, incomparable events—which, after all, they are—it also ranks only similar types of funds.

For example, each Canadian equity fund is ranked against other Canadian equity funds for as many years as the fund has been in existence—up to a maximum of ten years (far back enough to include two market cycles). Then we just average the ranks to find the Top Funds.

In the decathlon, the best athletes are those who are consistent. It's tough to win the decathlon with a first in jumps but a last-place finish in sprints. Likewise with mutual funds. It's better to do pretty well in most periods and eventually earn a rank that is better than most than it is to do spectacularly at some times then horribly in others.

So past performance, properly measured, really does provide useful clues about the future.

But is that all there is to finding tomorrow's best funds? Certainly not, although it's the first and most important step—if only because it eliminates over 80% of mutual funds from eligibility for *Top Funds 2002*. The result is that even before refining our shortlist with more qualitative tests (which we'll get to later), we now have a nucleus of funds that have proven themselves consistent performers and as such they represent strong investment choices.

research news

Why Consistency is Our Top Fund #1 Qualifier

We value the consistency of a fund's returns highly and here's why: Research published in the *Journal of Portfolio Management* concludes that consistency of returns is a good indicator of future performance. The researcher found that the key to consistent returns was diversification and, interestingly, high asset turnover. The conclusion was that "consistency, especially if measured over five-year periods, appears to be a successful tool for selecting managers who will offer superior performance in the future. Ranking solely by cumulative returns does not appear to offer predictability of future performance."

Scott D. Stewart, "Is Consistency of Performance a Good Measure of Manger Skill?" *Journal of Portfolio Management* 24, no. 3 (Spring 1998).

Assessing the Winners

Every fund within our Top Fund group can be quite justifiably described as a "winner" within its asset category. However, the funds vary considerably in terms of size, longevity, current security holdings, availability of other funds in the same fund family, and volatility.

Therefore, although our Multi-Period Composite analysis substantially delineates the winners, it would be simplistic to rate funds on this measure alone. Instead, we've supplemented our MPC analysis with other quantitative as well as qualitative reviews. We have categorized these qualifiers under the headings of consistency, risk, reward-to-risk relationship, efficiency, and style.

Top Fund Qualifier #1: Consistency

Consistency involves performance in both good and bad markets. It also considers the consistency of people—that is, the people at the helm of the fund. Ideally we're looking for no turnover at all (or very little turnover) among managers, research assistants, and others.

Let's examine each of these consistency factors in turn.

Performance

The MPC system evaluates a fund's performance history. Consequently, an older fund that had a few rough years in the beginning may not score as well as a younger fund—even if both funds performed equally well in more recent years. How do we overcome this "unfairness"? One way is to deconstruct the MPC formula, examining the performance rankings of each Top Fund relative to those in the same group for a given number of recent time periods.

For each category in the Top Funds listings, we provide comparative performance rankings for the years 1991 to September 30, 2001. This is shown graphically as a matrix consisting of 11 columns, each representing a year in the aforementioned time periods, and four rows, each representing the "performance quartile" for the time period. Consider the following example:

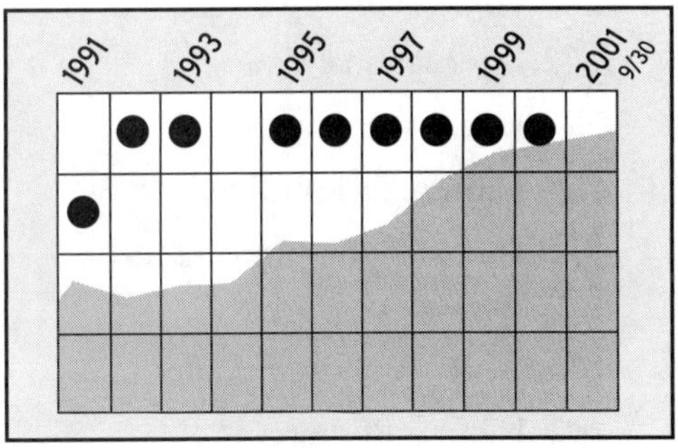

Here we see that in 1991, the fund started in the second performance quartile. In other words, it performed better than 50% of the funds (those in the third and fourth quartiles), but not as well as the 25% in the first quartile. In 1992, however, the fund moved up to the first quartile, outperforming 75% of funds in the same

top funds

close up

Why Rookies Don't Rate

There are many mutual funds available to Canadian investors that have great managers, wonderful performance, and impressive investment methodologies with one thing in common: They aren't eligible for *Top Funds 2002* consideration. We feel that performance data for anything less than 36 months is not sufficiently meaningful. Over the near term, luck can have a significant impact. Newspapers that run regular "investment challenges" invariably produce a Grade 6 student as the winner, handily outperforming the investment professionals. Similarly, a mutual fund universe of over 4,000 funds can easily produce a "winner" with stellar short-term performance based solely on a few lucky stock picks. We prefer to wait and see. If the performance continues to be superior, then, and only then, will we accept an entry for Top Fund consideration.

category. Any column with no data indicates either that the fund did not exist before this date, or that the number of funds in its category or "universe" was less than 20—quartile rankings are not meaningful below this number.

Another benefit of comparing performance over discrete (that is, non-overlapping) time periods is that it allows us to see how similar funds fared in both good and bad markets. Referring back to the figure above, note the shaded graph in the background, which indicates, in this example, the relative performance of the average Canadian equity fund.

We're using the new standardized 33 mutual fund categories as the basis for our background graphs. (The new standards replace the previous mutual fund industry practice whereby data providers created their own methods of categorizing mutual funds.) The standardized benchmarks allow "apples-to-apples" comparisons, which ensure that a fund is being assessed correctly.

The following is a list of the 33 standard categories:

1. Asia-Pacific Rim Equity
2. Asia Ex-Japan Equity
3. Canadian Tactical Asset Allocation
4. Canadian Balanced
5. Canadian Bond
6. Canadian Dividend
7. Canadian High-Income Balanced
8. Canadian Mortgage
9. Canadian Equity
10. Canadian Large-Cap Equity
11. Canadian Money Market
12. Canadian Short-Term Bond
13. Canadian Short/Mid-Cap Equity
14. Country Specific Equity
15. Emerging Markets Equity
16. European Equity
17. Foreign Bond
18. Foreign Money Market
19. Global Balanced & Asset Allocation
20. Global Equity
21. High-Yield Bond
22. International Equity
23. Japanese Equity
24. Latin American Equity
25. Labour-Sponsored Venture Capital
26. North American Equity
27. Natural Resources
28. Precious Metals
29. Real Estate
30. Science & Technology
31. Specialty/Miscellaneous
32. U.S. Equity
33. U.S. Small/Mid-Cap Equity

In our reviews of the 100 Top Funds, the shaded graph in the background is always the appropriate category average. This allows you to see how the particular fund category is performing. In the example shown above, we see that the fund's performance has been relatively consistent through a variety of market conditions.

Simply stated, the markets were bad in 1991 and 1994. So our hypothetical fund's first-quartile performance in both 1991 and 1994 demonstrates an impressive degree of consistency throughout changing market conditions.

Examining relative performance over successive time periods also allows us to note any meaningful trends that may not be obvious from a fund's MPC score alone. For example, the data may show that the performance of a highly ranked fund has declined marginally over the past few years, or that of a not-so-highly-ranked fund has improved. Either may have an effect on your investment decision.

Measuring Management Strength

Talent or Luck? Will a .400 batter hit the ball every time at bat? Probably not. And yet, such a hitter would be among the very best in the game.

Similarly, mutual fund managers provide no guarantees. But overall, a long-term investor will do well to stick with a manager or management team that has done well in the past (assuming a proper method of measurement, of course).

Poker, too, is a game of chance. On any given hand, a professional player is as likely to get a great hand as is a novice. And yet over time, the professional will win more frequently.

We think talent exists. We believe that over the long term it manifests itself in superior fund performance. How do we know that talent exists?

Well, let's take an example: Sir John Templeton turned $10,000 invested in the Templeton Growth Fund in 1954 into $5.4 million by April 30, 1999. George Soros, manager of the offshore-based Quantum

top funds

close up

Why Quartiles Change

Sharp-eyed readers have noticed that quartile rankings can change from year to year for mutual funds that are repeat Top Fund picks. A third-quartile performer for 2000 in *Top Funds 2001* may reappear this year with a second-quartile score for the same time period. Why? Blame it on the comparative fund universe, which is always evolving. Also blame it on fund mergers and consolidations, which also effects the quartile rankings. Fortunately, the new industry standards will help alleviate this problem. Funds that don't change their management style will stay in relatively static peer groups and the quartile rankings shouldn't change.

> research
> # news
> ### Fees *Do* Make A Difference
>
> The idea that mutual funds with low management expense ratios (MERs) should outperform their more expensive counterparts makes intuitive sense. Everything else being equal, lower fees should mean higher investor returns. We look at MERs when we pick our Top Funds and so should you. This information is readily available and indeed, much of the media coverage of the mutual fund industry focuses on the costs to investors of management fees and expenses.
>
> The problem is that there is a dearth of actual evidence in the real world. We haven't seen many research studies that support the "high-fees-equals-low-returns" hypothesis. Until now that is. A recent research study from the U.S. concluded that bond fund returns and expenses have a direct, one-to-one negative relationship. In other words, a 1% increase in fees results in a 1% decrease in bond fund returns. This relationship gets stronger as the investment horizon lengthens.
>
> Our own experience lends support to this research. We picked 11 Canadian bond funds as Top Funds in 2002 out of an eligible universe of 138 funds. Five of these Top Fund selections are among the ten cheapest bond funds available. Clearly, there's a relationship between costs and returns.
>
> William Reichenstein, "Bond Fund Returns and Expenses: A Study of Bond Market Efficiency," *Journal of Investing* 8, no. 4 (Winter 1999).

Fund turned U.S.$10,000 in 1969 (at the top of the market—just before the biggest bear market in history) into more than U.S.$20 million by 1996. Pure luck? We don't think so.

We believe that good managers (and good funds) can be identified by three fundamental characteristics:

1. They consistently beat the market;
2. They possess depth of talent in their management team;
3. They apply solid research in a clear process.

Many institutional investors have given up looking for good money managers who are capable of beating the market; they simply try to do as well as the market. These institutions are hiring "passive" money managers who simply "buy the market"—that is, they buy every stock that makes up the TSE 300 Composite Index (in the case of Canadian equity funds) or Standard & Poor's 500 Index (for U.S. equity funds) in proportion to the stock's weighting in that index.

Nevertheless, we believe that good managers can be identified on the basis of past performance. We think that reasonable judgment can determine whether a good manager still seems to have everything in place for future success. It is also possible to spot, and avoid, bad managers.

How do you spot bad fund managers? They exhibit opposite characteristics from the Top Funds managers:

- Their performance has been consistently below average or swings wildly between hot and cold;
- They experience high turnover of personnel because of poor environment, compensation, or structure;
- Their funds have high fees;
- They have no depth of personnel and few analysts, and usually rely on second-hand research from others instead of conducting their own.

Management Consistency. Since the performance of a mutual fund depends so much on its people, consistent management is one of the most important things to look for in a potential investment. After all, when you buy a mutual fund, you're essentially buying the talent of the team running it. If the team leaves, then everything that you've bought has changed.

In the "100 Top Funds" listing you'll find information about who manages each fund, and for how long they have done so. Investors should generally avoid those funds with recent, significant changes in management, and take the time to see how the new "hot shot" settles in.

Of course, as the saying goes, sometimes a change is as good as a rest. If there ever was a fund that would qualify for this mandate, it would be Spectrum United's Canadian Investment Fund. The oldest fund sold in Canada, it can trace its origins back to 1932, and its performance during the '70s and '80s could definitely be called sleepy. In 1996, however, Kim Shannon of AMI Partners took over the reins and used her fundamental value approach to kick-start the fund, which made its

research

news

Mutual Fund Performance Persistence: Explained at Last!

There is much debate about whether investors can create superior performing mutual fund portfolios simply by investing in last year's "hot" funds. Some studies suggest that this approach does pay dividends because fund performance does exhibit persistence from one time period to the next. Other researchers aren't convinced. Their analysis concludes that—just as the small print in the mutual fund advertisements cautions—"Past performance is not indicative of future returns." They feel that over the past decade, persistence has not persisted well.

Some new research offers support for both camps. The authors of the study conclude that persistence in fund returns disappears once the returns are adjusted for the size and style characteristics of the investments held in the fund. In other words, investors should focus on the size and style trends in the marketplace. If large caps are outperforming small caps or if growth investments are beating their value counterparts, then investors should select funds that have similar investment approaches.

F. Larry Detzel and Robert W. Weigand, "Explaining Persistence in Mutual Fund Performance," *Financial Services Review* 7, no. 1 (1998).

debut as a Top Fund in 1999. Ironically, in early 1999, Kim left AMI and joined Mercury Asset Management. Luckily for Canadian Investment Fund investors, she will continue to manage the fund.

For any Top Fund listed in this book, you can read our opinion about the management team and whether it's stable enough to make the fund a reasonable choice within its category. Other information that space does not allow us to include—but that you may wish to look into yourself—involves such facts as whether the fund manager owns a piece of the investment firm. Such managers tend to seek the best long-term results for the fund (and its investors), rather than shooting for a terrific quarter to make a good bonus.

Evaluating the Management Firm. Most often when we refer to a fund manager, we tend to think of an individual who makes all of the investment decisions. But even the most talented individuals rarely work alone; they are part of a team that works collaboratively within a management firm.

In addition to the qualities identified earlier, how do we identify a superior management firm?

- **It's been in business for 10-plus years.** Generally, it's a good sign if the firm has been in existence for at least 10 years.
- **It has a large asset base.** The firm should have enough assets under administration to buy and sell securities efficiently, and to attract the people that it needs. Look for total assets of $3 billion or more for bond managers, and $1 billion or more for equity managers.
- **It has a low turnover.** A firm should not lose more than one senior investment professional every five years. The reasons for any turnover should be closely investigated.
- **It has local expertise**. This characteristic is particularly important for specialized funds that buy stocks or bonds in overseas markets, where conditions are often quite different from those at home. Look for a firm that has investment management offices and/or advisors located in the markets where it does business.
- **It has efficient management structure.** Although difficult for nonprofessionals to measure, this factor is something we examine very closely. In an ideal situation, an individual fund manager should have full and immediate discretion—within the limits of the fund's overall investment objectives—to react to rapid market changes. In more bureaucratically structured firms, a

manager might have to wait for a committee meeting before taking action. Meanwhile, buying or selling opportunities could be missed.

Top Fund Qualifier #2: Risk

While properly constructed performance statistics provide a good measure of how well a fund has done (and may do), they're less informative about the likelihood of the fund doing badly at any given time. This type of worst-case evaluation is now being pioneered in the U.S. by academics and investment practitioners. It's called *downside risk*, and we believe that in a few years it will be as popular an investment buzzword as asset allocation is today.

In the *Top Funds 2002* listings we've laid out some easy-to-understand indicators of a fund's downside risk:

- How often a fund has beaten five-year GICs
- How often a fund has lost money
- A fund's worst annual return

Taken together, these indicators provide a more common sense picture of risk than accepted statistical measures such as standard deviation. And they're easier to understand!

Why Standard Deviation Isn't the Only Measure of Risk

The mutual fund industry is letting investors down. It's continuing to support the use of a one-risk measure—one that unknowingly misleads you by not telling you just how risky a fund really is. The measure in question is *standard deviation*, which shows how widely a fund's monthly returns vary, or deviate, from a calculated norm, usually over a three-year trailing period. Standard deviation is the basis of the volatility scale used in most newspapers' monthly mutual fund tables. It's so widely accepted that few question its validity or usefulness.

But standard deviation alone doesn't do the job. It fails to distinguish between volatility associated with making money (gains) and volatility associated with losses—punishing a fund that makes money equally with a fund that loses money.

Standard deviation rewards consistent losers and punishes erratic gainers. Academics think using it as the only risk measure for investment performance can be problematic unless its limitations are understood.

Don't believe us? There are dozens of high-end journal articles with powerful arguments against standard deviation. And of course, as the regulators say, "nobody understands risk."

Understanding risk, in our view, is the most important determinant of your performance as an investor. When you lose money in a fund that you didn't figure would go down—or go down by much—you're more likely to sell at the bottom. Why? Because all too often, investors buy at the peak and sell at the first setback. Dalbar Inc., a Boston-based consulting firm, has conducted one of the most comprehensive studies of investor behaviour. They found that investors underperform the market by as much as 40% due to the mistiming of their purchases and redemptions.

Should investors take all the blame for buying and selling at the wrong time, or could the industry be more helpful? Here's our suggestion: We recommend that the industry tell investors more about the risk of losing money, just like *Top Funds* has done for years—how much, how often, how long.

Cambridge Special Equity Fund, for example, is a Canadian small-cap equity offering for which these new measures of risk would be especially helpful. It has a standard deviation of 9.0, about double that of most similar funds, but it is not the riskiest fund of its type.

Wouldn't it be nice to be warned that this fund lost money in four years of its nine-year history? In three of those years, it lost more than 20%, and in its worst year (1990) it lost 34.8%. In only four of the nine years did it outperform GICs.

Which Fund Is Riskier?

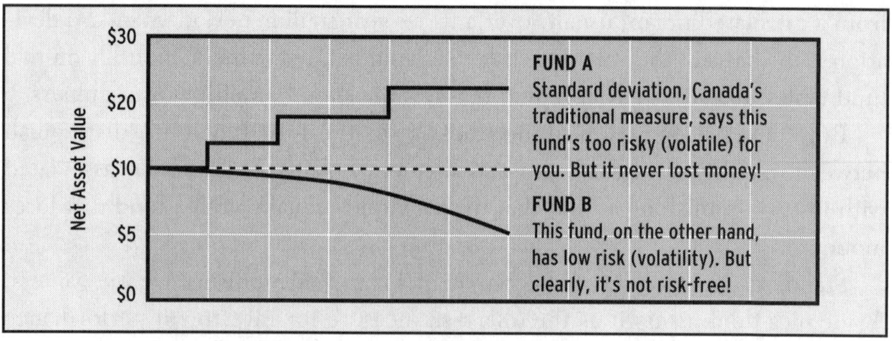

SOURCE: Assante Advisory Services

Measuring downside risk is the new wave in investment research. Downside risk is a broad term that can describe elaborate measures of a fund's likelihood of underperforming some minimum rate of return. Or it can calculate the average loss.

Overall, downside risk is a framework that often uses calculus to explain the potential for investment pain. We've used a greatly simplified downside risk framework in this book, making the concept easy to understand and calculate.

Being told in advance of the frequent, temporary set-backs that even good funds suffer might help people weather those downturns better. Or it might scare the nervous nellies away. Either result is a good thing for both the investor and the industry.

Making new risk measures mandatory won't solve all of the industry's problems. And these risk profiles will apply only to mature funds—those with a history of four or more years. A disclaimer would have to be drafted for newer funds.

But we believe the fund industry owes it to investors to better disclose past risk along with those seductive past returns it usually trumpets. And investors should start to demand more useful information about risk when they buy a fund.

Top Fund Qualifier #3: Reward-to-Risk Relationship

Despite its shortcomings, standard deviation does provide some insight into risk. Also, history (recent history, no less) has demonstrated that funds that soar upwards even for an extended period are capable of crashing when a bear market eventually comes along.

Thus, the degree to which a fund is volatile, even on the upside, provides insight into its inherent risk—a risk that is easily disguised in a long-running bull market.

Consequently, in *Top Funds 2002*, in addition to our measurement of downside risk, we've taken a hard look at volatility. But in our ongoing effort to provide increasingly research-driven data, we've gone one step further. Measuring risk is important, but on its own, it fails to consider the reward-to-risk relationship. Here's an example to demonstrate this important point.

Let's say Fund A was 25% riskier than the typical fund in its category as measured by standard deviation. Would you consider buying it? Well, it depends on your risk profile. Maybe you would and maybe you wouldn't.

Now, what if the same Fund A had earned a return 50% higher than the average fund over a prolonged period? Would that affect your decision? It very well might. In this example, Fund A is adding value in terms of return enhancement much greater than its risk increment. If you can handle the volatility, you might want to go ahead and invest—the managers are doing their job.

This method works for poorer performing funds as well. Let's say a fund provides a return 10% less than the average in its category, yet it does so at a 30% reduction in risk. For a conservative investor, this is a better choice than the average fund, despite its lower return; it has a better reward-to-risk relationship.

The point is that risk as measured in relation to return can impact your decision on how a fund meets your needs. Think of it like an airplane trip where there is both the smoothness of the flight (that is, the volatility or risk) and the speed of getting to your destination (the returns). Measuring them together helps you select the real winners—those who get you there faster (have higher returns) with less turbulence (below average volatility).

In order to measure the reward-to-risk ratio, we've relied on the Nobel Prize–winning work of Bill Sharpe. He has developed an equation called the *Sharpe Ratio*, which measures past return relative to risk that allows comparisons between mutual funds in a similar asset category. We've used the Sharpe Ratio to rate all of our Top Funds on a three- and five-year basis in terms of their reward-to-risk relationship, where this data was available.

Then in order to make it simpler for you, we ranked the funds within their respective categories in terms of their reward-to-risk capability. We used a quartile system, so the best 25% are in quartile 1, declining to the bottom 25% in quartile 4.

Morningstar Ratings

Last year we added the Morningstar Ratings tool to assist you in assessing risk to reward as you study possible additions and deletions to your portfolio. It's back in this edition and we think you'll find it very valuable.

In the U.S., the Morningstar Ratings system is arguably the best known and most highly respected fund rating method. To receive a five-star rating by

Morningstar is akin to a papal blessing, and a fund so blessed will almost invariably use its rating widely in promotional campaigns.

In order to be able to use the Morningstar Ratings effectively, you need to know what they do—and, equally important, what they do *not* do—and what their limitations are. First of all, the ratings are not intended to provide predictions—quite the opposite. They are intended to act as a report card, showing how the fund has performed in the past compared with its peers. Further, the components of the ranking are *entirely quantitative with absolutely no qualitative considerations*. We provide the qualitative component in our commentaries on the funds after taking all the quantitative and other considerations into account. That's the role a good financial advisor plays for clients.

The overall Morningstar Rating is a fund's risk-adjusted rating for three time periods (three, five, and ten years) combined to give an assessment of each fund's rating relative to other funds in its category. This ability is what has made Morningstar such a useful tool for investors in the U.S. and this ability is what we think will make it a useful tool for Canadian investors too.

A fund's overall ranking stems from a weighted average of up to three time periods. The ten-year statistics account for 50% of the overall score, the five-year figures for 30% of the overall score, and the three-year numbers for 20%. If only five years of history are available, the five-year period is weighted 60% and the three-year period 40%. If only three years of data are available, the three-year figures alone are used. Funds less than three years old are not rated.

In descending order, the categories are as follows: Highest (five stars), Above Average (four stars), Average (three stars), Below Average (two stars), and Lowest (one star). The ratings are recalculated monthly and the number of stars may increase or decrease as a result of the most recent data available.

It's important to realize that a fund's rating can also change for reasons that have little to do with its management or absolute performance. For example, Morningstar calculates star ratings for three-, five, and ten-year periods and combines these ratings to produce the overall star rating. Sometimes funds will lose a star when they celebrate their fifth (or tenth) birthday. Why? Well, until that point, a fund's star rating is based solely on the latest three (or five) years, and when a poor performance is suddenly picked up in the five-year (or ten-year) rating, the fund's overall rating may suffer. Conversely, some funds will see their rating improve at these milestones.

One of the other features of the Morningstar Ratings is a risk-adjusted look at returns, combing both returns and risk together in one convenient measure.

Morningstar Ratings

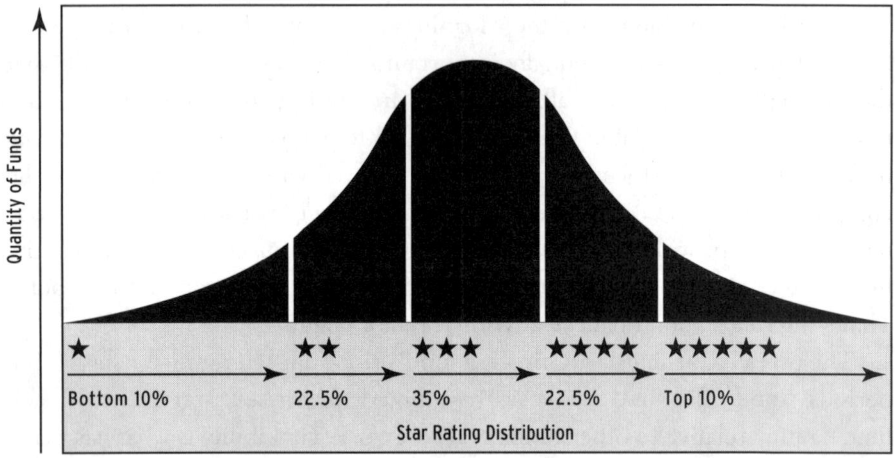

In this respect, it is similar to the Sharpe Ratio referred to earlier. That is to say, Morningstar believes, as we do, that the greatest fear for most investors is losing money (defined as underperforming the risk-free rate of return an investor can earn from guaranteed investments such as government Treasury bills). Thus, the Morningstar risk calculations focus on that downside risk only. To determine a fund's star rating for a given period (three, five, or ten years), the fund's Morningstar Risk score for that period is subtracted from its Morningstar Return score for that period.

The resulting number is plotted along a bell curve to determine that fund's rating for each time period. If the fund scores in the top 10% of the fund category it receives five stars; if it falls in the next 22.5%, it receives four stars; a spot in the middle 35% earns it three stars; those in the next 22.5% earn two stars; and those in the bottom 10% receive one star.

So, although it is critical to consider absolute performance potential and the downside risk when picking funds, it is also useful to measure the reward-to-risk relationship.

Top Fund Qualifier #4: Efficiency

The efficiency of a fund can be defined in many ways, but the term generally refers to fees and other expenses that are charged against a fund, thereby affecting its performance.

These fees are distinct from sales commissions, which are somewhat more difficult to compare, since different advisors provide different levels of service and, presumably, different levels of value for money. The bottom line is that we can't really compare the commissions paid on various funds. But we can speak about management fees.

Ultimately, it is much easier to predict a fund's fees than it is to predict a fund's investment returns. So if a fund's fees are reasonable, it is more likely—all else being equal—to do better in the future. This is especially true during periods when markets are relatively flat and every fraction of a percentage point gained or lost takes on a much greater significance.

In the *Top Funds 2002* listings we provide each fund's management expense ratio (MER), expressed as a dollar amount for every $100 in fund assets. (As you'll recall, the MER includes more than just management fees. It also includes all expenses charged to the fund, such as legal and accounting costs, custodial and safekeeping costs paid in carrying out the activities of the fund, and the costs of producing prospectuses and other reports.)

Since different types of funds require different levels of management activity, we should only compare MERs of similar funds. In the *Top Funds 2002* listings a circle accompanies each fund's MER Rating, indicating whether it is above average, average, or below average compared with similar types of funds.

research

news

Don't Confuse Me with the Facts!

Behavioural finance is a new discipline that attempts to explain the influence of human psychology on the investment process.

A recent study looked at the reasons why investors tend to sell their winning funds while simultaneously holding their losers and trading excessively. After reviewing over 88,000 randomly selected accounts at a national discount brokerage house, the authors found that newly-purchased securities underperformed recently sold securities by 3.6% over the next two years. The study also revealed that low turnover accounts produced annual returns of 18.5% while high turnover accounts returned only 11.4% annually.

The authors concluded that investor overconfidence was to blame for actively traded accounts. Investors trade because they feel that they have priviledged information or superior skills. Unfortunately, the data indicate that most investors have neither asset. The tendency to hold losers, on the other hand, is due to the "avoidance of regret" hypothesis. Most people want to avoid admitting mistakes and will therefore hold on to losing investments even when common sense dictates selling.

Brad M. Barber and Terrance Odean, "The Courage of Misguided Convictions," *Financial Analysts' Journal* 55, no.6 (November/December 1999).

How much importance should you assign to the MER rating? Chances are you won't mind paying relatively high management expenses if the investment returns are correspondingly high. But as we said earlier, a high MER can have a significant effect in poor markets.

Still, there are some real MER bargains to be had among the Top Funds. Phillips, Hager & North, for example, manage some outstanding funds with low management expense ratios.

Also consider the level of advice and service you want. Management expenses for many funds include a trailer or service fee payable to an advisor and the firm for the ongoing work on your portfolio. The majority of Canadians prefer this kind of advisory relationship, so just getting the cheapest MER isn't the goal. The objective is to obtain a portfolio of funds tailored to your needs, integrated into your tax and estate plans, and adjusted as both our dynamic world and your goals evolve.

Top Fund Qualifier #5: Style

Style—or, more specifically, investment style—refers to the basic approach that a fund's manager takes in constructing a portfolio. Among equity funds, for example, one fund manager may feel that stocks of large, established (or "blue chip") companies offer the best opportunities for returns. Another might prefer the growth potential of smaller, newer ("small cap" or "junior") enterprises. Yet another may look for stocks that, for various reasons, have been undervalued by the market. And so on.

Did we rank the Top Funds based on style? Not really, since there is no particular style that is, in all circumstances, better than the rest. Still, investment style is important to consider when selecting one or more funds to add to your portfolio. There are several reasons for this:

A fund's investment style should be compatible with yours. If you're the sort of person who would normally choose conservative stocks, then you'll probably feel uncomfortable with an aggressively managed fund that favours junior hi-tech or resource stocks, even if the fund has been remarkably successful with that approach.

A fund's investment style should complement those of other funds in your portfolio. Here we're talking about diversification: the process of spreading out your holdings to include a wide range of different investment types so that your overall risk is kept to a minimum. As we saw in Chapter 2, a good mutual fund portfolio will always contain some element of diversification, with assets allocated between cash (money market), fixed income, and equity investments. But within each of these investment types, you can (and should) diversify by investment style.

To illustrate why, let's say that you select three Top Funds with powerful performance, consistent management, low expenses, and a similar investment style. Now, the style of those funds may be "hot" when you buy the fund, but what happens when market and/or economic conditions change? Your entire portfolio will suffer.

On the other hand, if you diversify by investment style—by organizing your portfolio in two-fund pairs, where the style of one counterbalances the style of the other—you'll be less dependent on any given style, and your overall risk level will be reduced.

That's why, for each Top Fund—wherever possible—we've identified another Top Fund that will maximize your diversification within the asset category. That way you can still select top performers and ensure that you've got your risk reduced, not magnified, as you add more of them to your portfolio.

research
news

Barking up the Wrong Tree

Over the past few years, investors looking for a simple yet surefire method of beating the market have touted the "Dogs of the Dow" strategy. This investment approach involves investing in the top 10 dividend yielding stocks in the Dow Jones Industrial Average. A high dividend yield usually results when the price of a stock tumbles, thus the "Dogs of the Dow" moniker. The media has widely reported this phenomenon, books have been written about it, and it's a hot topic in Internet chat rooms. There is, however, a small problem: It doesn't work.

A study reviewed market data from 1961 to 1998. It concluded that the "Dogs" did indeed outperform the overall Dow, but by only 1.55% a year. Unfortunately, the capital gains taxes incurred from rebalancing plus transaction and brokerage costs and the income taxes from the higher dividends had an annual cost of 1.58%.

As an investment strategy, this one is, well...a dog.

Mark Hirschey, "The 'Dogs of the Dow' Myth," *Financial Review* 35, no. 2 (May 2000).

Understanding Equity Styles

Value. Managers with a value-based investment style usually use a "bottom-up" approach; that is, they pick securities using analyses of individual companies. Here managers look for companies with good products or services, as well as promising markets. They will (or should) perform detailed company reviews—perhaps even inspect the business onsite—spending a great deal of time looking at a company's financial situation, interviewing customers, and getting to know the business intimately. Ultimately, value managers find such information more important than "top-down" factors such as GDP growth, inflation rates, or industrial sector performance.

Typically, they look for stocks that sell cheap because, for any number of reasons, they have fallen out of favour with investors. (Here, "cheap" means that share prices are lower than what was expected, given the company's earnings or assets per share.) Sir John Templeton is a classic value investor.

Within the value category, there are subcategories:

- **Conservative value.** Portfolio managers employing this style will typically hold shares in companies with a very healthy financial position. Such companies will have substantial assets and little or no debt, as well as a solid earnings record—factors that are not reflected in share prices because of some other perceived weakness.
- **Aggressive value.** This type of stock portfolio acquires shares in companies that are being shunned by investors, and are therefore extremely cheap. The basic aim is to capitalize on an expected turnaround in the company. However, such a strategy comes with certain risks: The turnaround, if it happens at all, may be a long time in coming. For this reason, aggressive value managers typically hold stocks for long periods—often four years or more. So while the performance of such funds can be very good over the long term, there may be long periods of underperformance that can try the patience (and nerves) of many investors. Peter Cundill is a typical aggressive value investor, because he's a real contrarian.

Growth. Like their value-based counterparts, many growth managers also employ a "bottom-up" approach. But that's where the similarity ends. Growth managers buy shares in premium companies at premium prices. They look for companies that are doing things right: companies whose profits and sales are increasing rapidly, perhaps due to market expansion, new product development, or savvy packaging and service. For whatever reason, these companies are growing and their stocks trade at a premium because they are perceived as such.

Typically, growth companies provide a lower dividend yield to shareholders, since so much of their excess earnings is put back into the business. These are glamour stocks in the truest sense of the word. They are financially healthy and successful. For many investors, the idea of paying a premium for such a stock is very easy to accept.

Aggressive Growth. This portfolio management style tends to focus more on companies that are truly innovative within a specific area. They are therefore riskier, but this risk is offset to some degree by the companies' rapid sales and earnings momentum. Jim Broadfoot of Mackenzie's Universal group is typical of this style; he literally wrote the book on investing in emerging growth stocks.

surfing
the web

Even if you don't love analysis to paralysis, you're going to love this site. You can easily build a chart and compare it with anything in the investment world. BigCharts is a wealth of knowledge when it comes to investment research on the Internet. It provides access to professional-level research tools such as interactive charts, industry analysis, and market news and commentary. The graphics are superb and entertaining.

www.bigcharts.com

Sector Rotation. Managers with a sector rotation style frequently employ different types of inputs in their research and analysis, often using technical and macroeconomic research, with far less attention paid to company-specific data; they are "top-down" investors. Essentially, they look for broad trends in the economy—such as GDP growth, inflation, and major world developments in energy or population growth—and how these are likely to change various industrial sectors.

In general, a sector rotation manager will identify a number of sectors that appear to be most favourable, and will allocate the fund's portfolio accordingly. Within each sector, diversification is the key: rather than focusing on one or two "hot" companies within each sector, the manager will put money into a large number of stocks.

If the manager is successful in picking the right sectors, this approach can be very successful. In 1996, for example, just two sectors—oil and gas, and gold and silver—accounted for over 75% of the strong returns of the TSE 300. In fact, these two sectors nearly doubled in that one year. In 1996, small gold stocks were similarly ahead of the pack, pulling overweight managers up sharply, while in 1997, falling gold prices pummelled these same managers. Rising financial service stocks rewarded overweight funds during the same time frame.

As you might expect, the managers who correctly identified the right sectors came out of 1993 having done extremely well. And it would certainly have been tempting for investors to buy those winning funds. The problem is that economic forces change, and so does the relative strength of industry sectors. So it's never a great idea to load up on sector rotation funds exclusively. Sector rotation manager John Zechner of C.I. is an example of a hot manager from several years ago who has cooled recently. The key for him and for investors is consistency and patience.

The Equity Style Grid

As you've probably realized by now, classifying equity fund styles is not an entirely straightforward task. For example, a fund manager may be value oriented, but may also be inclined to growth stocks. Another may take the value approach, but specialize in small companies. A growth manager may prefer big blue chips. And so on.

To simplify the classification process, we have used a style grid to indicate the different approaches taken by different mutual fund managers. The style grid contains three columns, one for each general style category: value, growth, and sector rotation. The grid is also divided into three rows, each representing the size of companies the fund manager has tended to buy: large, medium, or small. So if a fund's portfolio contains mostly large (or big-cap) value companies, the box at the intersection of Value (column) and Large (row) will be filled in.

And what if, in our estimation, the fund manager uses a blended style, value and growth, for example? Simple. Both the Value and Growth squares will be filled in.

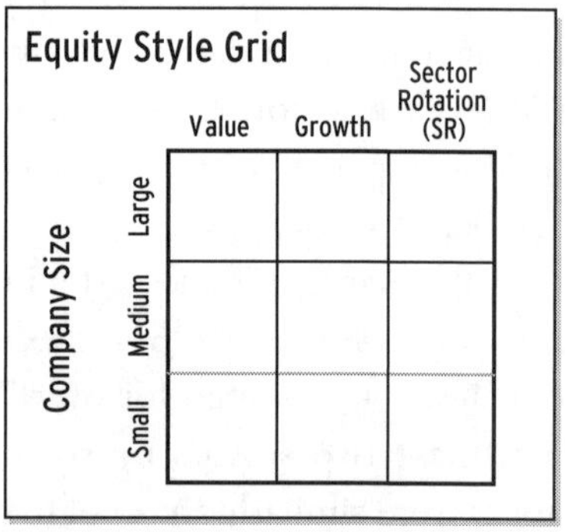

This visual approach offers a number of benefits in addition to simplicity. For instance, the relative aggressiveness of a fund manager can be identified just by looking at the position of the filled squares on the grid. More conservative companies will tend to be filled in on the upper left part of the grid. As you move right and down, you find funds that take a more specialized approach, which offers greater risks and rewards.

In the "100 Top Funds" section, we name the Top Fund in the same category that has been scientifically identified as the best correlated (and, therefore, most complementary) to the Top Fund described. We also name the Top Fund most similar to the Top Fund being discussed. The universes we use to select from and to compare with are Canadian equities, Canadian bonds, Canadian balanced, U.S. equities, international equities, international bonds, regional equities, sector equities, and international balanced funds; we're attempting to make reasonable apples-to-apples comparisons.

We think you'll find this to be a big help as you create your own portfolio.

Value or Growth Style: Which Is Better?

The debate over which style is "better" really heated up in early 2000. Previously, especially in Canada, the research was heavily in favour of value investing as the better or more successful style. But then, marginally in 1998 and spectacularly in 1999, growth stocks (heavily concentrated in the technology sector) went on an absolute tear, and trounced the returns earned by more traditional value stocks, including banking stocks.

Many suddenly knowledgeable investors pronounced that the old rules had changed and that this time it was different! And for several months, especially in late 1999 and the first couple of months of 2000, the evidence seemed to support them.

But in March of 2000, two events took place that began to turn the tide once again in favour of the value approach and against growth stocks. Abbey Joseph Cohen, a respected Wall Street analyst and pundit, made comments that were interpreted to mean that she felt many tech stocks were (surprise!) overvalued. At almost the same time, the U.S. government initiated action against Microsoft, declaring that it was attempting to create a monopoly and suggesting that Microsoft should be broken up into two stand-alone companies.

These events seemed to strike fear or to inject some common sense back into the markets, and we began to see a decline in the technology/growth market and a recovery in the value market as many fled from the previous high flyers to "quality" undervalued stocks, including banking stocks. By the end of May, the Nasdaq Index in the U.S. (home of many tech-based public companies) had closed at 3,300, wiping out much of the spectacular gain it had piled on from early November 1999 to March 10, 2000, when it peaked at slightly over 5,000.

Looking back from 1982 to 1999, the bar charts on the next page show that in Canadian equities, value outperformed growth 13 out of 18 years. On average, Canadian value style returned 12.47% over those years, while Canadian growth style returned 9.68%, despite growth's spectacular outperformance in 1999.

Barra Canadian Equity Value vs. Barra Canadian Equity Growth

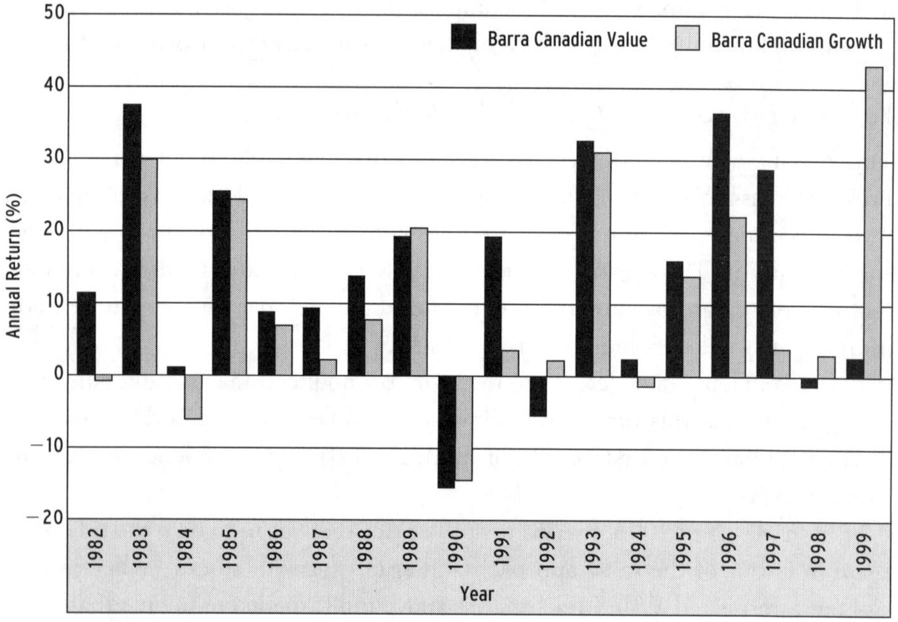

SOURCE: Assante Advisory Services

Annualized Return by Investment Style: 1982–1999

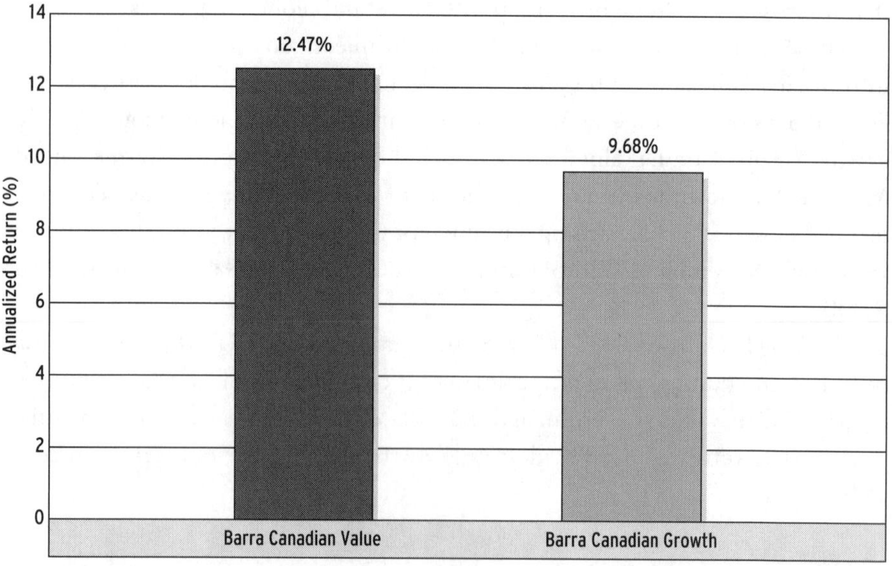

SOURCE: Assante Advisory Services

Barra U.S. Equity Value vs. Barra U.S. Equity Growth

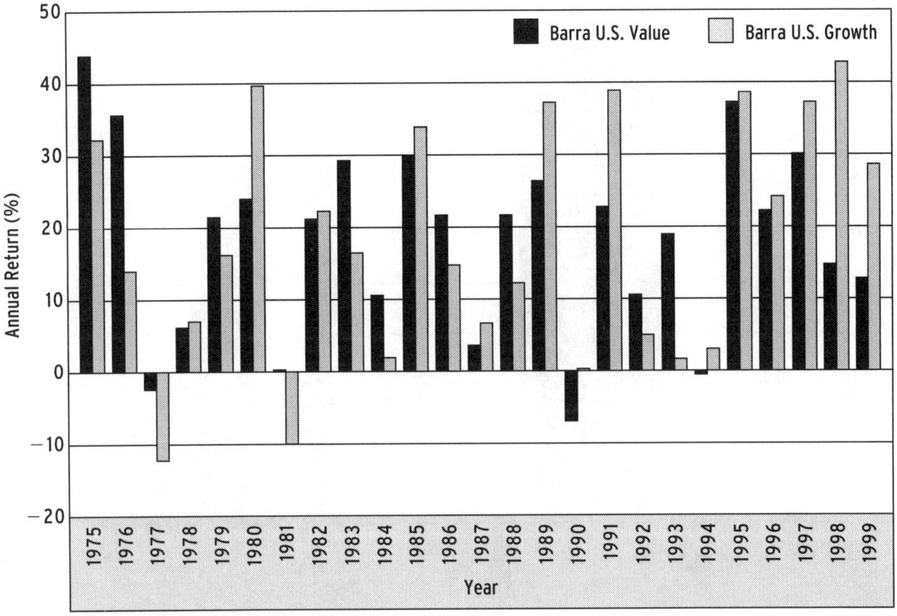

SOURCE: Assante Advisory Services

In the U.S., the difference between the two styles has been less obvious and spectacular. In fact, looking back over 26 years to 1975, we can see that on an annual basis, growth has outperformed value for 14 of 26 years and, notably, each and every year since 1994. On average, however, despite those six consecutive years of comparative underperformance, value's average return has been 17.30% compared with growth's average return of 16.76%.

So which style is "better"? The average return figures seem to suggest a slight advantage to value, but we think the question goes beyond historical performance. As we've said for years, a fund's management style should be compatible with yours, and it should complement the style of other funds in your portfolio. That's why from the first edition of *Top Funds*, we have provided our style grid as a means of assisting you to identify funds that are, from a style perspective, complementary to and funds that are similar to our identified Top Funds.

Finally, while using data from the past helps us to interpret the past, we have no idea whether similar patterns will develop into the future. Therefore, *we*

Annualized Return by Investment Style: 1975–1999

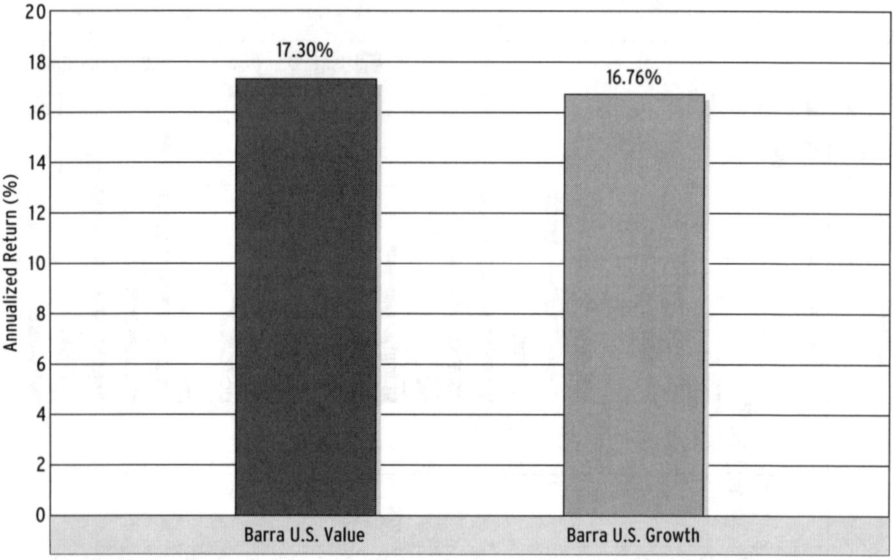

SOURCE: Assante Advisory Services

believe it's prudent to diversify by management style as well as diversification by asset category, geography, and security selection. It's a consistent, common sense approach to investing.

And we're not alone in our thinking. There is a growing demand for funds with a clear growth-management bias as investors become more aware of the existence of different management styles and—in the last few years—of the outstanding success achieved by growth managers. For their part, fund companies are responding and giving the customers what they want.

Perhaps the most obvious example of this development is the decision by Templeton Management in the spring of 2000 to offer a range of six growth-style funds to complement the renowned Templeton value management style. Developed by Templeton's partners, Franklin Mutual Advisors Inc., these funds include the Franklin U.S. Large-Cap Growth Fund, Franklin U.S. Aggressive Growth, and Franklin U.S. Small-Cap Growth RSP.

In addition, Franklin Templeton is also offering three growth management sector or theme funds—as are many other fund companies. These offerings include the Franklin World Telecom Fund, the Franklin Technology Fund, and the Franklin World Health Sciences and Biotech Fund. When we see staid, conservative old Templeton adding sizzling new growth-oriented options to their traditional fare, we know the world is changing!

Less surprisingly perhaps, but part of this growing trend to differentiate management styles, we note that Dynamic got a fairly early start by introducing their Power funds in 1998. Also, more recently, the proposed AIM merger with Trimark will give Trimark investors the choice of growth-style funds as part of an expanded family offering. As well, we see individual advisors constructing client portfolios with an eye to including both good value and growth managers.

So the question isn't "Which style is better?" Rather, it's "Does it make sense to limit ourselves to one management style?" We think the answer is "No," and therefore applaud the changes we see taking place in the industry.

Understanding Fixed Income Styles

There are two basic approaches to selecting bonds. One is *spread trading* and the other is *interest rate anticipation*. Each approach has its own distinctive flavour, and some managers use both approaches.

Spread Trading. Spread trading is the more conservative of fixed income styles, just as value is a more conservative equity strategy than sector rotation. Here, a manager tries to profit from small changes in the yields of various bonds or other debt instruments.

These funds aren't making big bets about the direction of interest rates. They profit most from changes in economic and cyclical factors affecting bonds. For example, as the economy has strengthened over the past year, and almost all of our provinces have actually begun to run budget surpluses, spread traders have profited from buying corporate and provincial bonds, which have risen relatively in price as company and government finances have improved (what Bay Streeters call *spread tightening*).

In most cases, however, spread traders don't need a major economic change to make a profit; even small, day-to-day changes in yields—often just a fraction of a percentage point—translate into big dollars when you deal in million-dollar bond transactions. Add to these incremental capital gains the coupon income (interest paid) on the bonds themselves, and you have the makings of a strong bond fund.

Interest Rate Anticipation. Interest-rate anticipation is a "big picture" strategy, where a manager uses macroeconomic analysis (among various other techniques) to predict changes in interest rates.

top funds

close up

Taxing Issues

Investors holding mutual funds outside their registered accounts should be aware of how tax efficient their funds are. Mutual funds distribute realized capital gains and interest income on a regular basis. These distributions are taxable and the investor could end up with a hefty tax bill at the end of the year, even if he or she didn't actually redeem any fund units. Watch out for funds that have an investment style that results in active trading or "turnover." While the investment returns can be appealing, the tax implications of constantly realizing capital gains can be less so. Luckily, many active managers are now structuring their portfolios to offset capital gains against capital losses whenever possible, and therefore are minimizing the tax problem. "Buy-and-hold" managers turn their portfolios over less often and so the tax issue doesn't come up as frequently. A caveat, though: You can't avoid the Canada Customs and Revenue Agency (CCRA) forever. Even buy-and-hold managers sell eventually, and the capital gain could create a whopping tax bill.

Generally, this comes down to a decision about whether to buy short- or long-term bonds. If the manager expects interest rates to rise, then it's short-term bonds, since they can be turned over relatively quickly and are the least sensitive to changes in interest rates. (Remember that when interest rates go up, bond prices go down.) If the manager anticipates that interest rates will fall, then it's long-term bonds; since their prices are the most sensitive to interest rates, they offer the best profit opportunity.

Successful rate anticipation can deliver some very hefty profits, as it did in the early 1990s when interest rates fell precipitously and bond fund investors enjoyed three years of 20% annual returns in some of the better funds.

Blend. Some managers use a blend of spread trading and rate anticipation—typically when the fund has an established policy of buying bonds with a particular term. If you think about it, you can see why. Let's say that a fund is mandated to buy long-term bonds. Clearly, the fund's style will be dictated by what's happening with interest rates; that is, if there's no money to be made from buying long-term bonds in anticipation of falling rates, the manager will have to resort to spread trading.

The Fixed Income Style Grid

The format of the style grid for bond (and other fixed income) funds is much like the one discussed earlier for equity funds. The difference is that the columns represent (from left to right) spread trading, blend, and rate anticipation styles. From top to bottom, the rows represent the term of bonds held in the fund.

Also like its equity counterpart, the bond style grid starts in the top left corner with the most conservative style, representing what should be an investor's core assets. These funds typically hold securities with a short-term average maturity. "Short" is anything between one year to just under four years.

Moving downward to the bottom right corner, we find the most aggressive, specialized types of funds. These typically hold longer-dated bonds ("long" defined as 10 years or more to maturity) with the aim of achieving capital gains on top of their interest income. While offering a higher potential return, these funds are appropriate only for someone with investment experience and sufficient assets diversified into other, less aggressive instruments.

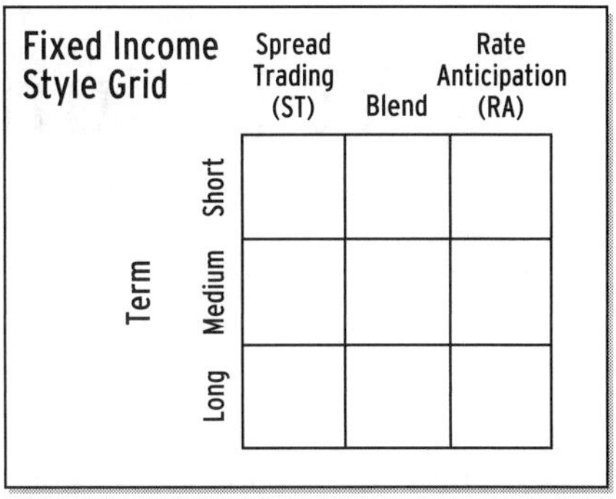

4

How They Rate: Top Funds 2002

Here's where it all comes together. The numbers have been crunched, the trends analyzed, and the final cuts made. What remains is an admittedly elite group: funds that have proven themselves the best of the best.

In this section, you'll find the 100 Top Funds selected for 2002, grouped according to fund category (this is indicated by a tab in the margin), and presented in alphabetical order.

The Top Funds Legend

Each full-page listing is provided in a concise, standardized format. Here's how to navigate your way through:

- **Fund Name** is the official name of the fund.
- **Fund Manager/Firm** (where applicable). The manager's name and the year when he or she assumed responsibility for the fund, plus the name of the fund management company. "Inception" means that the manager has looked after the fund since it began.
- **RRSP Eligibility.** An unstroked maple leaf indicates that the fund meets "Canadian content" rules of the Canada Customs and Revenue Agency, and can therefore make up to 100% of the total value of your RRSP or RRIF. A

maple leaf with an oblique stroke indicates that the fund is considered "foreign content" and therefore must not exceed 30% of the value of your RRSP or RRIF.

- **New Top Fund.** Funds listed for the first time in this 2002 edition are labelled "NEW."
- **Top Fund in Previous Year(s).** This indicates the year(s) in which the fund was on the *Top Funds* list.
- **Performance Trend.** This graph shows the fund's rankings by quartile for the calendar years where data was available from 1991 to September 2001.

  A first-quartile position indicates that the fund beat 75% of its direct competitors. A second-quartile ranking means that it beat 50% of the others, but was beaten by 25%.

  The shading in the background indicates the relative performance of the average mutual fund in that category.

  If a fund that you know has been in existence for a number of years is shown on the Performance Trend for fewer years, it is because there were less than four funds in the category for a period of time.
- **Risk indicators** are self-explanatory. The reference to the number of years is based on calendar years.
- **Reward-to-Risk Relationship/Sharpe Ratio Quartile Rankings/ Morningstar Ratings. The Sharpe Ratio** is a means of measuring risk-adjusted returns. It is the average annual return for three and five years less the three- and five-year average annual return of Government of Canada T-bills (a "risk-free" investment) divided by the annual standard deviation of the particular fund.

  To simplify, the chart shows how this fund compares with its peers with respect to the Sharpe Ratio. As with the performance trend, the higher the quartile ranking, the better. A first-quartile ranking is the most desirable while a fourth-quartile ranking is the least desirable. (Note that the chart shows comparative quartile performance rather than the more complicated Sharpe Ratio itself.)

  The Morningstar Five-Star Rating System. We believe that, assuming one is aware of the limitations and strengths of the Morningstar Ratings system, it is another valuable tool in the investor's arsenal and, along with the other "filters" we offer, can be useful in making those important selection decisions.

- **Efficiency/Management Expense Ratio (MER).** This is shown as the amount charged by the fund managers for every $100 in assets managed. Since different categories of funds require different levels of managerial effort, the model shows whether the MER for a given fund is high (above average) or low (below average) relative to other funds in the same category. If it's high, the "above average" circle is shaded; if it's average, the "average" circle is shaded; and if it's low, the "below average" circle is shaded.
- **Style Grid** categorizes the fund by investment style. In the example shown on page 111, the style leans towards medium companies with a growth approach. Note that this sample style is for funds that hold primarily equity or stock investments.

  A different grid is used for **fixed income** (bond, mortgage, money market) funds. Labels for this grid are shown here.

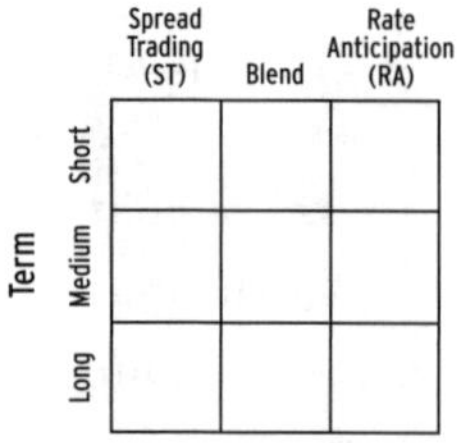

- Specific suggestions of a **complementary fund** and a **similar fund** are indicated.

Fund Name

Fund Manager/Firm

RRSP Eligibility

Top Fund in previous year(s)

New Top Fund

1995, 1996, 1997, 1998, 1999, 2000, 2001 RRSP

CANADIAN EQUITY

BISSETT CANADIAN EQUITY CLASS F FUND

Fred Pynn (1994)/Bissett Investment Management

Performance Trend

Consistency

Performance Trend

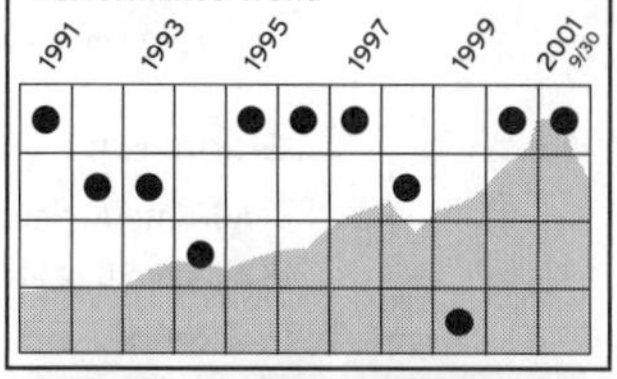

Risk Indicators

Risk

How often fund outperformed GICs	7 years in 9
How often fund lost money	1 year in 9
Worst year's rate of return	–15.02%

Risk-Adjusted Returns

Reward-to-Risk Relationship
Sharpe Ratio Quartile Rankings

3-Year	1
5-Year	1

Morningstar Rating

Morningstar Rating

★★★★★

Management Expenses (MER)

Efficiency/MER

Management expense/$100

$1.26

○ above average
○ average
● below average

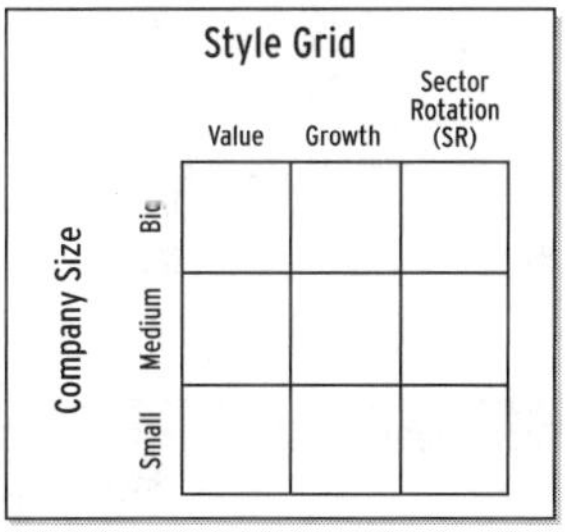

Style

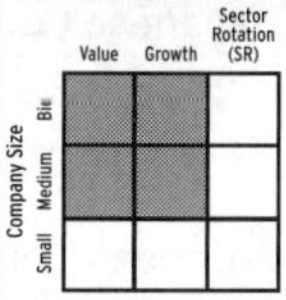

Complementary Fund:
PH&N Dividend Income

Similar Fund:
Fidelity True North

The takeover of Bissett & Associates Investment Management by Franklin Templeton Investments last year holds both good and bad news. The bad news is that one of Canada's finest independently owned mutual fund companies was purchased by a foreigner, albeit a foreigner with an excellent pedigree. We had visions of wholesale manager firings and fund consolidations. The good news is that Franklin Templeton didn't buy the firm in order to dump its most valuable assets; the Bissett funds are still available and the original managers are still managing.

Manager Fred Pynn's Bissett Canadian Equity Fund has been a Top Fund choice for eight years in a row. His GARP (growth-at-a-reasonable-price) investment style blends the best of both the growth and value worlds. The result is a 15-year compound annual rate of return of 11.4%, the third best in the Canadian Equity category. Bissett Canadian equity's only losing calendar year was 1994, when the fund declined by 2.3%.

Bissett feels that economically sensitive companies offer the best opportunities for investors when markets rebound. The largest holding in his 90-position portfolio is a 3.1% weighting in Power Financial. Alberta Energy, Magna International, Suncor Energy, and CAE make up the rest of the top five.

The "F" class units represent the original, no-load version of the fund. They are still offered by Franklin Templeton, but most mutual fund dealers will offer the "F" class units only to fee-based clients. The "A" units will be more widely available, but the management expense ratio is 1.06% higher and investor annual returns will therefore be lower by that percentage.

THE 100 TOP FUNDS OF 2002

The following is a list of the 100 Top Funds of 2002, arranged by category and in alphabetical order within each category. An (✓) beside a fund indicates that it is a NEW Top Fund in 2002.

1999, 2000, 2001 RRSP

AIC DIVERSIFIED CANADA FUND

Jonathan Wellum (1990)/Georgian Capital Partners Inc.

Consistency

Performance Trend

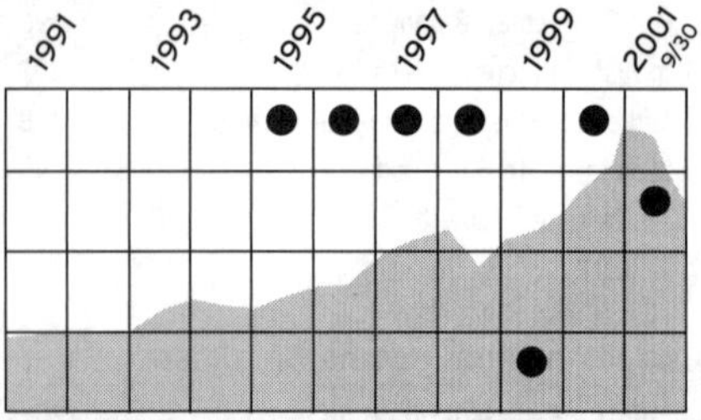

Risk

How often fund outperformed GICs	5 years in 5
How often fund lost money	1 year in 5
Worst year's rate of return	−15.1%

Reward-to-Risk Relationship

Sharpe Ratio Quartile Rankings

3-Year	3
5-Year	1

Morningstar Rating

★★★★

Efficiency/MER

Management expense/$100

$2.45

○ above average
● average
○ below average

Style

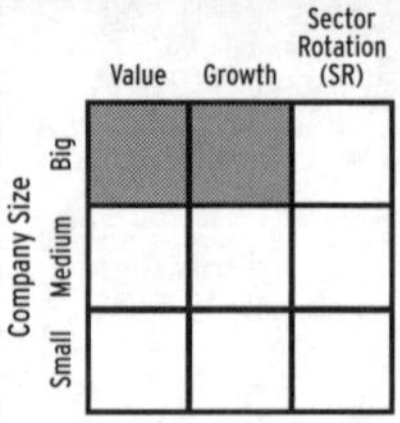

Complementary Fund:
PH&N Dividend Income

Similar Fund:
Investors Summa

One of the challenges we face when picking our Top 100 funds each year is determining whether the light at the end of the tunnel is actually an oncoming locomotive. Put another way, we have to decide if any short-term performance issues are due to market changes or a manager's losing the magic touch. Is the fund suffering because there actually is a new paradigm afoot or because the management style is briefly out of fashion?

AIC Diversified Canada is a case in point. We've always been impressed with this fund and are comfortable with AIC's investment philosophy and discipline. In 1999, performance suffered when investors embraced the growth style and we admittedly did take a second look at the fund when we put together *Top Funds 2001*.

This year we will modestly state that we made the right decision to keep AIC Diversified Canada on our list. The fund has gained 12.9% over the past year, compared with a 6.3% loss for the average Canadian equity fund. The longer-term picture is even better: a five-year compounded annual rate of return of 9.5%.

The portfolio has only 25 names. The largest individual holding is Toronto Dominion Bank, which represents just under 9.0% of fund's assets. Bombardier, Loblaws, Thomson Corp., and DuPont Canada round out the top five. AIC managers have always been bullish on the wealth management and financial services sector and AIC Diversified Canada's 39% weighting to this sector confirms that their view hasn't changed. Technology issues are underweighted, but manager Jonathan Wellum continues to be very high on the fund's sole technology holding, Celestica Inc.

New

RRSP

AIM CANADIAN FIRST CLASS FUND

Roger Mortimer (1997), Ronald Sloan (1997)/AIM Capital Management

CANADIAN EQUITY

Consistency

Performance Trend

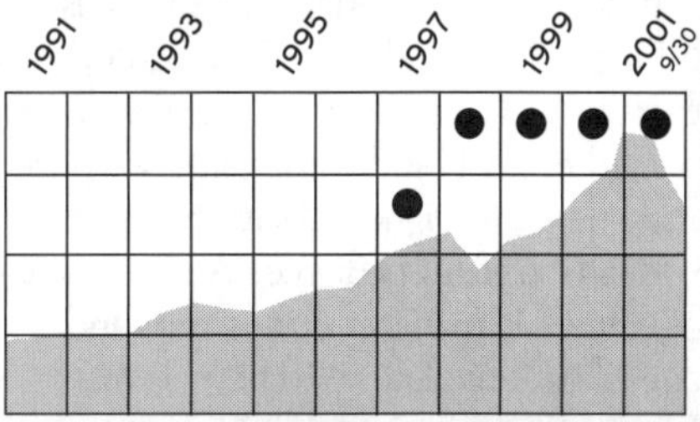

Risk

How often fund outperformed GICs	2 years in 2
How often fund lost money	1 year in 2
Worst year's rate of return	–13.07%

Reward-to-Risk Relationship
Sharpe Ratio Quartile Rankings

3-Year	1
5-Year	N/A

Morningstar Rating

★★★★★

Efficiency/MER

Management expense/$100

$2.79

- above average (marked)
- average
- below average

Style

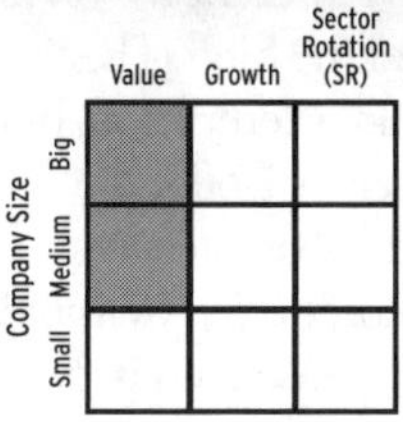

Complementary Fund:
PH&N Dividend Income

Similar Fund:
CI Harbour Fund

Manager Roger Mortimer likes the concept of "unlocking true value." As a value manager, he uses traditional valuation methods to choose investments: P/E and P/B ratios, dividend yield, cash flow, and historical earnings all play an important role in his decision-making process. However, Mortimer feels the key is finding a catalyst that will unlock the true value of a stock.

A good example of his theory is Canadian Pacific Ltd., the largest holding in the portfolio. In the case of this stock, the corporate decision to break the company up into separate businesses was the key. In Mortimer's opinion, the sum of the value of each business wasn't reflected in the price of the stock and the market needed news of the breakup to push the stock price to its true value. The stock was trading in the $40 range before word of the breakup hit, and since then has traded as high as $66.95. Mortimer also likes Onyx Corp. This holding company has a large position in Celestica Inc. and he feels that the Celestica investment alone accounts for most of the value of Onyx shares.

AIM Canadian First Class has returned 15.7% a year over the past three years and has eked out a 2.1% gain over the past twelve months. By comparison, the average Canadian equity fund grew 4.4% a year over the past three years and lost 6.3% over the past year.

This fund was formerly the AIM Canada Value Class Fund.

1995, 1996, 1997, 1998, 1999, 2000, 2001 RRSP

BISSETT CANADIAN EQUITY CLASS F FUND

Fred Pynn (1994)/Bissett Investment Management

Consistency

Performance Trend

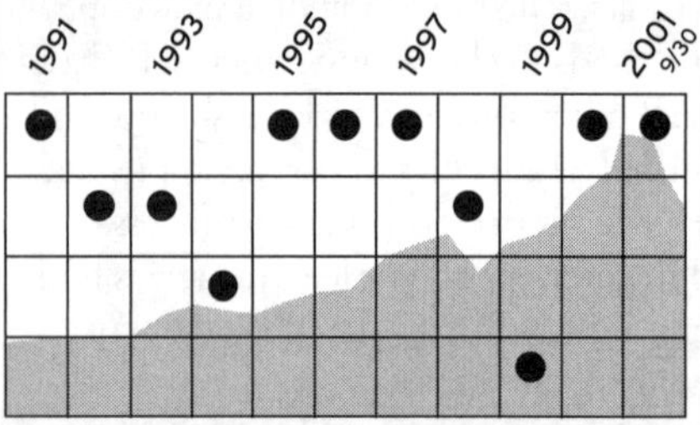

Risk

How often fund outperformed GICs	7 years in 9
How often fund lost money	1 year in 9
Worst year's rate of return	−15.02%

Reward-to-Risk Relationship

Sharpe Ratio Quartile Rankings

3-Year	1
5-Year	1

Morningstar Rating

★★★★★

Efficiency/MER

Management expense/$100

$1.26

○ above average
○ average
● below average

Style

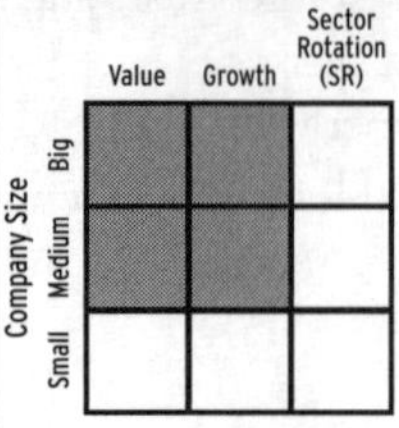

Complementary Fund:
PH&N Dividend Income

Similar Fund:
Fidelity True North

The takeover of Bissett & Associates Investment Management by Franklin Templeton Investments last year holds both good and bad news. The bad news is that one of Canada's finest independently owned mutual fund companies was purchased by a foreigner, albeit a foreigner with an excellent pedigree. We had visions of wholesale manager firings and fund consolidations. The good news is that Franklin Templeton didn't buy the firm in order to dump its most valuable assets; the Bissett funds are still available and the original managers are still managing.

Manager Fred Pynn's Bissett Canadian Equity Fund has been a Top Fund choice for eight years in a row. His GARP (growth-at-a-reasonable-price) investment style blends the best of both the growth and value worlds. The result is a 15-year compound annual rate of return of 11.4%, the third best in the Canadian Equity category. Bissett Canadian equity's only losing calendar year was 1994, when the fund declined by 2.3%.

Bissett feels that economically sensitive companies offer the best opportunities for investors when markets rebound. The largest holding in his 90-position portfolio is a 3.1% weighting in Power Financial. Alberta Energy, Magna International, Suncor Energy, and CAE make up the rest of the top five.

The "F" class units represent the original, no-load version of the fund. They are still offered by Franklin Templeton, but most mutual fund dealers will offer the "F" class units only to fee-based clients. The "A" units will be more widely available, but the management expense ratio is 1.06% higher and investor annual returns will therefore be lower by that percentage.

1999, 2000 RRSP

CHOU RRSP

Francis Chou (1986)/Chou Associates Management Inc.

Consistency

Performance Trend

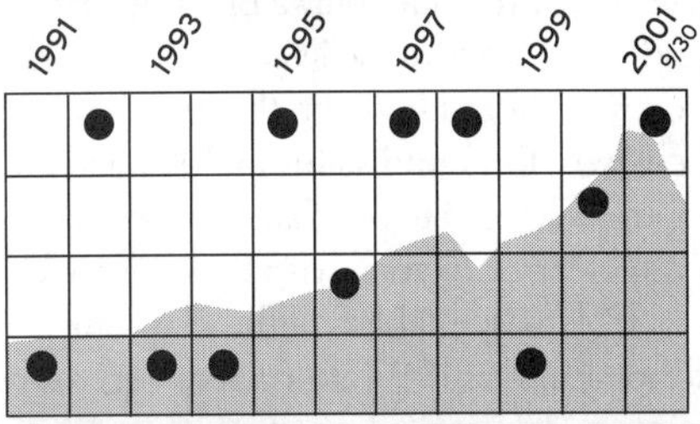

Risk

How often fund outperformed GICs	6 years in 8
How often fund lost money	2 years in 8
Worst year's rate of return	–13.89%

Reward-to-Risk Relationship

Sharpe Ratio Quartile Rankings

3-Year	2
5-Year	1

Morningstar Rating

★★★★★

Efficiency/MER

Management expense/$100

$2.11

○ above average

○ average

● below average

Style

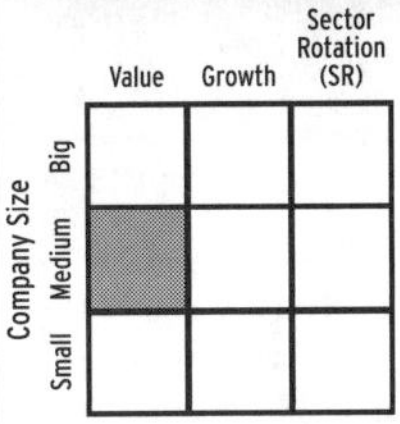

Complementary Fund:
PH&N Dividend Income

Similar Fund:
Saxon Small Cap

Francis Chou is a rarity in the mutual fund world. He doesn't aggressively market his funds, he doesn't give media interviews, and he doesn't cater to the independent advisor network. Chou makes up for these "deficiencies" by simply giving his investors superior returns.

Chou RRSP returned 24.3% over the past 12 months and has averaged 13.6% a year over the past 10 years. Chou's disciplined value style kept him away from the technology sector and he has avoided the declines that many Canadian equity funds have experienced over the past two years.

The Chou RRSP Fund's five-year Sharpe ratio ranks the highest of any Canadian equity fund in our Morningstar database, which confirms our opinion of the excellent risk/reward characteristics of this fund.

CANADIAN EQUITY

New

RRSP

CI HARBOUR FUND
Gerry Coleman (1997)/C.I. Mutual Funds Inc.

Consistency

Performance Trend

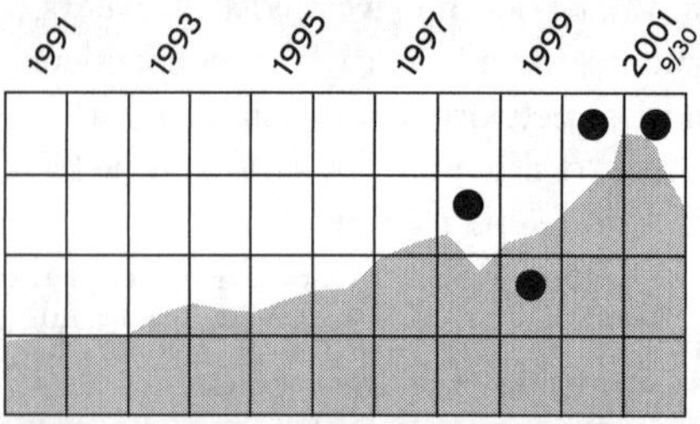

Risk

How often fund outperformed GICs	2 years in 3
How often fund lost money	0 years in 3
Worst year's rate of return	−13.13%

Reward-to-Risk Relationship
Sharpe Ratio Quartile Rankings

3-Year	1
5-Year	N/A

Morningstar Rating

★★★★★

Efficiency/MER

Management expense/$100

$2.46

- ○ above average
- ● average
- ○ below average

Style

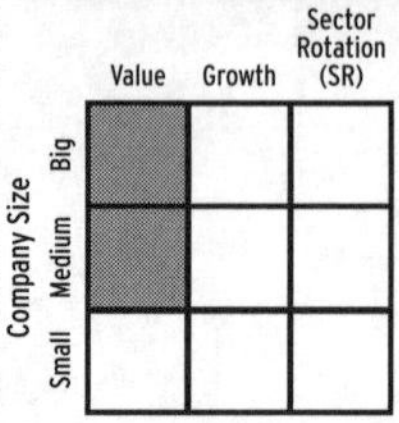

Complementary Fund:
PH&N Dividend Income

Similar Fund:
CI Signature Select Canadian

Back in 1998, we named this fund as one of our "up and comers." At that time, the Harbour Fund had only a brief history and was therefore ineligible for Top Fund consideration. However, the fund has achieved Top Fund status in 2002 and we're delighted to see that industry veteran Gerry Coleman hasn't lost his touch.

Coleman established the Harbour fund family in 1997 after a very successful stint at Mackenzie running the Ivy Canadian Fund with Jerry Javasky. His style is value orientated, but his real strength is the ability to create concentrated portfolios that will be held for a long time. For example, he has only 33 stocks in his portfolio and his turnover rate in 2000 was only 34%.

Coleman continues to favour oil and gas and financial stocks. In his view, these sectors still offer good fundamentals and attractive prices. His largest position is a 6.2% weighting to Bank of Montreal. Talisman Energy and Royal Bank each represent 4.3% of the fund. Currently, the P/E ratio of his portfolio is only 13.3, which is almost half of the 26.3 weighted P/E of the TSE 300.

Harbour Fund has a large cash position of 26.4%. It provides both a downside cushion and proof that Coleman won't be pressured to invest just because he has the cash available.

New

RRSP

CI SIGNATURE SELECT CANADIAN FUND
Eric Bushell (1998)/C.I. Mutual Funds Inc.

Consistency

Performance Trend

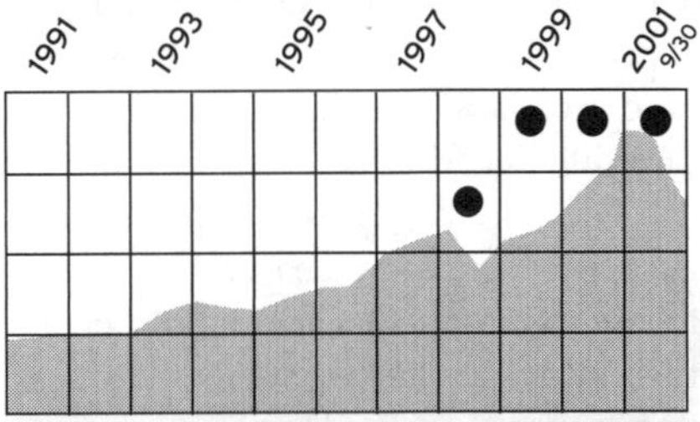

Risk

How often fund outperformed GICs	2 years in 2
How often fund lost money	0 years in 2
Worst year's rate of return	1.54%

Reward-to-Risk Relationship
Sharpe Ratio Quartile Rankings

3-Year	1
5-Year	N/A

Morningstar Rating

★★★★★

Efficiency/MER

Management expense/$100

$2.56

○ above average
● average
○ below average

Style

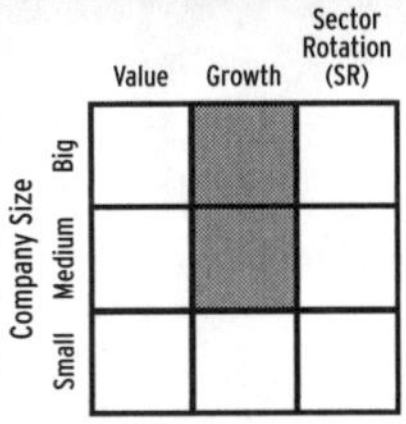

Complementary Fund:
PH&N Dividend Income

Similar Fund:
CI Harbour Fund

Lots of equity funds made money in 1999. Lots of equity funds made money in 2000. Unfortunately, not many funds made both lists but the CI Signature Select Canadian Fund is one of them. In fact, the fund has a cumulative return over the past three years of 74.6%, which is the highest of any Canadian equity fund that is eligible for inclusion in *Top Funds*. This result translates to an average annual return over three years of 20.4%. By comparison, the average Canadian equity fund grew by only 4.4% a year over the same period.

Manager Eric Bushell is a GARP manager. He picks securities based on the growth-at-a-reasonable-price philosophy, which theoretically prevents him from getting carried away when growth stocks start to get pricey. He overlays this approach with an analysis of global economic and financial market trends, allowing him to identify investment themes.

His portfolio holds many of the usual suspects: CIBC, Toronto Dominion Bank, RBC, Canadian Pacific, BCE, etc. There are a couple of interesting holdings among the 66 names in his portfolio, however. One of these names is CHC Helicopter Corp., a transportation service company specializing in the oil and gas industry, which is usually seen in small-cap or resource funds. Another is Manitoba Telecom Services, a utility with a reliable record of consistent dividends.

New

RRSP

CUNDILL CANADIAN SECURITY SERIES B

Peter Cundill (1997), Alan Pasnik (1998)/The Cundill Group

Consistency

Performance Trend

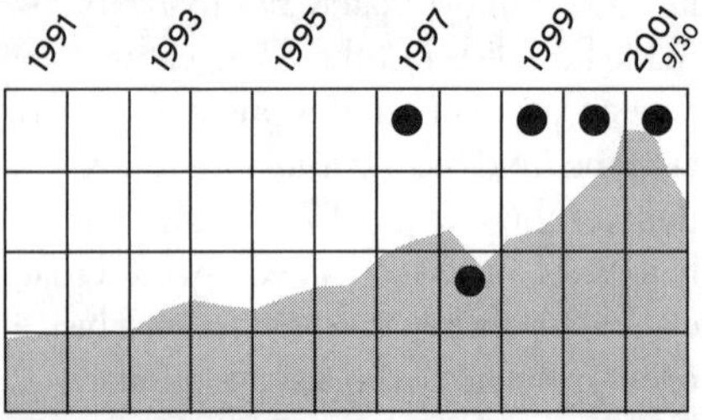

Risk

How often fund outperformed GICs	3 years in 3
How often fund lost money	0 years in 3
Worst year's rate of return	–2.43%

Reward-to-Risk Relationship

Sharpe Ratio Quartile Rankings

3-Year	1
5-Year	N/A

Morningstar Rating

★★★★

Efficiency/MER

Management expense/$100

$2.53

- ○ above average
- ● average
- ○ below average

Style

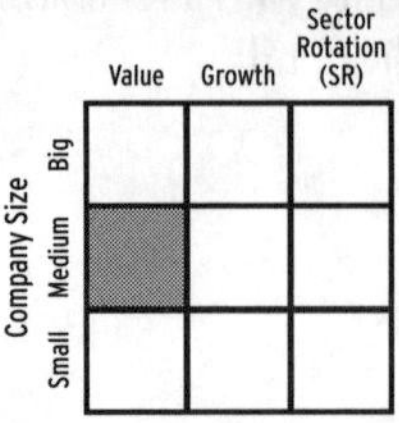

Complementary Fund:
Mac Universal Feature

Similar Fund:
CI Signature Select Canadian

Technically, this is the first appearance for Cundill Canadian Security in *Top Funds*. The Series "A" version, however, did appear in 1998 and Canadian investors have been fans of the Cundill approach to investing since 1974.

The Cundill approach is the contrarian approach. Lead manager Alan Pasnik focuses on stocks that are trading below their intrinsic value. He wants securities that are unappreciated by the markets, but that have excellent long-term prospects. The fund typically has a low correlation with the TSE 300 and is therefore an excellent choice to complement to a more traditional large-cap equity fund. Of course, a 16% allocation to Japan helps to explain the lack of similarity to the TSE! In fact, three of the top ten holdings are non-Canadian equities.

The fund has gained 20.5% over the past twelve months and 12.4% a year over the past three years. The three-year standard deviation of returns is only 12.5, which is the sixth best of any Canadian equity fund eligible for *Top Funds*.

2001 RRSP

FIDELITY TRUE NORTH FUND

Alan Radlo (1996)/Fidelity Management & Research Co.

Consistency

Performance Trend

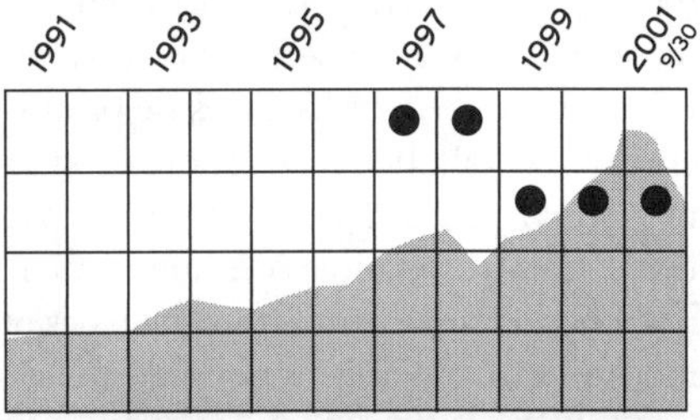

Risk

How often fund outperformed GICs	3 years in 4
How often fund lost money	0 years in 4
Worst year's rate of return	−16.62%

Reward-to-Risk Relationship

Sharpe Ratio Quartile Rankings

3-Year	1
5-Year	1

Morningstar Rating

★★★★★

Efficiency/MER

Management expense/$100

$2.50

○ above average
● average
○ below average

Style

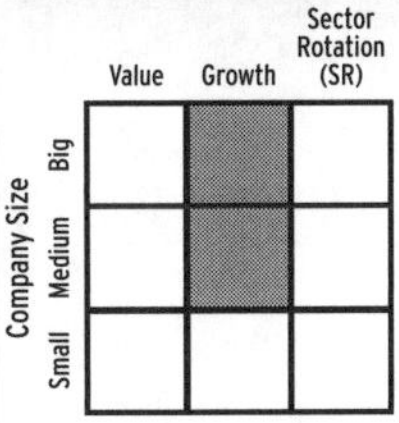

Complementary Fund:
BMO Dividend

Similar Fund:
Synergy Canadian Momentum Class

Fidelity True North has been featured in this book for three years now. In 2000, the fund wasn't yet three years old and was therefore ineligible for consideration in *Top Funds*, but we did mention it as an up-and-comer. Last year, it was a Top Fund and is again this year.

Manager Alan Radlo has put together a fund that we feel could be a core Canadian equity holding for investors. His approach is to seek companies that continue to increase their revenues, cash flow, and shareholder value, and he will generally select investments based on their fundamental value. He doesn't have a specific growth or value bias, however, and his asset mix is an eclectic collection of stocks that meet his criteria. He doesn't have a specific market capitalization mandate and can hold small-, mid-, or large-cap stocks.

True North has been a first-quartile performer over both two and three years. Over the past year, the fund slipped 0.9% versus a 6.59% decline for the fund's benchmark, the TSE 300 Capped Index, and a 6.3% decline for the average Canadian equity fund.

Radlo holds 94 securities in the portfolio. He is underweight in utilities, financials, and pipelines, although his two largest holdings, National Bank of Canada and Sun Life, are in the financial sectors. The fund is also underweight in technology, which has also helped performance. By contrast, last year Radlo had Nortel and JDS Uniphase in his portfolio, but we see no record of these two stocks in his current top holdings. He likes oil and gas, merchandising, transportation, and environment. Bombardier, CP, and Penn West Petroleum make up the balance of his top five positions.

1999, 2000, 2001 RRSP

INVESTORS SUMMA FUND

Scott Morrison/Investors Group

Consistency

Performance Trend

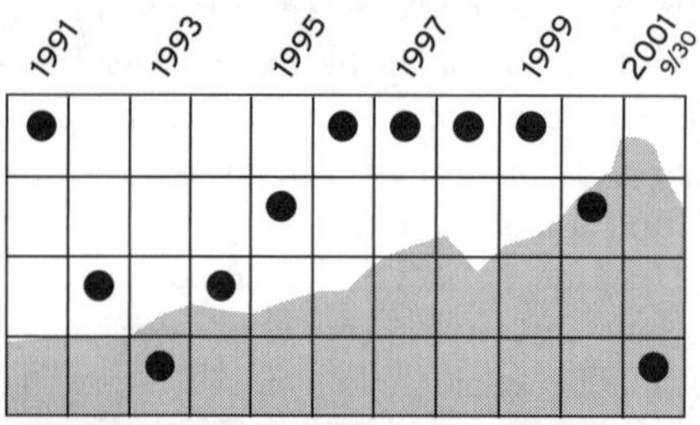

Risk

How often fund outperformed GICs	7 years in 9
How often fund lost money	1 year in 9
Worst year's rate of return	−29.34%

Reward-to-Risk Relationship

Sharpe Ratio Quartile Rankings

3-Year	2
5-Year	1

Morningstar Rating

★★★★

Efficiency/MER

Management expense/$100

$2.96

● above average
○ average
○ below average

Style

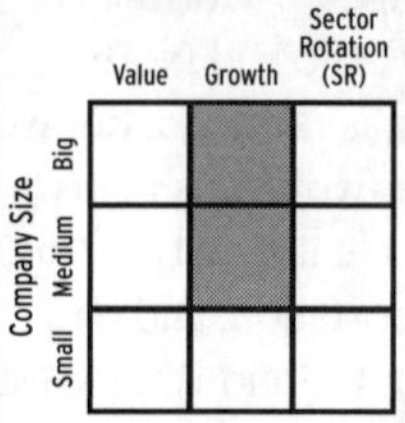

Complementary Fund:
PH&N Dividend Income

Similar Fund:
Synergy Canadian Momentum Class

Many funds with a socially responsible mandate put up some great numbers in the late '90s. The argument has been made that socially responsible companies have fewer expensive liabilities (legal and environmental), better and more productive employees, and products and services that socially responsible consumers want. The counter argument is that the types of industries that socially responsible investment (SRI) funds gravitate towards, such as financial services and technology, were simply the "hot" sectors at the time.

A look at the top holdings of Investors Summa supports the latter argument: 12 of the top 15 are financial services and technology names. Performance has suffered over the past 12 months with a loss of 12.4% versus a 6.3% decline for the average Canadian equity fund.

The longer-term numbers are a different story, however. Investors have earned an average of 13.3% a year over ten years and 16.6% over five years. Although Investors Summa is more a bit more volatile than the average fund in the Canadian equity category and the management expense ratio is also higher than average, this fund has appeal for investors. They can sleep soundly at night, knowing that being socially responsible and making money aren't mutually exclusive endeavours.

1998, 1999, 2000, 2001 RRSP

IVY CANADIAN FUND

Jerry Javasky (1993), Chuck Roth (1993)/Mackenzie Financial Corp.

Consistency

Performance Trend

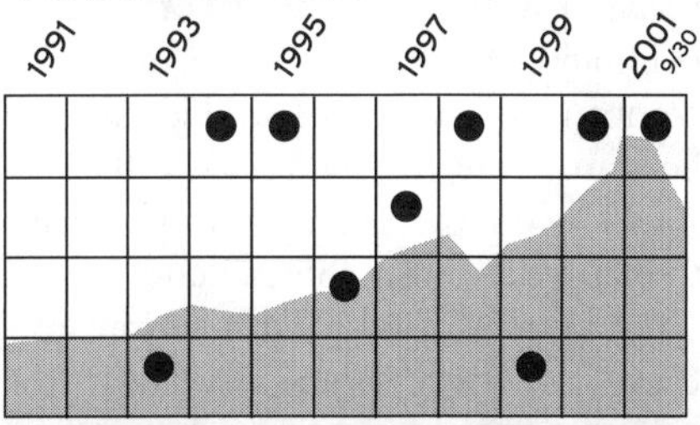

Risk

How often fund outperformed GICs	5 years in 8
How often fund lost money	0 years in 8
Worst year's rate of return	–3.65%

Reward-to-Risk Relationship

Sharpe Ratio Quartile Rankings

3-Year	1
5-Year	1

Morningstar Rating

★★★★

Efficiency/MER

Management expense/$100

$2.47

- ○ above average
- ● average
- ○ below average

Style

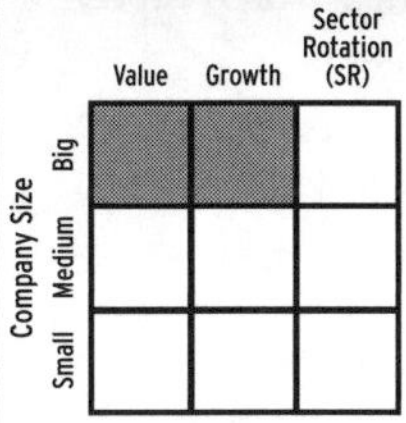

Complementary Fund:
Saxon Small Cap

Similar Fund:
Standard Life Canadian Dividend

In last year's edition of this book, we made the observation that we were "going out on a limb" by continuing to make Ivy Canadian a Top Fund. We're glad that we did. Ivy Canadian gained 6.7% over the past 12 months versus –6.3% for the average Canadian equity fund. Over five years, the fund has returned 11.5% a year compared with 9.6% a year for the average fund in the category.

This flagship Mackenzie fund, the largest Canadian equity fund in the land, has become an investor favourite because of an unwavering approach to stock selection. The fund has only 36 stocks in the portfolio, which is remarkable given its size, and there seems to be no hurry to spend the cash that frequently builds up.

Javasky and Roth make no attempt to forecast or time the market. There is a long-term outlook to their stock selections, which are made using a blended value/growth style. Capital preservation is paramount and the fund has never lost money over any calendar year. Ivy Canadian makes sense for risk-adverse investors and is an excellent core portfolio holding.

New

RRSP

SAXON STOCK FUND

Richard Howson (inception)/Howson Tattersall Investment Counsel Ltd.

Consistency

Performance Trend

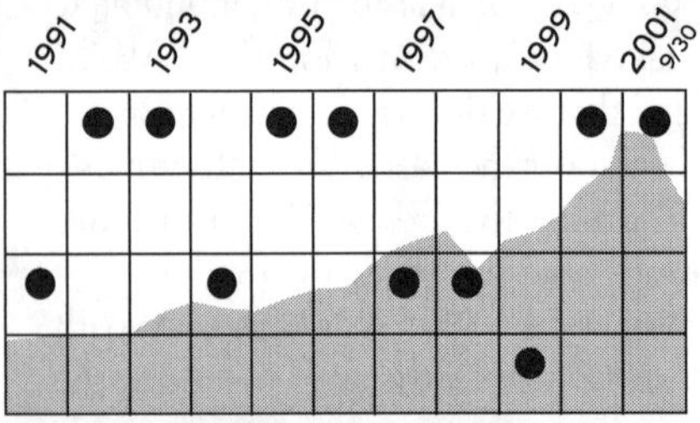

Risk

How often fund outperformed GICs	7 years in 8
How often fund lost money	2 years in 8
Worst year's rate of return	–13.34%

Reward-to-Risk Relationship

Sharpe Ratio Quartile Rankings

3-Year	1
5-Year	1

Morningstar Rating

★★★★★

Efficiency/MER

Management expense/$100

$1.75

○ above average
○ average
● below average

Style

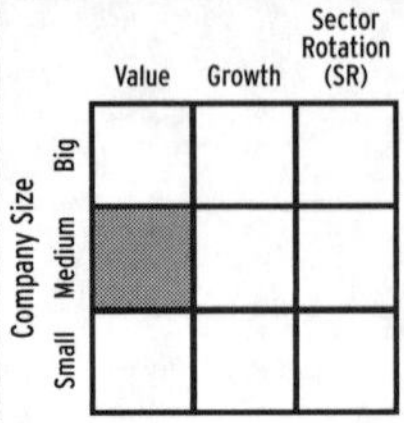

Complementary Fund:
AIC Diversified Canada

Similar Fund:
Spectrum Canadian Investment

Howson Tattersall Investment Counsel Ltd. is a smallish Toronto-based money manager with a proud record of manager continuity. For example, manager and company co-owner Richard Howson has been managing this fund since 1989.

Howson uses a contrarian approach to manage the Saxon Stock Fund. He can invest in small-, mid-, and large-cap Canadian companies and is willing to hold his selections for a long time. In fact, the average hold period of each security is four to five years, as Howson understands that it may take the market quite some time to realize the intrinsic value of his holdings. This approach makes Saxon Stock attractive for the non-RRSP portion of an investor's portfolio; low turnover means that taxable gains are triggered less often.

Howson notes that many of the same companies hitting 12-month lows this year are the same names that hit 12-month highs a year earlier. Although stocks hitting new lows are usually candidates for purchase by value managers, Howson says that few have attractive valuations or financial numbers. As a result, he still has little exposure to the Internet or wireless sectors. His largest weighting is a 32% exposure to industrial products, followed by a 26% weighting to financial services. The largest individual security holding is Goldcorp Inc., which represents 4% of the fund assets.

2000, 2001 RRSP

STANDARD LIFE CANADIAN EQUITY FUND
Management Team (inception)/Standard Life Investments Inc.

Consistency

Performance Trend

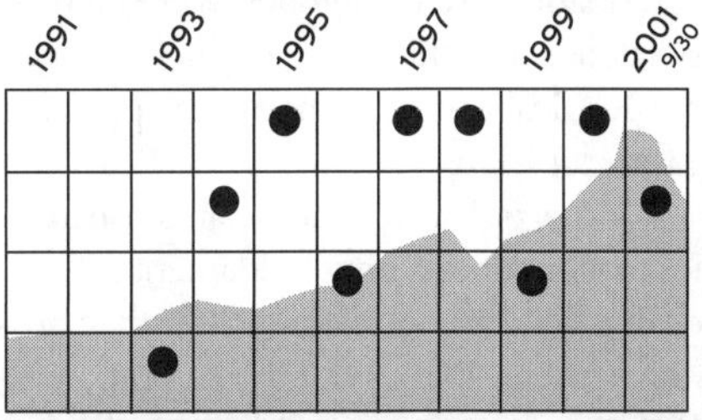

Risk

How often fund outperformed GICs	6 years in 8
How often fund lost money	0 years in 8
Worst year's rate of return	−16.43%

Reward-to-Risk Relationship
Sharpe Ratio Quartile Rankings

3-Year	2
5-Year	1

Morningstar Rating

★★★★

Efficiency/MER

Management expense/$100

$2.00

○ above average
○ average
● below average

Style

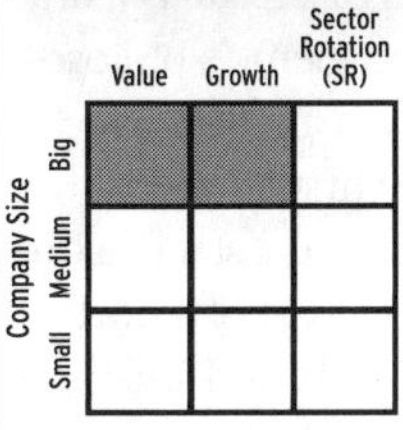

Complementary Fund:
BMO Dividend

Similar Fund:
Fidelity True North

Fundamental independent research is the "cornerstone" of Standard Life's investment philosophy, and over 75% of its research is internally generated. Its investment strategy is top-down in approach and is based on forecasts for interest rates, economic conditions, and capital markets growth. Standard Life also stresses teamwork with a committee-based structure that ensures a centralized approach to decision making. Rock star managers or investment gurus need not apply.

This fund, like many of Standard Life's equity portfolios, had a hefty exposure to Nortel Networks over the past two years. A 12.4% Nortel weighting on December 31, 2000 was reduced to only 4.3% by June 30, 2001. However, prudent stock selection and sector allocation decisions have offset much of the damage that Nortel has inflicted. The fund has fallen only 4.6% over the past 12 months and still has returned an average compounded annual rate of 14.2% over five years.

The management team has overweighted the energy and financial sectors, steering away from technology, gold, and transportation. The largest holding in the portfolio is a 4.3% weighting to CIBC.

2001 RRSP

SYNERGY CANADIAN MOMENTUM CLASS FUND

David Picton (1997)/Synergy Mutual Funds

Consistency

Performance Trend

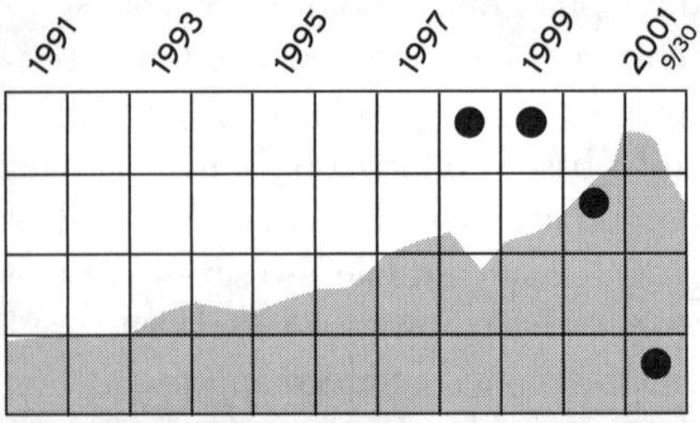

Risk

How often fund outperformed GICs	3 years in 3
How often fund lost money	0 years in 3
Worst year's rate of return	−32.83%

Reward-to-Risk Relationship
Sharpe Ratio Quartile Rankings

3-Year	2
5-Year	N/A

Morningstar Rating

★★★★

Efficiency/MER

Management expense/$100

$2.94

- ● above average
- ○ average
- ○ below average

Style

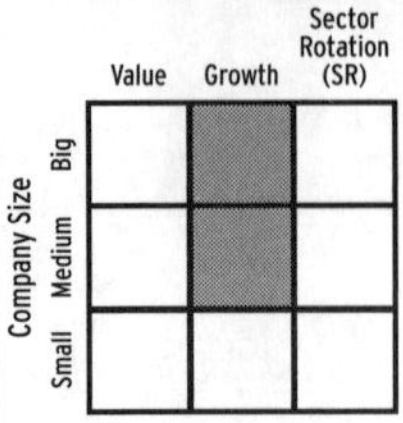

Complementary Fund:
BMO Dividend

Similar Fund:
E&P Dividend Canadian Equity Class

We're intrigued by this fund. Many funds and many managers claim to use research and quantitative techniques to create their portfolios, but this is one of the few funds to specifically use a momentum approach to stock picking.

Manager David Picton wants companies that are undergoing fundamental changes and are improving faster than anyone expects. To root out these companies, Picton uses a computer-driven model that analyses four change factors: (1) accelerating earnings/revenues, (2) positive estimate changes, (3) positive earnings surprises, and (4) strong relative price strength. After suitable candidates are identified, Picton then uses traditional fundamental analysis to narrow the list down further. He can't be characterized as a buy-and-hold manager. If a company doesn't meet his four criteria, he'll sell the stock.

The fund attempts to maximize its allowable foreign content for RRSP purposes, with 26.6% of the assets invested in foreign equities, mostly in the Synergy Global Momentum Fund. The largest single equity holding is a 4.8% exposure to CIBC.

Unfortunately, momentum can work both ways. Technology stocks met most of the momentum criteria in 2000 and an overweighting to that sector contributed to a decline of 15.4% over the past 12 months. But an average annual rate of return over three years of 12.0% is a first-quartile performance. Synergy's philosophy is style diversification and the company would be the first to admit that this fund makes no sense as a stand-alone investment. However, as part of a portfolio that has value, growth, and small-cap components, it makes perfect sense.

2001 RRSP

UNIVERSAL FUTURE FUND
John Rohr (1993)/Mackenzie Financial Corp.

Consistency

Performance Trend

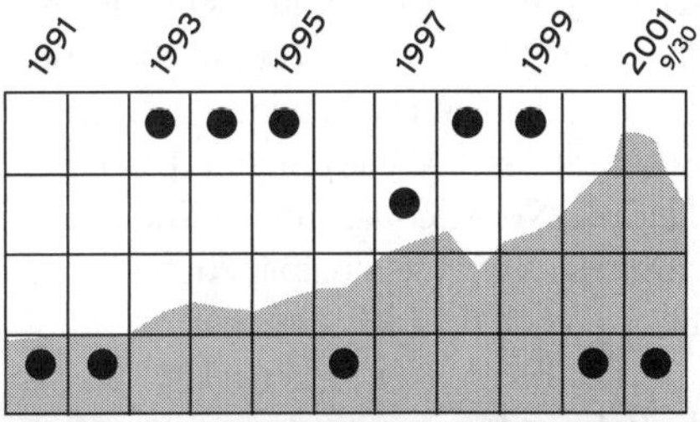

Risk

How often fund outperformed GICs	5 years in 8
How often fund lost money	2 years in 8
Worst year's rate of return	–31.36%

Reward-to-Risk Relationship
Sharpe Ratio Quartile Rankings

3-Year	2
5-Year	2

Morningstar Rating

★★★★

Efficiency/MER

Management expense/$100

$2.48

○ above average
● average
○ below average

Style

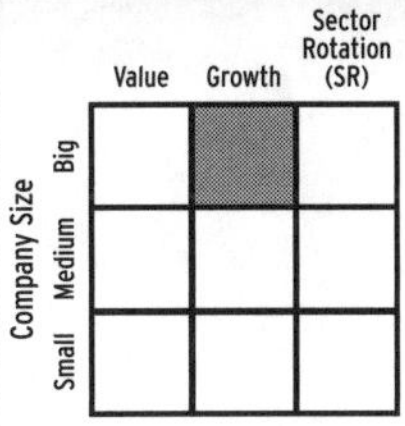

Complementary Fund:
BMO Dividend

Similar Fund:
Synergy Canadian Momentum Class

John Rohr's Universal Future Fund is a hybrid. Although the mandate is to invest at least half of fund assets in technology stocks on both sides of the border, Rohr also has significant "old economy" holdings in the oil and gas and automotive sectors. There is also a hefty 17.4% cash position.

Eight of the top ten holdings are non-technology stocks, although one can argue that many of those holdings have become industry leaders because of their use of technology. For example, Bombardier and Magna utilize cutting edge technologies in their manufacturing processes. Nonetheless, these non-technology investments have provided some welcome downside protection over the past 12 months. The Nasdaq Index is down 50.0% and the average science and technology fund has fallen 39.9%, while Universal Future Fund has dropped 21.9%. It's a big loss in absolute terms, but rather small relative to the losses many other investors experienced. Rohr also benefited from avoiding the high concept/no revenue Internet and software stocks that have fallen particularly hard. He prefers companies in industries with high barriers to entry because of advanced technological requirements.

Rohr is confident that there will be a recovery in the technology sector in 2002. The current valuations provide investors with a "much sounder investment window" and he feels that the technology sector still offers the greatest long-term opportunities for Canadians.

New

RRSP

CLARINGTON CANADIAN EQUITY FUND
Peter Marshall (1996)/Seamark Asset Management

Consistency

Performance Trend

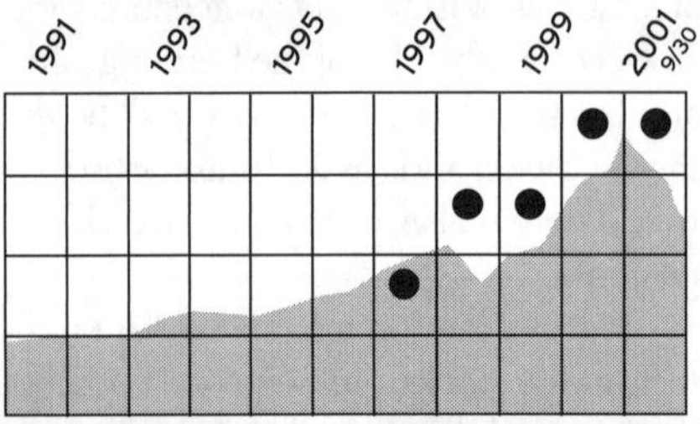

Risk

How often fund outperformed GICs	3 years in 4
How often fund lost money	0 years in 4
Worst year's rate of return	−17.25%

Reward-to-Risk Relationship
Sharpe Ratio Quartile Rankings

3-Year	1
5-Year	1

Morningstar Rating

★★★★★

Efficiency/MER

Management expense/$100

$2.90

● above average
○ average
○ below average

Style

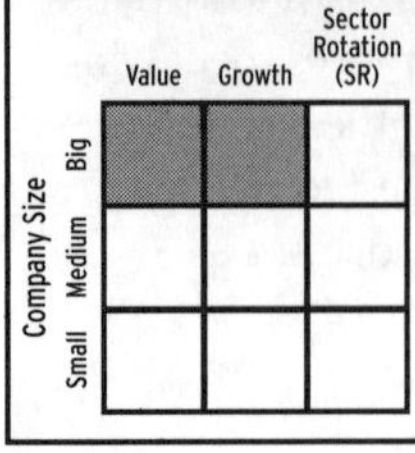

Complementary Fund:
PH&N Dividend Income

Similar Fund:
CI Signature Select Canadian

The top performing Canadian large-cap equity fund over the past three years, Clarington Canadian Equity Fund is proof that Bay Street isn't necessarily the centre of the Canadian investment universe. Seamark Asset Management is based in Halifax, Nova Scotia, and continues to impress us with its disciplined, fundamental approach to stock selection.

The firm uses a "Master List" that contains at least five years of corporate information and financials. Along with a commitment to personally meeting the management teams of the candidate firms, this database allows fund manager and Seamark founder Peter Marshall to determine whether there is a gap between the current market price and the three- to five-year price outlook. Three of the top four holdings in the ninety-position portfolio are Canadian banks, although the low valuations in some technology issues are starting to interest Marshall.

This approach is obviously successful. Clarington Canadian Equity has gained 3.7% over the past twelve months and 12.7% a year over the past three. Nortel's fall from grace continues to affect the Canadian large-cap sector as the average fund in the category lost 8.1% over the past twelve months and has gained only 4.0% annually over the past three years.

2001 RRSP

ELLIOTT & PAGE CABOT CDN EQUITY CLASS A FUND

Shauna Sexsmith (1999)/Altamira Management Ltd.

Consistency

Performance Trend

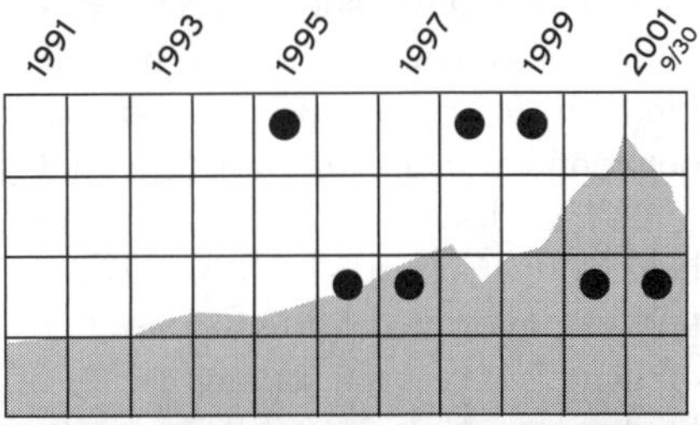

Risk

How often fund outperformed GICs	5 years in 6
How often fund lost money	0 years in 6
Worst year's rate of return	−28.96%

Reward-to-Risk Relationship

Sharpe Ratio Quartile Rankings

3-Year	1
5-Year	1

Morningstar Rating

★★★★

Efficiency/MER

Management expense/$100

$2.71

- ○ above average
- ● average
- ○ below average

Style

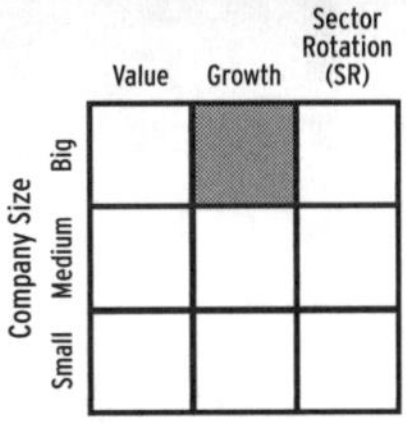

Complementary Fund:
BMO Dividend

Similar Fund:
Synergy Canadian Momentum Class

The "Class A" version of the E&P Cabot Canadian Equity Fund is the no-load, low fee fund that is sold through Manulife advisors. The "Advisors" version is available through independent financial planners and mutual fund salespeople. The MER of this version is 2.83% versus 2.71% for its "Class A" counterpart. The difference rates of return for the two versions should therefore be negligible.

Manager Shauna Sexsmith is a growth manager and therefore has suffered from the collapse of Nortel. Even now, her top 10 list shows Nortel as the second largest holding in the portfolio at 4.0%. This would explain the 15.2% decline in the fund over the past 12 months. By comparison, the average large-cap fund fell only 8.1%. The fund has posted first-quartile numbers over three and five years, however.

The fund usually holds 50 or so securities chosen from the top 150 companies on the TSE 300. Sexsmith typically focuses on certain sectors, although she currently has no significant sector bets. She is slightly overweight in financial services and oil and gas, but is well diversified across 13 of the 14 TSE subindices.

Sexsmith is fully invested, with only a 5.7% cash cushion. Unlike many Canadian equity managers, she doesn't hold any foreign holdings and makes no attempt to maximize the 30% foreign content that RRSP eligible funds are currently allowed.

2000, 2001 RRSP

ROYAL & SUN ALLIANCE EQUITY FUND

Brad Cann (2000)/Royal & Sun Alliance Investment Management

Consistency

Performance Trend

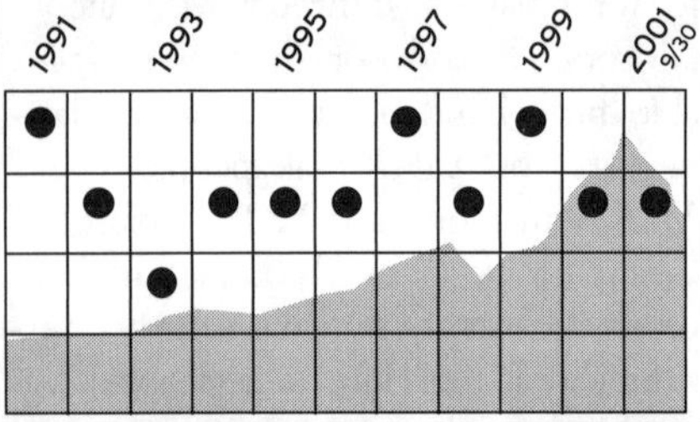

Risk

How often fund outperformed GICs	7 years in 8
How often fund lost money	2 years in 8
Worst year's rate of return	–18.39%

Reward-to-Risk Relationship

Sharpe Ratio Quartile Rankings

3-Year	1
5-Year	1

Morningstar Rating

★★★★★

Efficiency/MER

Management expense/$100

$2.65

○ above average
● average
○ below average

Style

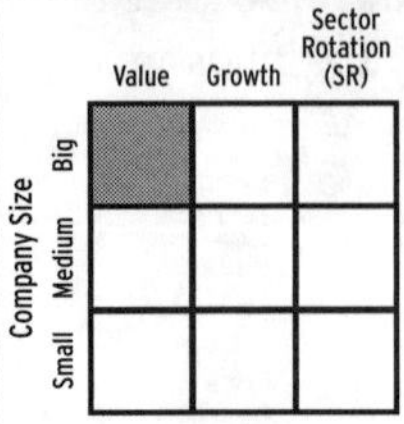

Complementary Fund:
BMO Dividend

Similar Fund:
E&P Cabot Canadian Equity Class A

In last year's edition of *Top Funds*, we mentioned that manager Brad Cann was new to the fund but we didn't expect any problems with performance or style. The fund remains a Top Fund pick this year, so our confidence in Cann wasn't misguided.

A Canadian large-cap fund that didn't hold Nortel Networks in the past is a rare find and unfortunately this fund isn't one of them. Last year, a whopping 14.7% of fund assets were in Nortel. This year, the company represents only 2.3% of the fund. The largest holding is a 4.7% exposure to CIBC; in fact, five of the top seven holdings are Canadian banks.

The fund has returned 14.5% a year over five years and 11.9% over ten years—both are first-quartile numbers. It has lost 9.5% over the past 12 months versus a 8.1% decline for the average Canadian large-cap fund.

1999, 2000 RRSP

SPECTRUM CANADIAN INVESTMENT FUND
Kim Shannon (1999)/Mercury Asset Management

Consistency

Performance Trend

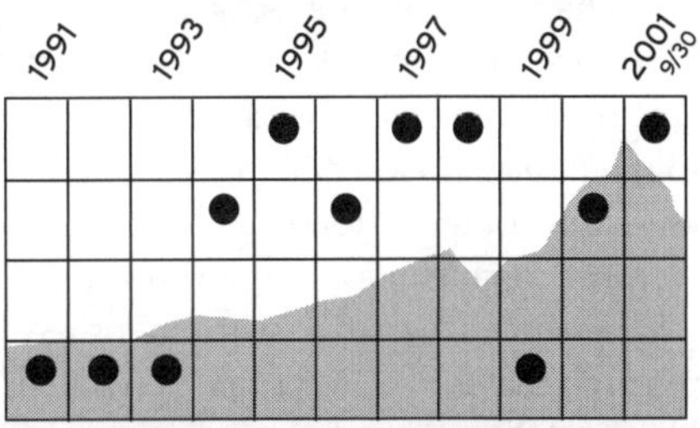

Risk

How often fund outperformed GICs	6 years in 8
How often fund lost money	2 years in 8
Worst year's rate of return	−8.77%

Reward-to-Risk Relationship
Sharpe Ratio Quartile Rankings

3-Year	1
5-Year	1

Morningstar Rating

★★★★

Efficiency/MER

Management expense/$100

$2.52

○ above average
● average
○ below average

Style

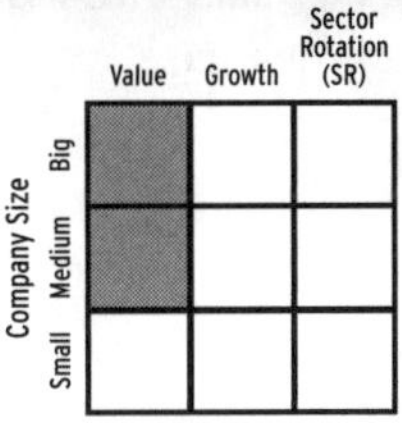

Complementary Fund:
Saxon Small Cap

Similar Fund:
Maxxum Dividend

Kim Shannon has actually been at the helm of this fund since 1996. In early 1999, she left AMI Partners—the manager of the fund at that time—and joined Mercury Asset Management. Six months later, Spectrum hired Mercury Asset Management—and Kim Shannon—to manage the fund.

Quite frankly, we made a mistake by leaving this fund out of our Top 100 last year. We're big proponents of the value style and Shannon's value approach to investment management paid off big time when investors went looking for blue chip investments in the aftermath of the technology stock collapse. Over the past 12 months, the fund has gained 13.8% versus a 23.1% loss for the TSE 300. A two-year average annual return of 13.5% and a five-year annual average return of 14.6% confirm that the fund also offers a low level of volatility to investors. In fact, our Morningstar database reveals that Spectrum Canadian Investment has the lowest standard deviation of returns of any Canadian large-cap equity fund over the past five and ten years.

Shannon owns no technology stocks and is proud of that fact. In her view, investors are still willing to pay high multiples for technology issues in anticipation of an expected earnings recovery in 2002. The problem is that 2002 earnings are anticipated to reach only 2000 levels. She still feels that the "old economy" is the place to be. Her holdings are a blue chip "who's who" of the Canadian economy: RBC, Magna, Bank of Montreal, CNR, and Alcan make up her top five names.

New

RRSP

BEUTEL GOODMAN SMALL-CAP FUND
Dennis Marsh (1997)/Beutel Goodman Managed Funds Inc.

Consistency

Performance Trend

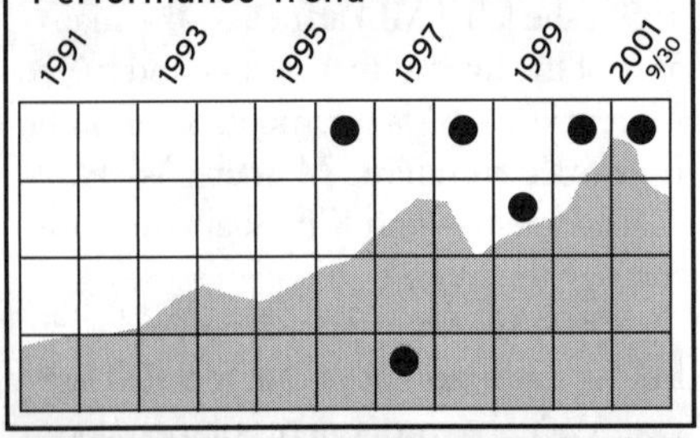

Risk

How often fund outperformed GICs	3 years in 4
How often fund lost money	1 year in 4
Worst year's rate of return	–16.87%

Reward-to-Risk Relationship
Sharpe Ratio Quartile Rankings

3-Year	1
5-Year	1

Morningstar Rating

★★★★★

Efficiency/MER

Management expense/$100

$1.39

○ above average
○ average
● below average

Style

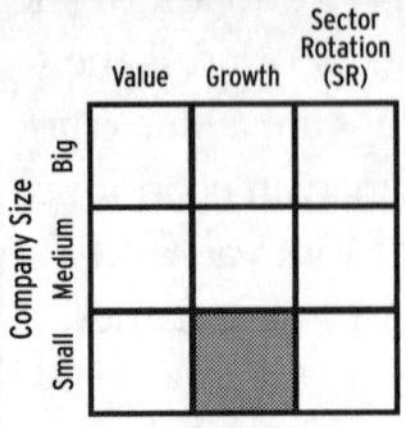

Complementary Fund:
PH&N Dividend Income

Similar Fund:
E&P Cabot Canadian Equity Class A

This fund is a bit of an anomaly in the Canadian small-cap world. Most of these funds have volatile returns, with home run years offset by strike out years. Most are growth oriented, with a technology focus. Beutel Goodman Small-Cap follows none of these trends. Manager Dennis Marsh employs a bottom-up, value-oriented approach with extensive research that is 90% internally generated. His portfolio names do include some technology companies, but he also has a hefty weighting to both the real estate and natural resources sectors. The average P/E and P/B ratios of the 45 companies in the portfolio are lower than average, while the dividend yields are higher than average. This is, of course, characteristic of the value management style.

The largest holding in the portfolio is a 7.2% weighting in Mosaic Group. Beutel Goodman managers like to have focused portfolios, with meaningful positions in their investments. It's therefore noteworthy that the fund has provided investors with consistent returns. The three-year standard deviation of returns is much lower than average and the fund has only lost money in one calendar year, 1998, when it declined by 2.7%.

Marsh feels that small-cap investments will continue to outperform their large-cap counterparts over the next two to three years. As a result, he is fully invested for the first time in many quarters.

New

RRSP

NATIONAL BANK SMALL CAPITALIZATION FUND
Benoit Durand (1988)/Natcan Investment Management Inc.

Consistency

Performance Trend

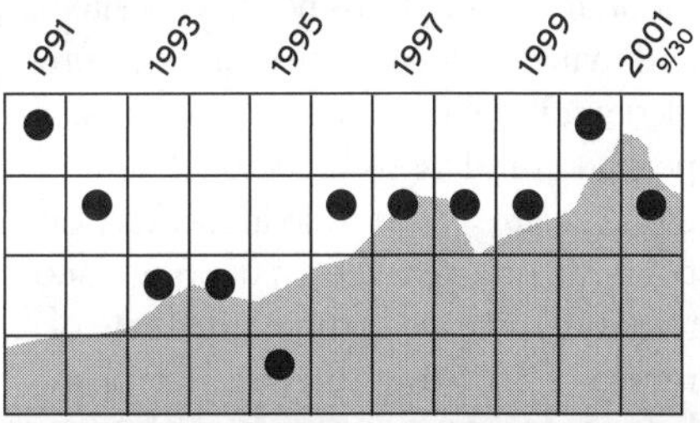

Risk

How often fund outperformed GICs	7 years in 8
How often fund lost money	2 years in 8
Worst year's rate of return	−21.76%

Reward-to-Risk Relationship
Sharpe Ratio Quartile Rankings

3-Year	1
5-Year	1

Morningstar Rating

★★★★

Efficiency/MER

Management expense/$100

$2.35

○ above average
● average
○ below average

Style

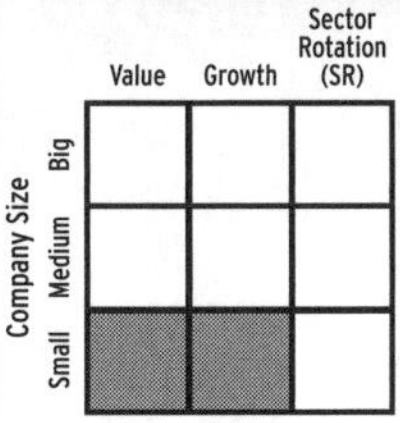

Complementary Fund:
PH&N Dividend Income

Similar Fund:
Fidelity True North

We're impressed with this fund. Manager Benoit Durand has produced excellent returns with lower-than-average volatility. The fund has gained 18.7% over the past 12 months versus a 5.3% loss for the benchmark BMO Nesbitt Burns Small-Cap Index. Equally impressive is the fact that the fund has beaten the Index in each of the past five calendar years.

Durand's portfolio has a value bias, with P/E and P/B ratios that are lower than average and dividend yields that are higher than average. His largest equity holding is a 3.7% weighting to Van Houtte Ltee. The top 15 holdings represent just over 40% of the 63 stock portfolio, which is average for the category. Durand's focus is on the communications and media sectors, consumer products and distribution. He likes Leitch Technology (a digital television company and the third biggest name in his portfolio), Axcan Pharma and Theratechnologies.

2001 RRSP

RESOLUTE GROWTH FUND

Tom Stanley (1993)/Thomson Kernaghan & Co. Ltd.

Consistency

Performance Trend

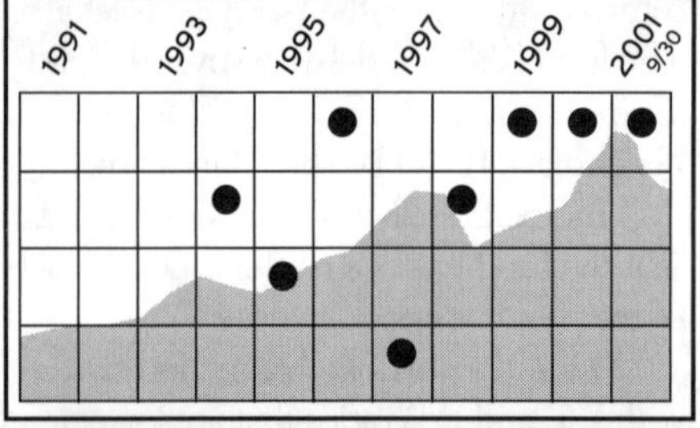

Risk

How often fund outperformed GICs	4 years in 4
How often fund lost money	3 years in 4
Worst year's rate of return	−17.66%

Reward-to-Risk Relationship

Sharpe Ratio Quartile Rankings

3-Year	1
5-Year	1

Morningstar Rating

★★★★★

Efficiency/MER

Management expense/$100

$2.09

- ○ above average
- ○ average
- ● below average

Style

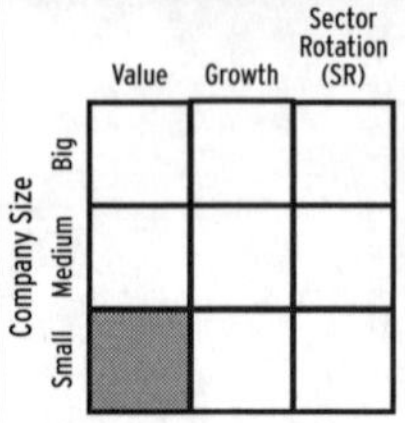

Complementary Fund:
PH&N Dividend Income

Similar Fund:
Saxon Small Cap

Last year we picked Resolute Growth Fund as an entry that didn't get the recognition it deserved. It's now a year later, and manager Tom Stanley has been profiled in one of Canada's national newspapers and fund assets have doubled. We didn't realize we were so influential! Of course, a one-year return of 36.6% and an annual average compounded rate of return of 36% over three years probably helped.

Stanley likes to focus his investments on his best ideas and the result is a concentrated portfolio of only 16 stocks. The largest holding, Cangene Corp., composes over 19% of the portfolio. Stanley is a long-term investor and a self-described skeptic who looks for investments that make sense from both growth and value perspectives. His current focus is on oil and gas, despite acknowledging that short-term price fluctuations are unpredictable. Long term, he expects the demand for oil to grow and energy higher prices to spur exploration and development.

The small number of holdings mean volatility; in fact, the fund has lost money in three of the past eight years. However, investors with a long time horizon and an interest in diversifying into small Canadian companies should consider this fund.

New

RRSP

SAXON SMALL-CAP FUND

Robert Tattersall (inception)/Howson Tattersall Investment Counsel Ltd.

Consistency

Performance Trend

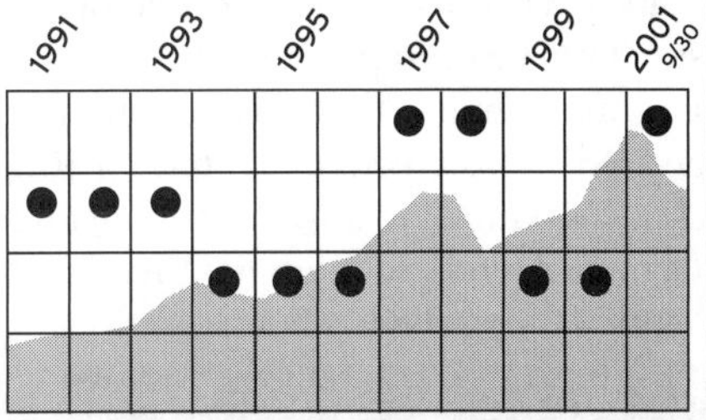

Risk

How often fund outperformed GICs	7 years in 9
How often fund lost money	1 year in 9
Worst year's rate of return	–14.82%

Reward-to-Risk Relationship

Sharpe Ratio Quartile Rankings

3-Year	1
5-Year	1

Morningstar Rating

★★★★

Efficiency/MER

Management expense/$100

$1.75

- ○ above average
- ○ average
- ● below average

Style

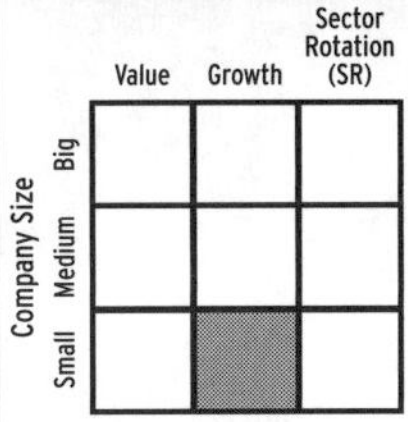

Complementary Fund:
PH&N Dividend Income

Similar Fund:
National Bank Small Capitalization

Industry veteran Bob Tattersall is a recognized expert in the small-cap stock area. He has a strict "value" philosophy and feels that patience is the key to successful value investing. It takes time for the market to appreciate the intrinsic value of the stocks that Tattersall likes to own, which is something he's learned through 30 years of bull and bear markets.

His portfolio consists of companies listed on the Toronto Stock Exchange (TSE) with a market capitalization of less than $300 million. The valuations of his holdings compare very favourably with those of the TSE 300. The portfolio price-to-book value of 1.09 is less than half the 2.31 P/B ratio of the TSE. Similarly, his price-to-cash flow ratio is 5.38 versus 9.5 for the broader market.

The Saxon Small-Cap Fund has averaged 17.0% a year over the past five years and 15.1% a year over ten years. Impressively, these returns have been achieved at levels of volatility lower than both the average small-cap equity fund and the TSE 300 itself.

2001 RRSP

DYNAMIC VENTURE OPPORTUNITIES FUND

Ray Benzinger (1996)/Goodman & Company Investment Counsel

Consistency

Performance Trend

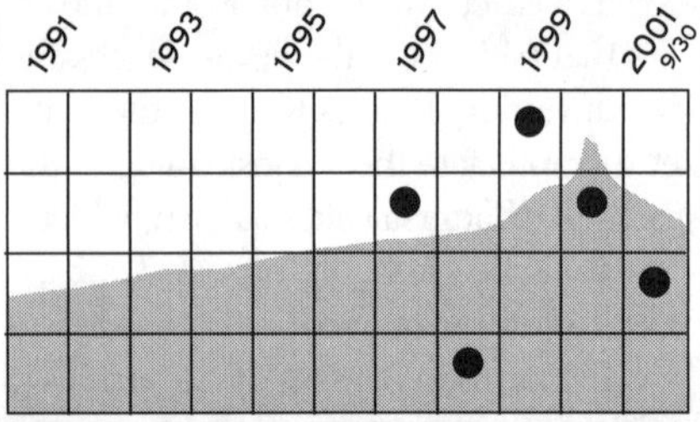

Risk

How often fund outperformed GICs	2 years in 3
How often fund lost money	3 years in 3
Worst year's rate of return	–28.36%

Reward-to-Risk Relationship

Sharpe Ratio Quartile Rankings

3-Year	1
5-Year	1

Morningstar Rating

N/A

Efficiency/MER

Management expense/$100

$5.32

● above average
○ average
○ below average

Style

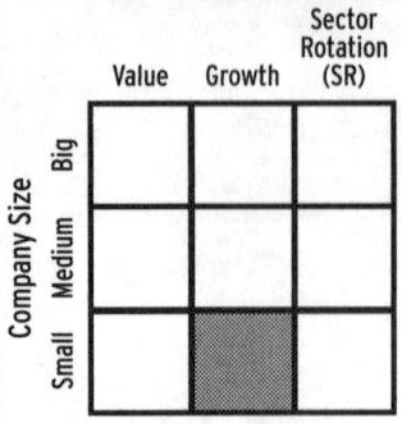

Complementary Fund:
N/A

Similar Fund:
N/A

An investment that posts an annual compound rate of return of 24.3% over three years or 11.3% over five years is impressive. Even more impressive is that investors continue to receive provincial and federal tax credits to the tune of 30% as an "incentive" to invest in venture capital mutual funds, such as the Dynamic Venture Opportunities Fund.

The irony is that over the past two years, Canadian investors needed little incentive to invest in venture capital situations. Unfortunately, they didn't know it was venture capital investments they were making at the time. The resulting market correction left investors disillusioned. Many small companies have also been left without a source of capital. Valuations have recently become more reasonable, however, and manager Ray Benzinger feels that there are many excellent opportunities available for his fund. He currently has a huge cash position—over 52% of the fund assets—and he will continue to seek out real companies with real products and real profit possibilities. His top five holdings are AirIQ Inc., Dimethaid Research Inc., PetHealth Inc., Shopsy's Hospitality, and Nu-Gro Corporation.

New

RRSP

WORKING OPPORTUNITY BALANCED FUND
Management Team (inception)/Growth Works Capital Ltd.

Consistency

Performance Trend

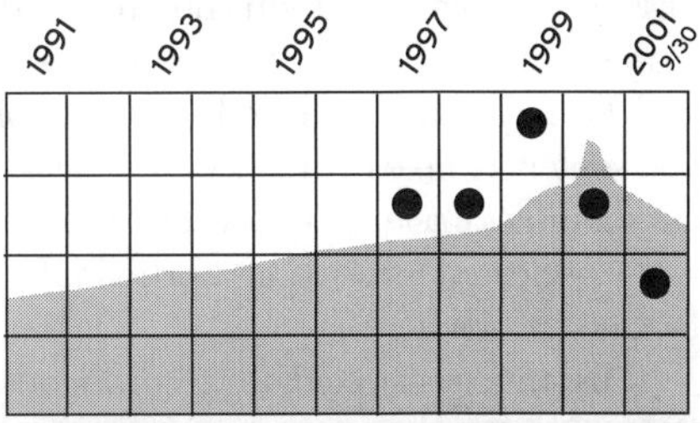

Risk

How often fund outperformed GICs	4 years in 8
How often fund lost money	0 years in 8
Worst year's rate of return	−14.15%

Reward-to-Risk Relationship
Sharpe Ratio Quartile Rankings

3-Year	1
5-Year	1

Morningstar Rating

N/A

Efficiency/MER

Management expense/$100

$2.40

○ above average
○ average
● below average

Style

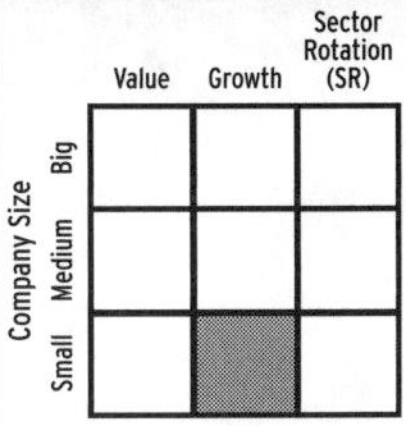

Complementary Fund:
N/A

Similar Fund:
N/A

We shouldn't be talking about this fund, as it is only available for sale in British Columbia and we normally like our Top Fund picks to be available across the country. However, there are so many things we like about Working Opportunity Balanced that we're including it anyway.

The first thing we like is the low management expense ratio. An MER of 2.4% may not seem that low, but it is for a labour-sponsored venture capital fund. Incredibly, nine labour-sponsored funds have MERs that are greater than 5.0% and one charges 7.16%! The second thing we like is that the fund is actually investing in venture capital situations. A visit to the excellent Working Opportunity Web site (another thing we like about the fund) offers profiles of the companies into which the fund has invested. One of the main criticisms of labour funds has been that cash often sits in bonds and T-bills; that isn't the case with this fund.

Finally, the fund has been good to its investors. It has averaged 34% a year over the past two years and its average annual return of 14.3% over five years is tops in the category. It's a great fund that, unfortunately, most Canadians can't purchase.

2000, 2001 RRSP

BMO DIVIDEND FUND
Michael Stanley (1994)/Jones Heward Investment Counsel

Consistency

Performance Trend

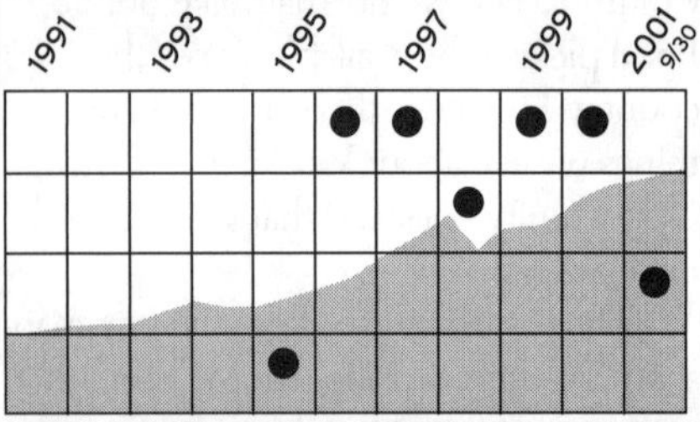

Risk

How often fund outperformed GICs	4 years in 6
How often fund lost money	0 years in 6
Worst year's rate of return	−8.37%

Reward-to-Risk Relationship
Sharpe Ratio Quartile Rankings

3-Year	1
5-Year	1

Morningstar Rating

★★★★★

Efficiency/MER

Management expense/$100

$1.80

○ above average
○ average
● below average

Style

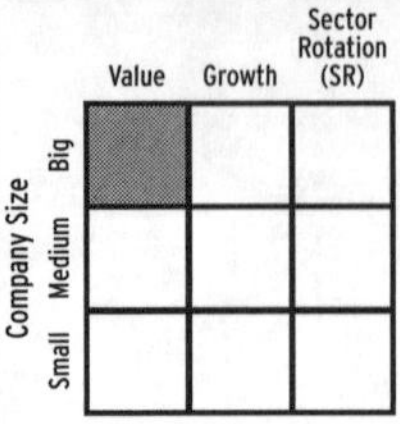

Complementary Fund:
Mac Universal Future

Similar Fund:
PH&N Dividend Income

The mandate of Michael Stanley's BMO Dividend Fund is to invest "primarily in dividend-yielding common and preferred shares of established Canadian companies." Disregard the preferred share part of that sentence. Like many successful dividend fund managers, Stanley doesn't have many preferred issues in his portfolio. In fact, he has none.

His strategy has paid, um. . .dividends. BMO Dividend has returned 23% over the past twelve months, 10.4% over three years, and 20.0% over five years. A lower-than-average management expense ratio of 1.77% (versus 2.29% for the average Canadian dividend fund) certainly helps, but Stanley's focus on common shares can be credited for his success. The "search for quality" in the wake of the technology meltdown also helped, as shell-shocked investors found comfort in the large, blue chip Canadian companies that Stanley likes. He doesn't invest in U.S. or international stocks, so investors hoping to gain the 30% foreign exposure that most RRSP eligible funds have should look elsewhere. By contrast, the average Canadian dividend fund has 11.8% of fund assets in non-Canadian equities.

1996, 1997, 1998, 1999, 2000, 2001 RRSP

MAXXUM DIVIDEND FUND
Bill Procter (2001)/Mackenzie Financial Corp.

Consistency

Performance Trend

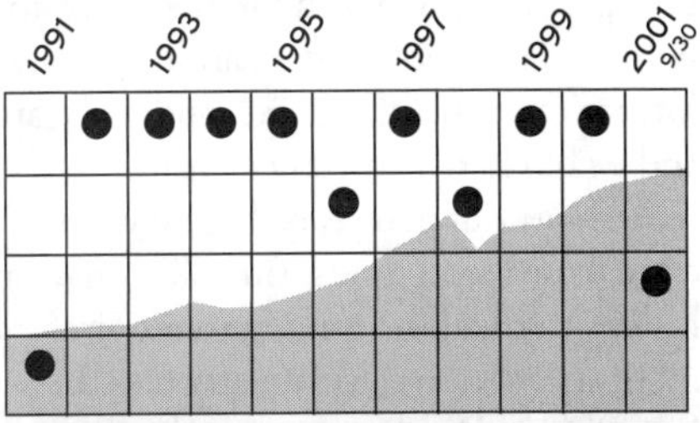

Risk

How often fund outperformed GICs	7 years in 10
How often fund lost money	0 years in 10
Worst year's rate of return	–10.49%

Reward-to-Risk Relationship
Sharpe Ratio Quartile Rankings

3-Year	1
5-Year	1

Morningstar Rating

★★★★

Efficiency/MER

Management expense/$100

$2.40

- ○ above average
- ● average
- ○ below average

Style

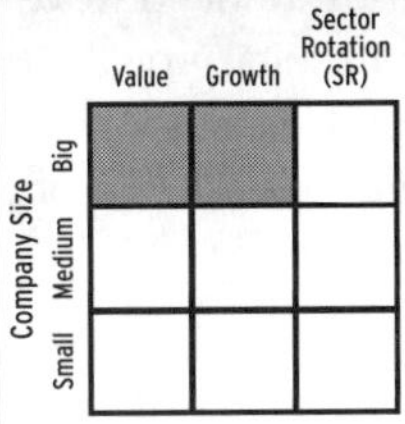

Complementary Fund:
Saxon Small Cap

Similar Fund:
Standard Life Canadian Dividend

No, it isn't a typo. Jackee Pratt is out and Mackenzie's Bill Procter is in. In July of this year, Mackenzie Financial announced that they would be replacing all of the MAXXUM fund managers with Mackenzie managers. The decision to have all the funds sold by independent advisors placed under Mackenzie's control (made by Mackenzie's parent, Investors Group) makes business sense, but we are still leery. Despite assurances from Mackenzie that fund mandates won't change, we're from Missouri on this one: you'll have to show us.

Pratt's approach was to focus on good quality, blue chip firms with above average dividend yields. She favoured common shares over preferred issues. Five of her top ten holdings were banks and both bank stocks and preferred issues share one important characteristic: they both are susceptible to interest rate risk; when rates go up, bank stocks and preferred stocks go down.

MAXXUM Dividend Fund has been a first-quartile performer over three, five, and ten years. We, however, are withholding our recommendation of this fund to new investors. Don't get us wrong: Bill Procter is a good manager. In fact, his Industrial Income Fund is a Top Fund this year. Jackee Pratt, however, is a great manager and she'll be missed.

1996, 1997, 1998, 1999, 2000, 2001 RRSP

PHILLIPS, HAGER & NORTH DIVIDEND INCOME FUND

Dale Harrison (1999)/Phillips Hager & North Investment Management

Consistency

Performance Trend

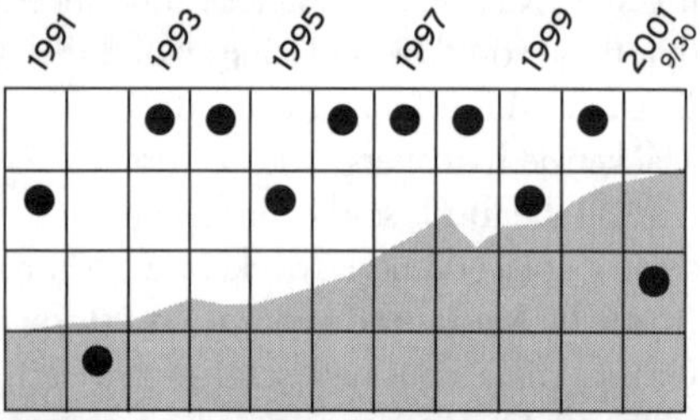

Risk

How often fund outperformed GICs	6 years in 9
How often fund lost money	1 year in 9
Worst year's rate of return	–6.93%

Reward-to-Risk Relationship

Sharpe Ratio Quartile Rankings

3-Year	1
5-Year	1

Morningstar Rating

★★★★★

Efficiency/MER

Management expense/$100

$1.21

○ above average
○ average
● below average

Style

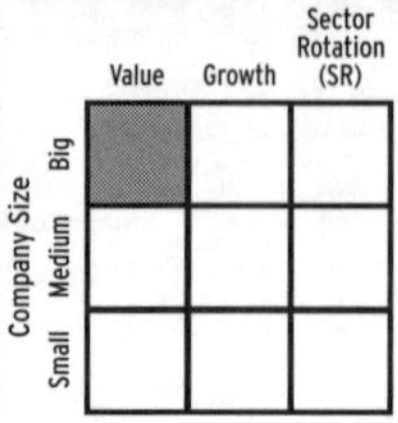

Complementary Fund:
Saxon Small Cap

Similar Fund:
BMO Dividend

Investors with $25,000 to invest in a dividend fund should look seriously at the Phillips, Hager & North Dividend Income Fund. It has been a first-quartile performer over one, three, five, and ten years and would have posted first-quartile returns over fifteen years if there were enough dividend funds with a fifteen-year history to meet the minimum requirements needed to calculate quartiles. In fact, PH&N Dividend Income has the second highest average annual rate of return over fifteen years (14.3%) of any Canadian equity fund.

Manager Dale Harrison's economic outlook is for modest growth, continued low inflation and low interest rates. He credits a relatively large exposure to manufacturing, utility, and financial services stocks for the fund's recent superior performance. He's also underweight in oil and gas and technology stocks. In fact, most of the PH&N Canadian equity funds have benefited from an underweight position in Nortel. Harrison feels that the prospects for continued high energy prices aren't good and has been taking profits on his oil and gas positions.

Harrison's investment approach is to focus on attractively valued, mature, well-managed, and highly profitable growth companies. Most of his holdings are the common shares of blue chip companies, which offer both superior dividend yields and the opportunity for capital growth. The largest position in the 32-stock portfolio is a 7.5% exposure to RBC. Five of the top ten holdings are the Big Five banks.

2000, 2001 RRSP

STANDARD LIFE CANADIAN DIVIDEND FUND

Management Team (inception)/Standard Life Investments Inc.

Consistency

Performance Trend

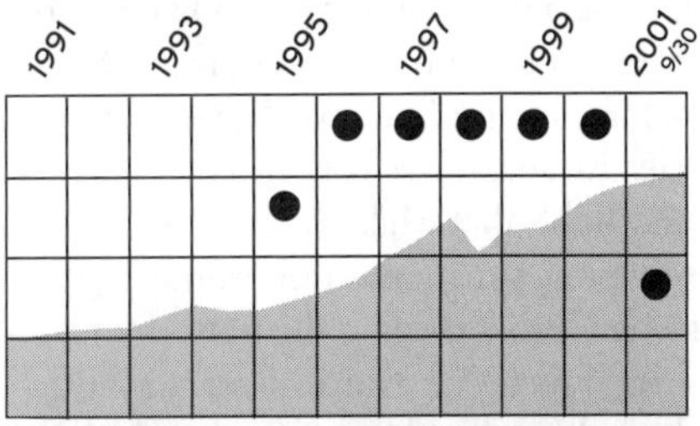

Risk

How often fund outperformed GICs	5 years in 6
How often fund lost money	0 years in 6
Worst year's rate of return	−9.23%

Reward-to-Risk Relationship

Sharpe Ratio Quartile Rankings

3-Year	1
5-Year	1

Morningstar Rating

★★★★★

Efficiency/MER

Management expense/$100

$1.50

○ above average
○ average
● below average

Style

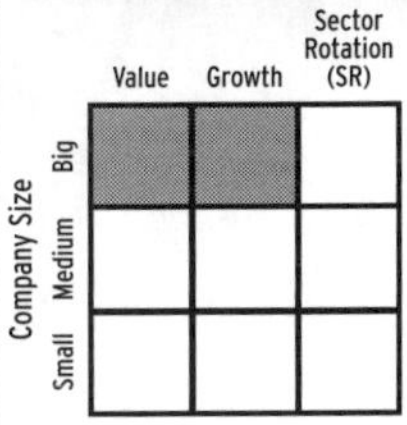

Complementary Fund:
Saxon Small Cap

Similar Fund:
BMO Dividend

Standard Life is proud of its disciplined approach to equity portfolio construction. The first step with this strategy is to establish sector weightings based on their 12- to 18-month outlook. Next, security weights for each sector are determined, with predetermined limits set for individual stocks and cash. An equity team of 13 managers and analysts then identifies possible investment opportunities within each sector. A written research report must accompany each recommendation before a senior vice-president approves it. Finally, all trades and activity reports are monitored by the entire investment team.

This rigorous approach has been successful: The Standard Life Canadian Dividend Fund has been a first-quartile performer over one, two, three, and five years. In fact, the average annual rate of return of 21.5% a year over the past five years is the eighth best of any mutual fund sold in Canada.

The equity allocation is 55% interest sensitive stocks and 45% economy sensitive stocks. Cash has been invested into banks and other cyclical issues. A small Nortel position resulting from the Bell spin-off was finally sold after Nortel eliminated the dividend on the stock. The largest holding, representing 6.6% of the portfolio, is Scotiabank. TD Bank, CIBC, BCE, and RBC make up the rest of the top five.

2001 RRSP

HSBC U.S. EQUITY FUND
Management Team/HSBC Asset Management (Americas) Inc.

Consistency

Performance Trend

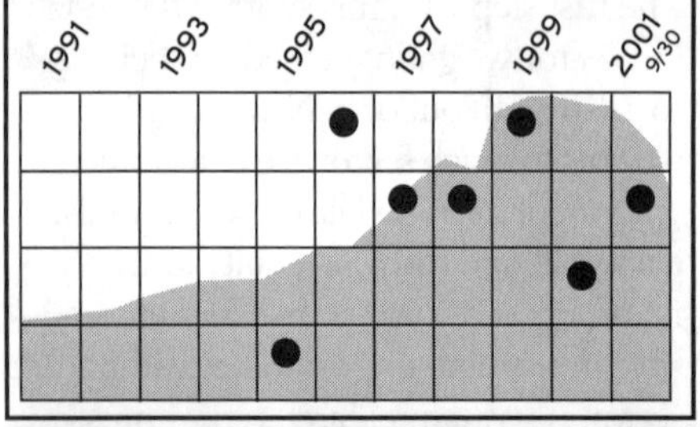

Risk

How often fund outperformed GICs	5 years in 5
How often fund lost money	1 year in 5
Worst year's rate of return	−28.52%

Reward-to-Risk Relationship
Sharpe Ratio Quartile Rankings

3-Year	1
5-Year	1

Morningstar Rating

★★★★

Efficiency/MER

Management expense/$100

$2.25

- ○ above average
- ○ average
- ● below average

Style

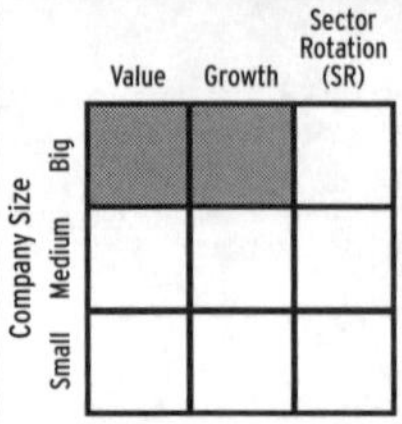

Complementary Fund:
Investors U.S. Large Cap Value

Similar Fund:
TD U.S. Index

This fund is managed with a "big picture" style. The management team uses an approach that blends a top-down macro review of economic conditions, technical factors, and business cycle analysis, with selective security selection. Their current view holds that while the U.S. short-term economic situation is not promising, they feel the economy is at the bottom of a U-shaped recovery. The analysts at HSBC also believe the U.S. market has the best positioning for a rebound in world markets.

The fund is fully invested, with only a 0.9% cash reserve. The largest holding in the 62-stock portfolio is a 4.5% exposure to Microsoft. American International Group and Exxon Mobil Corp. are the next two largest positions. Compared with the average U.S. equity fund, HSBC U.S. Equity is overweighted to technology and healthcare. Of course, this weighting isn't surprising given the fund's orientation to growth stocks.

This growth stock focus explains the performance over the past 12 months: the fund lost 20.0% last year, but has returned a first-quartile 14.7% a year over 5 years.

There is an RRSP eligible version of this fund available.

New

RRSP

INVESTORS U.S. LARGE-CAP VALUE FUND

Terry Wong (1998)/Investors Group

Consistency

Performance Trend

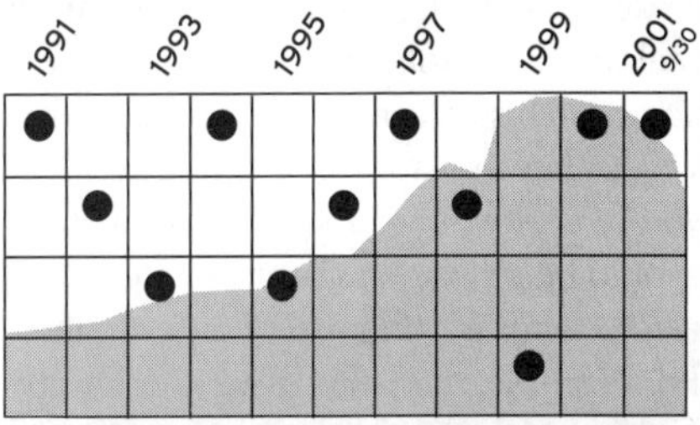

Risk

How often fund outperformed GICs	8 years in 9
How often fund lost money	1 year in 9
Worst year's rate of return	–17.96%

Reward-to-Risk Relationship

Sharpe Ratio Quartile Rankings

3-Year	1
5-Year	1

Morningstar Rating

★★★★★

Efficiency/MER

Management expense/$100

$2.94

● above average
○ average
○ below average

Style

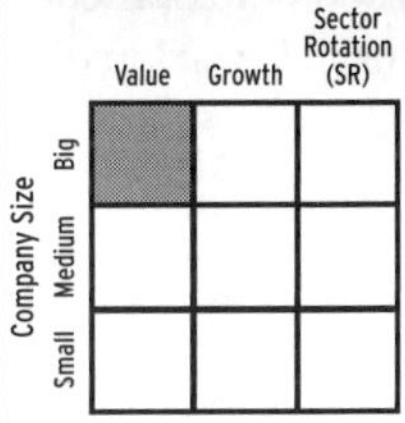

Complementary Fund:
HSBC U.S. Equity

Similar Fund:
Fidelity Small Cap America

Manager Terry Wong is happy that 1999 is long gone. As a value manager who invests in companies with good cash flows and management that is shareholder focused, Wong avoided technology and the fund's performance suffered. It lost 10.2% in an environment that rewarded growth and technology investors. Two years later, of course, things are different. Investors U.S. Large-Cap Value gained 26.7% in calendar 2000 and has eked out a 0.8% return in the year to date. By comparison, the average U.S. equity fund lost 4.4% in 2000 and has slipped 8.2% in the year to date. Long term, the fund has averaged an impressive 19.6% a year over five years and 18.5% a year over ten years.

Wong is seeing value in health care and consumer products. He feels the large pharmaceuticals are underpriced and believes some of the large brandname companies, such as Procter & Gamble and Gillette, are also excellent long-term investments. Not surprisingly, he also has a 4.1% weighting in his portfolio to Warren Buffett's Berkshire Hathaway.

There is an RRSP eligible version of this fund available.

2001 RRSP

JANUS AMERICAN EQUITY FUND
Warren Lammert (1997)/Janus Capital Corp.

Consistency
Performance Trend

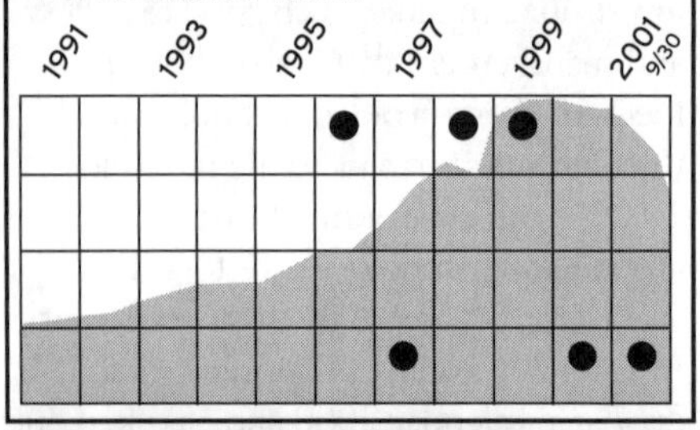

Risk

How often fund outperformed GICs	4 years in 4
How often fund lost money	1 year in 4
Worst year's rate of return	−46.28%

Reward-to-Risk Relationship
Sharpe Ratio Quartile Rankings

3-Year	1
5-Year	1

Morningstar Rating
★★★★

Efficiency/MER
Management expense/$100

$2.90

● above average
○ average
○ below average

Style

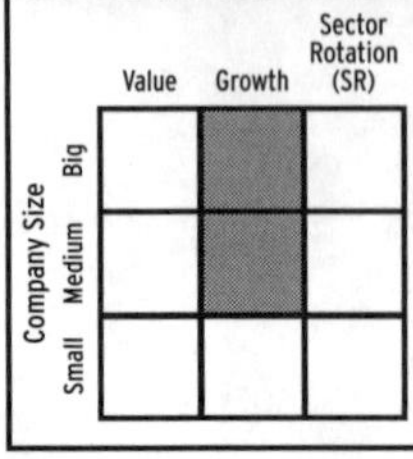

Complementary Fund:
Investors U.S. Large Cap Value

Similar Fund:
TD U.S. Index

"Informational risk" is a term the investment analysts at Janus Capital Corp. use to describe the biggest risk they face when building a portfolio: not knowing enough about each stock and each company into which they invest. They also feel that if you're performing unique research, it should be reflected in your portfolio. As a result, Janus portfolios are concentrated. For example, the Janus American Equity Fund holds only 67 securities.

The downside of this approach is higher volatility. Over the past 12 months, Janus American Equity has lost 31.2% of its value. The upside is that long-term results should be superior, which is the case with this fund: the 21.7% compound annual rate of return over five years is the highest of any U.S. equity fund sold in Canada. In 1999, the fund rose 76.9% after climbing 67.8% in 1998.

Manager Warren Lammert's focus is on large-cap growth stocks and many of his top holdings are the technology names that have suffered badly over the past two years. A full 34% of his portfolio and eight of his top ten are technology companies. His largest holding is Nokia, the Finnish cellular phone and wireless infrastructure giant. Lammert still likes this stock. Nokia is the world's number five brand and Lammert believes its dominant market share translates into lower costs and big advantages in research and development.

There is an RRSP eligible version of this fund available.

2000, 2001 RRSP

MCLEAN BUDDEN AMERICAN GROWTH FUND

Management Team (inception)/McLean Budden Ltd.

Consistency

Performance Trend

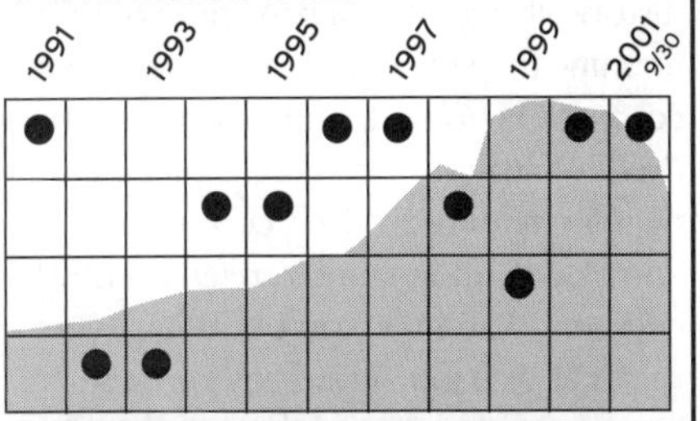

Risk

How often fund outperformed GICs	8 years in 10
How often fund lost money	0 years in 10
Worst year's rate of return	−15.25%

Reward-to-Risk Relationship

Sharpe Ratio Quartile Rankings

3-Year	1
5-Year	1

Morningstar Rating

★★★★★

Efficiency/MER

Management expense/$100

$1.29

- above average
- average
- below average (selected)

Style

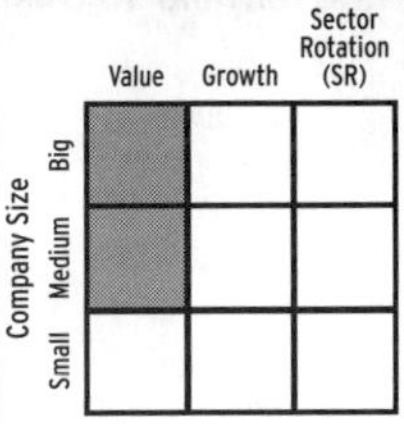

Complementary Fund:
AGF Aggressive Growth

Similar Fund:
TD U.S. Index

We like stability. In our view, it translates into consistently superior performance. McLean Budden has been in the investment business since 1947 and they are proud of the fact that their portfolio management teams have an average 15 years' experience in the industry.

The McLean Budden American Equity Fund has a growth stock orientation, but the fund has managed to avoid most of the pain that growth equity funds have suffered over the past two years. A 12-month loss of only 1.4% compares favourably with a 13.9% decline for the average U.S equity fund. In fact, the fund has been a first-quartile performer over one, two, three, five, and ten years. A management expense ratio of only 1.60% certainly helps, but so does a growth-at-a-reasonable-price (GARP) style that allows lead manager Bruce Murray to avoid many of the really overpriced issues that led last year's correction.

The portfolio is fairly concentrated, with only 50 equity positions. Murray feels that the technology sector has bottomed out, but doesn't think its recovery will be rapid. He's overweight in technology, healthcare, and industrials. The largest holding is a 3.9% exposure to United Technologies. Procter & Gamble and American Home Products are the next biggest positions.

1996, 1997, 1999, 2000, 2001 RRSP

TD U.S. INDEX FUND

Tim Thompson (1992), Craig Gaskin/TD Asset Management Inc.

Consistency

Performance Trend

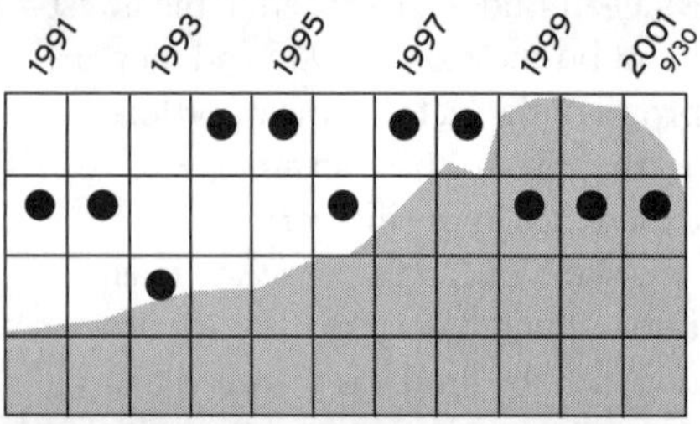

Risk

How often fund outperformed GICs	8 years in 9
How often fund lost money	1 year in 9
Worst year's rate of return	–23.23%

Reward-to-Risk Relationship

Sharpe Ratio Quartile Rankings

3-Year	2
5-Year	1

Morningstar Rating

★★★★★

Efficiency/MER

Management expense/$100

$0.62

○ above average
○ average
● below average

Style

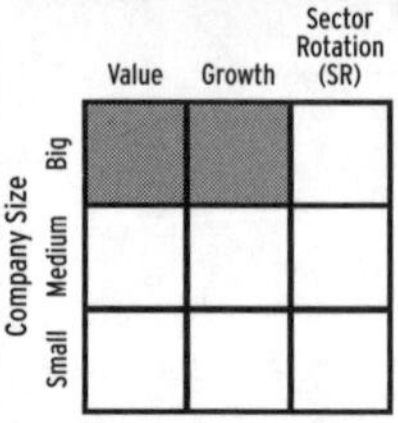

Complementary Fund:
Investors U.S. Large Cap Value

Similar Fund:
HSBC U.S. Equity

We've had mixed feelings about index funds in the past. Active fund managers historically have had a hard time outperforming the efficient U.S. market. Every company is under the microscope of hundreds of analysts and there is precious little information that isn't common knowledge. Index funds are an acknowledgment that if you can't beat 'em, you might as well join 'em. Fees for these funds are very low and the mandate is to simply match the performance of the applicable index. In our view, index funds make sense for U.S. markets. In other markets, however, there are inefficiencies that can be exploited and active managers do add value.

Over the past 10 years, the TD U.S. Index Fund has averaged 17.1% a year versus 18.4% for the S&P 500 Index, the fund's benchmark, and only 13.5% for the average U.S. equity fund. Performance has been aided by a low management expense ratio, only 0.63% versus 2.52% for the average U.S. equity fund. There are, of course, no high-priced analysts or economists required to decide which stocks to buy or when to buy them. Low fees make tracking the S&P 500 an easier proposition.

This fund makes a good core holding in a portfolio and is a fine complement to an actively managed U.S. equity fund.

An RRSP eligible fund, similar to this fund, is also available.

2001 RRSP

AGF AGGRESSIVE GROWTH FUND

Richard Driehaus (1993)/Driehaus Capital Management

Consistency

Performance Trend

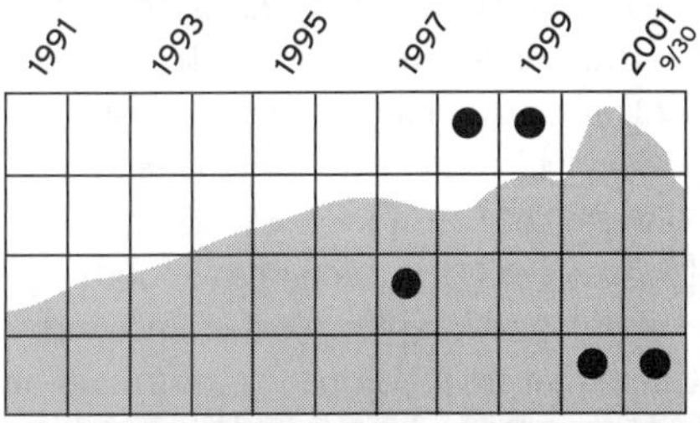

Risk

How often fund outperformed GICs	4 years in 5
How often fund lost money	2 years in 5
Worst year's rate of return	–63.29%

Reward-to-Risk Relationship
Sharpe Ratio Quartile Rankings

3-Year	1
5-Year	2

Morningstar Rating

★★★★

Efficiency/MER

Management expense/$100

$2.45

○ above average
● average
○ below average

Style

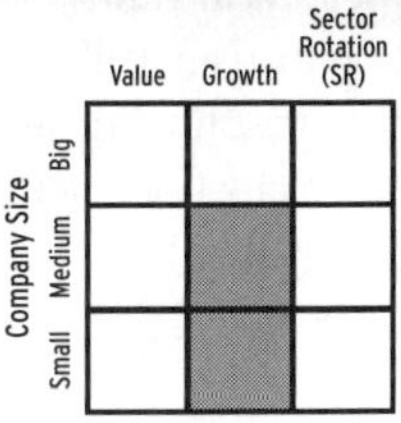

Complementary Fund:
McLean Budden American Growth

Similar Fund:
Fidelity Small Cap America

When manager Richard Driehaus is good, he's very, very good. Case in point: the 195.1% return the AGF Aggressive Growth achieved in 1999. Unfortunately, when he's bad…

We're not being fair to Richard Driehaus. He's acknowledged as one of the premier momentum managers, and notwithstanding his 14.2% loss in 2000 and a 33.5% year-to-date decline, we still like him—and his fund. Driehaus has been in the business for over 30 years and has been consistent in his approach.

Momentum managers believe in buying high and selling higher. Portfolio turnover is high and capital gains are therefore quickly realized.

Driehaus leans towards small-to-medium-sized companies in the U.S. His portfolio of 125 securities currently focuses on healthcare and technology, composing 50% of the total. Top holdings include Barnes & Noble, Varian Medical Systems, IVAX Corp, and our personal favourite, Krispy Kreme Doughnuts.

AGF Aggressive Fund would be an excellent complement to a large cap, blue chip US equity fund. Volatility is high, but as the 195.1% return two years ago reminds us, so are the opportunities.

New

RRSP

FIDELITY SMALL-CAP AMERICA FUND
James Harmon (2000)/Fidelity Management & Research Co.

Consistency

Performance Trend

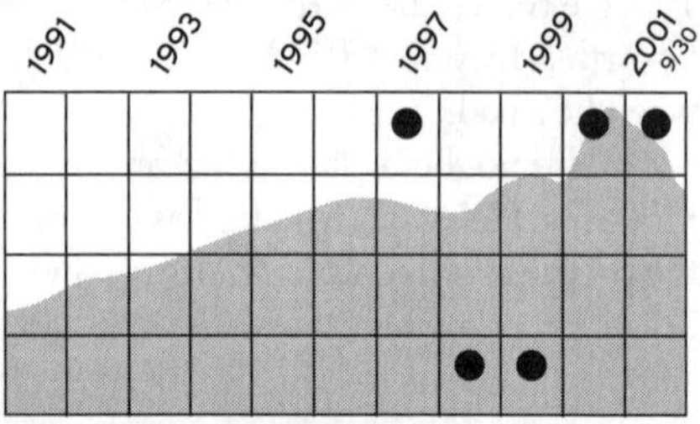

Risk

How often fund outperformed GICs	4 years in 6
How often fund lost money	0 years in 6
Worst year's rate of return	–20.03%

Reward-to-Risk Relationship
Sharpe Ratio Quartile Rankings

3-Year	1
5-Year	1

Morningstar Rating

★★★★

Efficiency/MER

Management expense/$100

$2.64

○ above average
● average
○ below average

Style

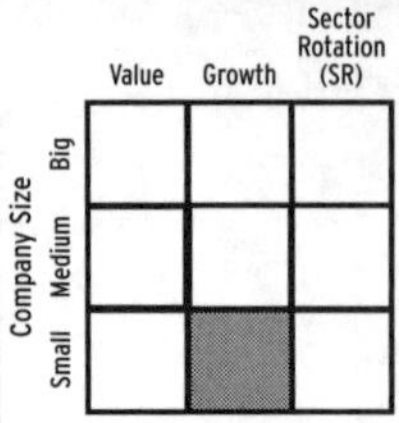

Complementary Fund:
Investors U.S. Large Cap Value

Similar Fund:
AGF Aggressive Growth

Over the past five years, the U.S. small-cap sector has underperformed relative to the large-cap market. The Russell 2000, a benchmark for small-cap stocks, gained 12.0% a year while the Dow Industrials Index, which consists of the 30 largest U.S. stocks, rose 15.6% a year. This performance was recorded despite both research and long-term experience indicating that small company investments are riskier and therefore should offer higher returns.

Things seem to be returning to normal, however, at least for Fidelity Small-Cap America. The fund has gained 43.3% over the past twelve months, 17.2% a year over three years and 20.7% a year over five years. With apologies to manager James Harmon, we feel that Fidelity's research capabilities can take the credit for these sparkling numbers. One can argue that with so many analysts covering large U.S. companies, all the factors effecting the share price are in the public domain. Therefore, share prices should always be at their "correct" level. This principle is known as the "efficient market hypothesis." Smaller companies aren't so well researched and it's possible to discover undervalued firms that the rest of market isn't familiar with. Based on the performance of Small-Cap America, Fidelity is obviously skilled at doing just that.

Harmon likes the health care and education sectors, feeling they are still relatively inexpensive. His largest holding is Strayer Education, followed by Carreker (an information technology firm) and Cima Labs.

1998, 1999, 2000, 2001 RRSP

GLOBAL EQUITY

AGF INTERNATIONAL VALUE FUND

Charles Brandes, Jeff Busby (1994)/Brandes Investment Partners

Consistency

Performance Trend

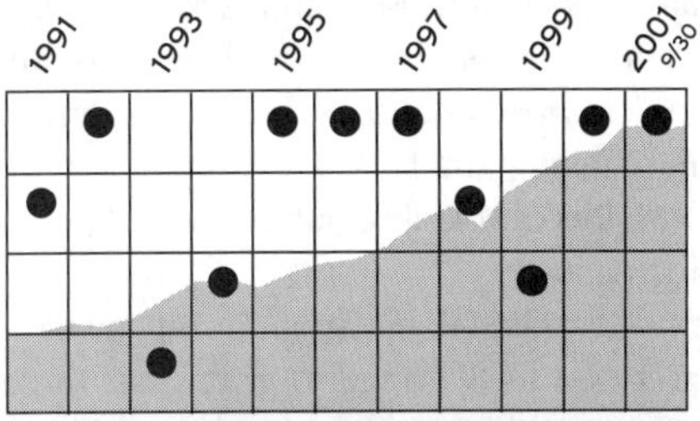

Risk

How often fund outperformed GICs	9 years in 10
How often fund lost money	0 years in 10
Worst year's rate of return	−5.14%

Reward-to-Risk Relationship

Sharpe Ratio Quartile Rankings

3-Year	1
5-Year	1

Morningstar Rating

★★★★★

Efficiency/MER

Management expense/$100

$2.79

○ above average
● average
○ below average

Style

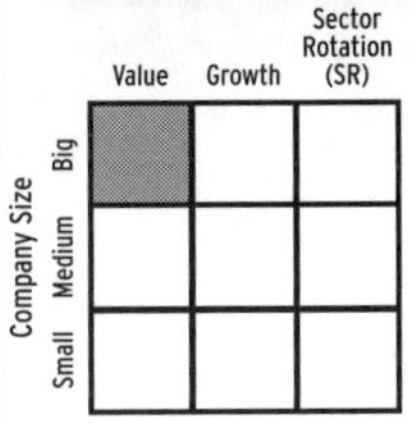

Complementary Fund:
Orbit World

Similar Fund:
Trimark Fund

The AGF International Value Fund has achieved Top Fund status for the past five years and it continues to impress us. Indeed, it is one of the few funds we would consider for a core holding in almost anyone's portfolio.

The numbers are compelling: AGF International Value has been a first-quartile performer over one, three, five, and ten years, and the long-term investor would have been rewarded with an average annual compound rate of return of 16.6% over the past decade. The performance hasn't been at the expense of stability, either. Over the past 10 years, the fund has never lost money in any one calendar year.

Charles Brandes and Jeff Busby utilize four elements in their value approach to investing. They conduct in-depth, company specific financial research that allows them to identify a firm's intrinsic value and set an initial "sell" price target. They also take a long-term view, usually three to five years and establish a margin of safety in the creation of the portfolio. The stock selection process then begins with a database of over 13,000 companies that is reduced to 2,500 after a preliminary screening, then is reduced again to a 700-stock universe approved by an investment committee. The end portfolio consists of only 35 to 75 stocks. Finally, the margin of safety requirement is met by stipulating a maximum 5% exposure to one security, and predetermined maximum country and industry weightings.

There is an RRSP eligible version of this fund available.

New

RRSP

ALTAMIRA GLOBAL SMALL COMPANY

Charles Bastyr (inception)/Altamira Management Inc.

Consistency

Performance Trend

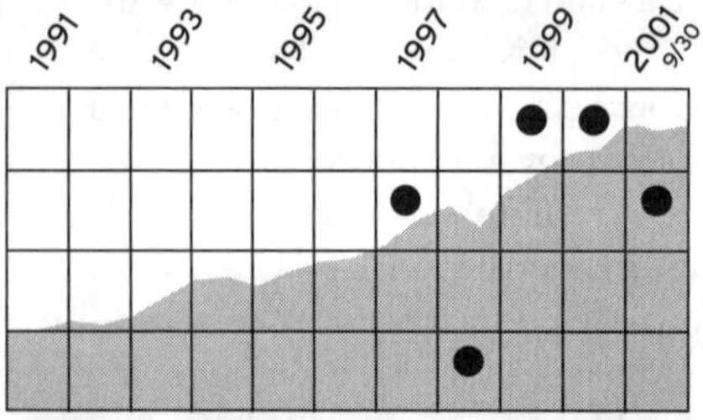

Risk

How often fund outperformed GICs	4 years in 4
How often fund lost money	0 years in 4
Worst year's rate of return	−25.25%

Reward-to-Risk Relationship

Sharpe Ratio Quartile Rankings

3-Year	1
5-Year	1

Morningstar Rating

★★★★★

Efficiency/MER

Management expense/$100

$2.53

○ above average
● average
○ below average

Style

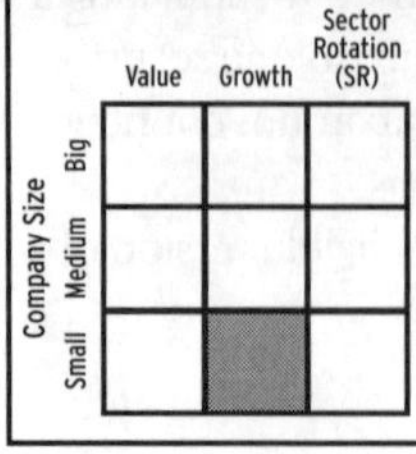

Complementary Fund:
Merrill Lynch Select Int'l Growth

Similar Fund:
Mawer World Investment

The mandate of manager Chuck Bastyr is to invest in global small companies, which are defined as those with market capitalizations of less than U.S.$2 billion, located in developed countries. He can also invest in emerging markets. The result is a fund with lots of volatility, but also lots of performance.

Altamira Global Small Company has averaged 14.8% a year over the past three years, but the fund has also dropped 8.9% of its value in the past twelve months. The 86 holdings in the portfolio are well diversified by sector and country. U.S. stocks represent 24% of total fund assets, followed by the U.K. and Japan. Altogether, the fund has invested in 22 countries around the world.

Bastyr is a bottom-up manager and selects companies that have the best combination of relative valuation, growth potential, competitive positioning, and management ability. His top holding is a 2.6% position in Huaneng Power International Inc.

2001 RRSP

CI GLOBAL FUND
Bill Sterling (1980)/C.I. Global Advisors LLP

Consistency

Performance Trend

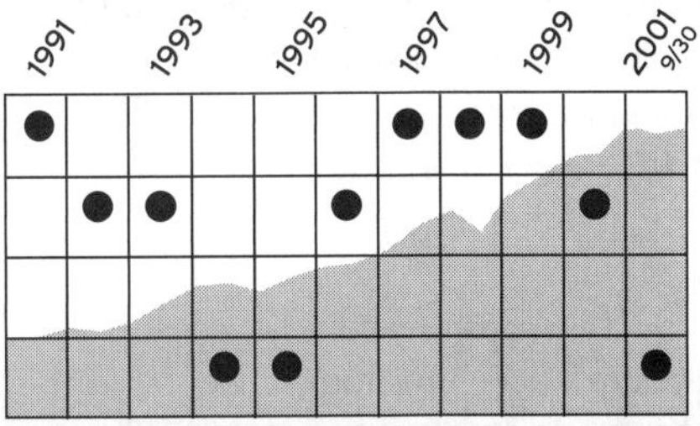

Risk

How often fund outperformed GICs	7 years in 8
How often fund lost money	2 years in 8
Worst year's rate of return	−38.82%

Reward-to-Risk Relationship
Sharpe Ratio Quartile Rankings

3-Year	3
5-Year	2

Morningstar Rating

★★★

Efficiency/MER

Management expense/$100

$2.52

○ above average
● average
○ below average

Style

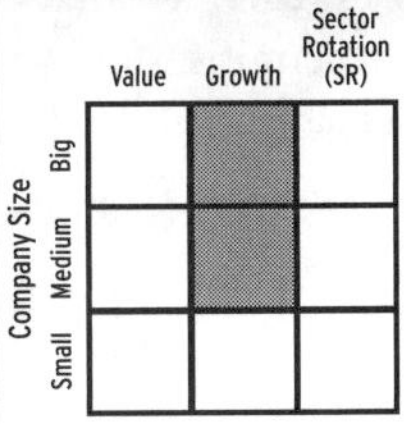

Complementary Fund:
Mac Cundill Value Series B

Similar Fund:
Great-West Life International Eq(P)

The last year hasn't been kind to manager Bill Sterling. He admits that he made two mistakes: the first was believing that the markets would react more positively to the Federal Reserve's initial rate cuts; the second was using a securities selection process that favoured growth stocks. As result, CI Global Fund was only a third-quartile performer last year, losing 22.5% over the past 12 months. The fund still has been a superior long-term performer, however, and we still like this fund.

Sterling is generally optimistic about the prospects for his fund. Most world markets are at or close to their lows. Although corporate earnings are still disappointing, he feels that a recovery in early 2002 is likely. In fact, he believes that selected technology stocks may be coming back and he is currently moderately overweight.

Although he tends to be more industry orientated than country focused, he likes Japan and emerging markets. His current weighting is 57.4% to the U.S., 12.5% to Japan, 8.5% to developed Europe, and 10.4% to Asia and emerging markets.

Sterling uses a blended approach to investment management. He is renowned for his reports on global macroeconomic trends, but also uses a bottom-up process to pick stocks that offer superior growth characteristics. He has 170 securities in his portfolio; the biggest name, Citigroup, represents only 2.3% of the total holdings.

There is an RRSP eligible version of this fund available.

New

RRSP

CUNDILL VALUE SERIES B

Peter Cundill (1997), Tim McElvaine (1997), David Briggs (1996)/The Cundill Group

Consistency

Performance Trend

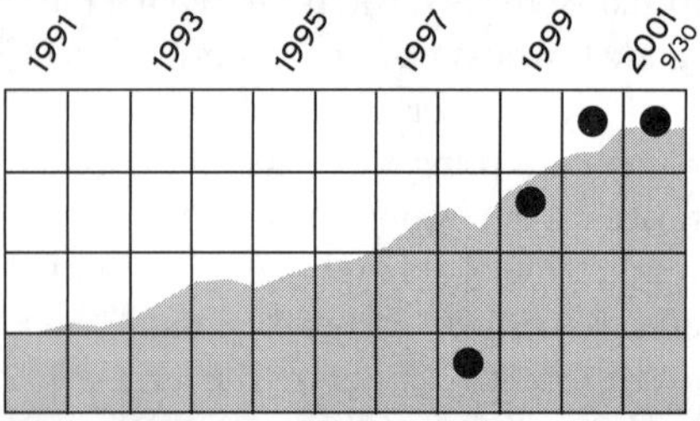

Risk

How often fund outperformed GICs	2 years in 2
How often fund lost money	1 year in 2
Worst year's rate of return	−18.52%

Reward-to-Risk Relationship
Sharpe Ratio Quartile Rankings

3-Year	1
5-Year	N/A

Morningstar Rating

★★★★★

Efficiency/MER

Management expense/$100

$2.56

○ above average
● average
○ below average

Style

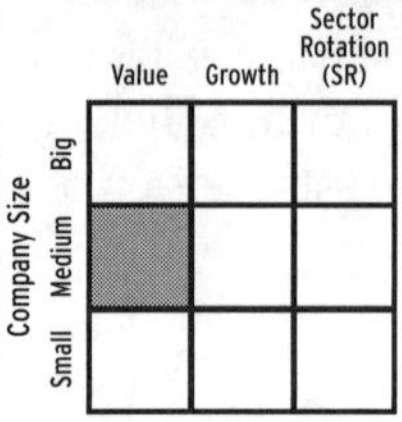

Complementary Fund:
Orbit World

Similar Fund:
Janus Global Equity

The mandate of this fund is to seek long-term growth by investing in a broad range of undervalued, unappreciated, and generally unloved global equities. This approach emphasizes companies that trade below their intrinsic or breakup values, and therefore have little downside risk.

This management style requires patience from investors, as well as confidence in the skill of Messrs Cundill, McElvaine, and Briggs. The fund has no sector or country limits, nor do the managers try to forecast corporate earnings or economic conditions. The result can be a portfolio that doesn't seem to follow the rules. For example, the fund currently has a 43% exposure to Japanese markets and six of the top ten holdings are Japanese firms. The average global equity fund has only a 7.1% exposure to Japan and many investors avoid this market. In fact, the average *Japanese* equity fund has only a 65% weighting to Japanese stocks. The Cundill team, however, feels that many Japanese stocks have been unfairly tainted by all the bad news coming from that country and there are numerous companies that meet their investment criteria.

This fund has averaged 18.0% a year over the past three years, although the "A" series version of this fund has averaged 11.6% a year over fifteen years. It's an excellent fund for the patient investor.

There is an RRSP eligible version of this fund available.

2001 RRSP

JANUS GLOBAL EQUITY FUND
Helen Young Hayes (1997)/Janus Capital Corp.

Consistency

Performance Trend

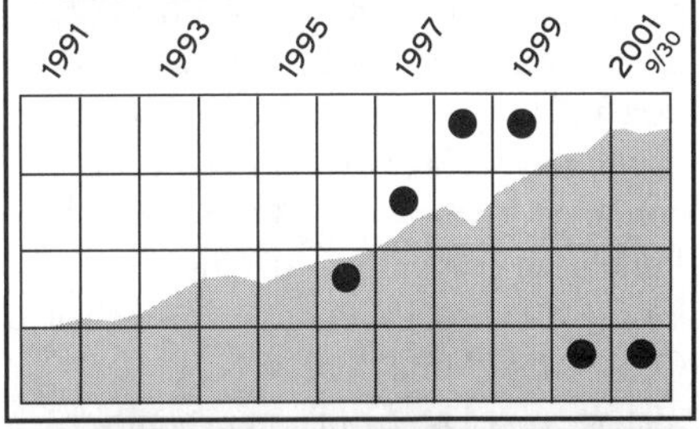

Risk

How often fund outperformed GICs	4 years in 4
How often fund lost money	1 year in 4
Worst year's rate of return	−36.83%

Reward-to-Risk Relationship
Sharpe Ratio Quartile Rankings

3-Year	2
5-Year	2

Morningstar Rating

★★★

Efficiency/MER

Management expense/$100

$2.90

● above average
○ average
○ below average

Style

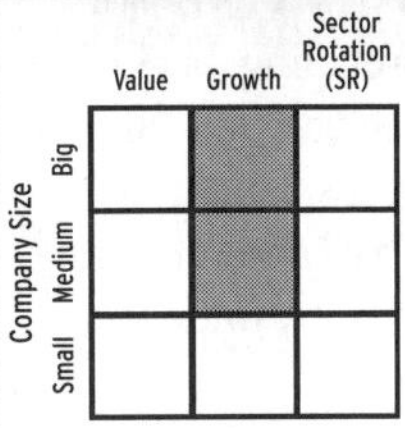

Complementary Fund:
Merrill Lynch Select Int'l Growth

Similar Fund:
Altamira Global Small Company

The buy-and-hold approach doesn't seem to be a philosophy that Helen Hayes believes in. The manager of Janus Global Equity had an 83% turnover rate last year. In our experience, most equity fund managers turn their portfolios over between 30% to 40% a year.

Country allocations are the result of a bottom-up stock selection process. U.S. stocks represent 34% of total fund assets, which actually is an underweight position compared with the benchmark MSCI World Index. Japan is the second largest country with a 7.7% weighting, also an underweighting to the index. Telecommunications and information technology stocks compose just over 25% of the portfolio. It's therefore no surprise that Janus Global Equity Fund has faltered over the past 12 months. The fund fell 27.4% compared with a 19.4% decline for the index and a loss of 14.9% for the average global equity fund.

There is an RRSP eligible version of this fund available.

2001 RRSP

ORBIT WORLD FUND

David Marvin (1995)/Marvin & Palmer Associates

Consistency

Performance Trend

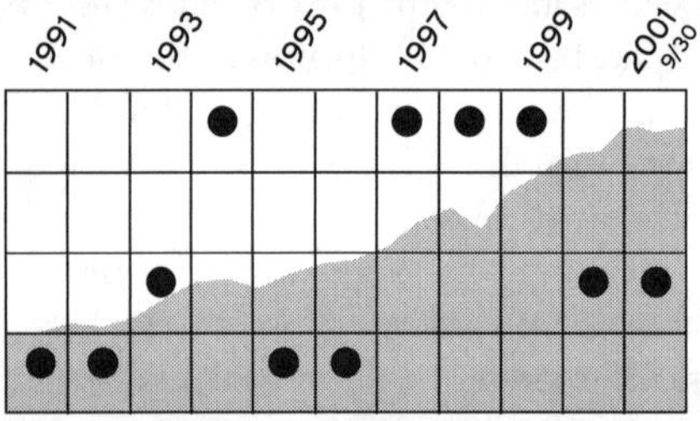

Risk

How often fund outperformed GICs	5 years in 8
How often fund lost money	2 years in 8
Worst year's rate of return	−27.25%

Reward-to-Risk Relationship

Sharpe Ratio Quartile Rankings

3-Year	1
5-Year	1

Morningstar Rating

★★★★★

Efficiency/MER

Management expense/$100

$2.75

○ above average
● average
○ below average

Style

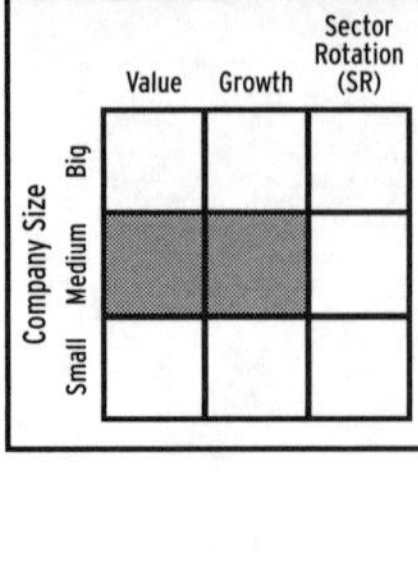

Complementary Fund:
Mac Cundill Value Series B

Similar Fund:
Great-West Life International Eq(P) A

In the investment business, being smart enough to know that you're not the smartest player is a key determinant of success. In other words, do what you do best and hire others who are smarter than you in their area of expertise. The folks running Montreal-based Orbit Mutual Fund Management Ltd. did just that by hiring Marvin & Palmer to manage their Orbit World Fund. Marvin & Palmer manage over U.S.$7 billion in equity investments for pension, institutional, and mutual fund clients worldwide. They're equity managers only—they oversee no bonds or money markets.

Orbit World is big on performance and small on assets. With only $34.9 million in assets, it's dwarfed by the venerable Templeton Growth Fund's $9.82 billion in assets. Performance, however, is another matter. Orbit has averaged 22.5% a year over the past five years, while Templeton Growth gained only 9.0% over the same time period. (But we will give credit where credit is due: Templeton's average annual compound rate of return of 14.6% a year over 27 years will never, ever be matched.)

Marvin is a top-down manager. He makes his country, sector, and currency decisions before he makes his individual stock selections. Marvin's current country allocation is relatively neutral compared with the benchmark index. His major sector emphasis is on retailing, healthcare, and media stocks. Financials and information technology issues have a neutral weighting, while materials and telecommunications are significantly underweighted.

1995, 1996, 1997, 1998, 1999, 2000 RRSP

TRIMARK FUND

Judith Adams (1999), Bill Kanko (1999), Tye Bousada (2001)/AIM Funds Mgmt Inc.

Consistency

Performance Trend

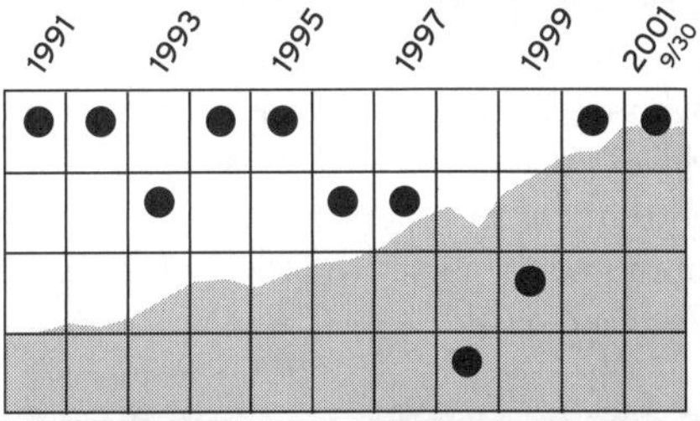

Risk

How often fund outperformed GICs	10 years in 10
How often fund lost money	0 years in 10
Worst year's rate of return	–13.38%

Reward-to-Risk Relationship
Sharpe Ratio Quartile Rankings

3-Year	1
5-Year	1

Morningstar Rating

★★★★★

Efficiency/MER

Management expense/$100

$1.62

○ above average
○ average
● below average

Style

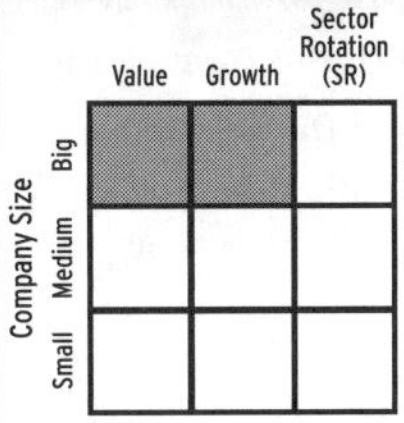

Complementary Fund:
Orbit World

Similar Fund:
AGF International Value

Over the years, Trimark Fund has been a model of consistency. It's been a Top Fund for seven of the past eight years and has rewarded investors with an average 13.7% annual return over the past fifteen years. A $1,000 investment at the end of June 1986 would be worth over $6,830 today.

The fund is focused on the U.S. market with a 63% exposure to U.S. stocks. Nine of the top ten holdings are U.S. issues; Japan's Canon Inc. is the exception. In fact, 13% of fund assets are in Japanese stocks. The fund is underweighted to the technology, media, and telecom sectors, and currently has a 11% cash reserve.

Trimark's founder, Bob Krembil, espouses a team-based investment philosophy and the inevitable manager changes that have occurred over the years haven't effected either the stability of the investment approach or the performance of the fund. The standard deviation of the fund's returns is much lower than the average global equity fund over both three and five years. The fund lost 9.9% in 1990, but has provided double-digit returns to investors in every other year, with the exception of 1998. That year, the fund gained only 6.4% and many industry observers felt that stodgy old Trimark was starting to lose its way. They were wrong.

New

RRSP

AGF INTL STOCK CLASS-INTL GROUP FUND

Charles Brandes (1997), Jeff Busby (1997)/Brandes Investment Partners

Consistency

Performance Trend

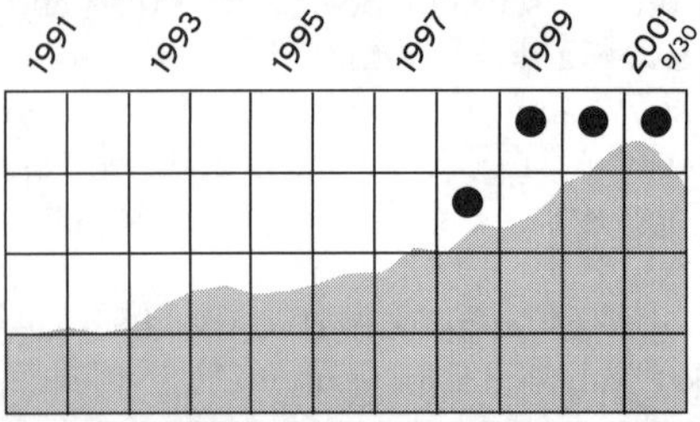

Risk

How often fund outperformed GICs	2 years in 3
How often fund lost money	0 years in 3
Worst year's rate of return	−14.6%

Reward-to-Risk Relationship

Sharpe Ratio Quartile Rankings

3-Year	1
5-Year	N/A

Morningstar Rating

★★★★★

Efficiency/MER

Management expense/$100

$2.71

○ above average
● average
○ below average

Style

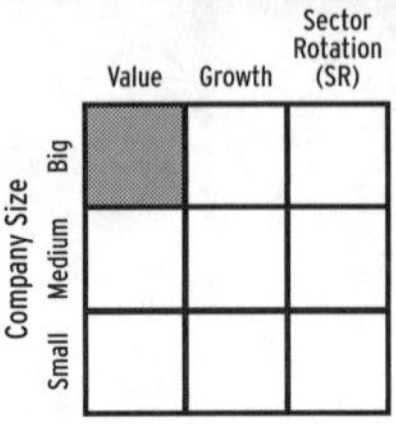

Complementary Fund:
Orbit World

Similar Fund:
Mawer World Investment

Fund managers Charles Brandes and Jeff Busby are traditional bottom-up, value-style stock pickers. In fact, Brandes was acquainted with Benjamin Graham, whose seminal work entitled *Security Analysis* influenced a whole generation of investment managers. Brandes himself has authored the highly regarded book, *Value Investing Today*.

The mandate of AGF International Stock Class is to invest in international equities excluding North America. It is therefore a sensible choice for investors with Canadian and U.S. equity stocks who want international exposure without the risk of duplicating some of their existing holdings.

The managers look for companies that are trading at a discount to their intrinsic value or are operating in an industry that is out of favour. There are no specific country allocations; these are determined simply by where the investments are domiciled. Currently, 26% of the holdings are located in the United Kingdom, 20% are in Japan, and 8% are in France. The largest single holding is a 3.1% allocation to Telefonos de Mexico SA, followed by a 3.0% stake in Unilever PLC.

The date of inception for AGF International Stock Class was June 1997. Normally, we'd be leery about recommending a fund with only a four-year history, but Brandes's success in managing AGF International Fund prompts us to have no reservation about making this fund a Top Fund selection this year.

1999, 2000, 2001 RRSP

GREAT-WEST LIFE INTERNATIONAL EQUITY (P) FUND

John Storkerson (1994)/Putnam Investment Management

Consistency

Performance Trend

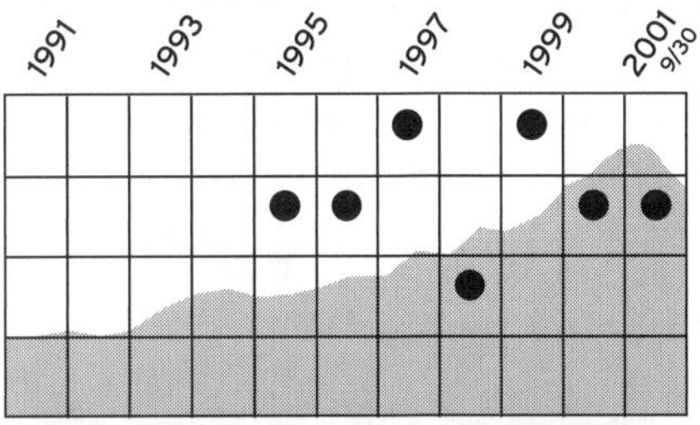

Risk

How often fund outperformed GICs	4 years in 5
How often fund lost money	1 year in 5
Worst year's rate of return	−25.9%

Reward-to-Risk Relationship

Sharpe Ratio Quartile Rankings

3-Year	1
5-Year	1

Morningstar Rating

★★★★★

Efficiency/MER

Management expense/$100

$2.67

- ○ above average
- ● average
- ○ below average

Style

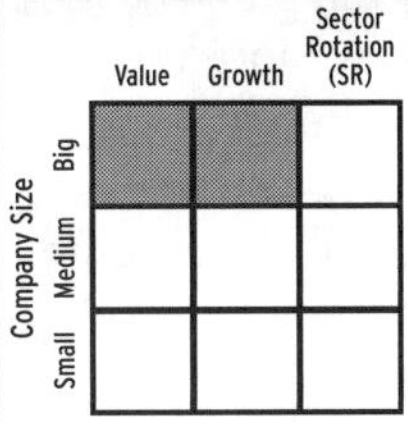

Complementary Fund:
Mac Cundill Value Series B

Similar Fund:
AGF Intl Stock Class, Intl Group

Putnam Investment Management is one of the best investment managers that you have never heard of. South of the border, the 64-year-old firm has an enviable reputation as one the country's finest institutional money managers.

Putnam's investment philosophy is based on style consistency. This fund has a growth mandate and current market dissatisfaction with that style won't influence its investment approach. Storkerson does not discriminate by sector or country, although the fund is restricted to only non-North American stocks. The fund currently is represented in 29 countries. The largest country exposure is a 25% allocation to U.K. stocks. France is the surprising second position at 16%, and Japan represents 14.4% of the total. No other country has more than 8% of fund assets.

Storkerson is overweighted to energy stocks and underweighting to technology helped the fund to beat the index last year. Unfortunately, that's faint praise for investors who saw the fund fall 21.9% in a difficult year for foreign markets. Longer-term results have been impressive, however, with a 10.8% annual return over five years. By contrast, the average international fund rose only 5.8% over the same time period.

2000 RRSP

MAWER WORLD INVESTMENT FUND

Gerald Cooper-Key (inception)/Mawer Investment Management

Consistency

Performance Trend

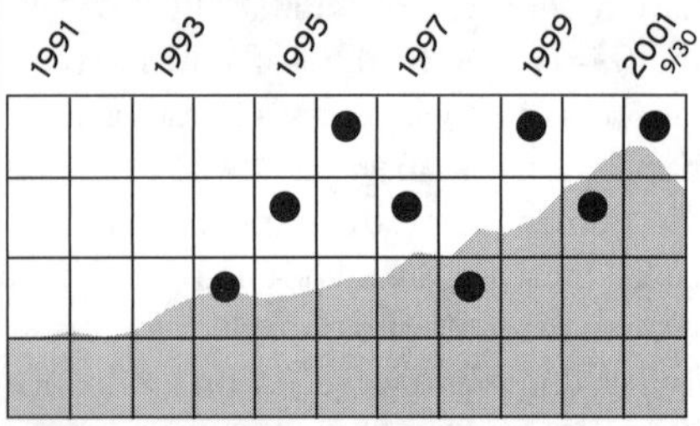

Risk

How often fund outperformed GICs	6 years in 9
How often fund lost money	1 year in 9
Worst year's rate of return	−22.43%

Reward-to-Risk Relationship

Sharpe Ratio Quartile Rankings

3-Year	1
5-Year	1

Morningstar Rating

★★★★★

Efficiency/MER

Management expense/$100

$1.55

○ above average
○ average
● below average

Style

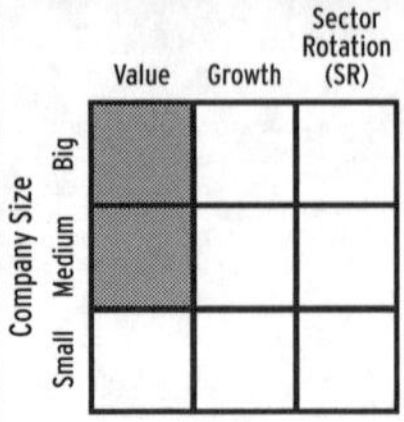

Complementary Fund:
Merrill Lynch Select Intl Growth

Similar Fund:
AGF Intl Stock Class, Intl Group

Calgary-based Mawer Investment Management has caught the rest of the investment world's eye. In 2001, Nelson Information awarded the Mawer World Investment Fund with the "Nelson's World's Best Money Manager" designation. Nelson provides investment information and software to institutional money managers and ranks over 1,500 managers and 4,500 portfolios on a quarterly basis.

Manager and company chairman Gerald Cooper-Key uses bottom-up fundamental analysis to identify companies trading at a discount to their North American counterparts. He focuses on industries that exist outside of North America and companies whose value has not yet been fully recognized by investors. The portfolio is also diversified by region, company type, and capitalization. Europe represents 67% of the fund assets, followed by a 15% exposure to emerging markets, 11% to Japanese stocks, and 3% to other Pacific Rim countries.

Residents of Alberta and Saskatchewan can purchase this and other Mawer funds either directly from Mawer Investment Management with a minimum initial purchase of $25,000 (per client), or through brokers and investment dealers with a minimum initial purchase of $5,000 (per fund). Residents in the rest of the country can purchase the funds directly from Mawer Investment Management with a minimum purchase of $100,000 (per client), or through major dealers and financial planners with a minimum initial purchase of $5,000 (per fund).

2001 RRSP

MERRILL LYNCH SELECT INTL GROWTH FUND

David Marvin (1995)/Marvin & Palmer Associates

Consistency

Performance Trend

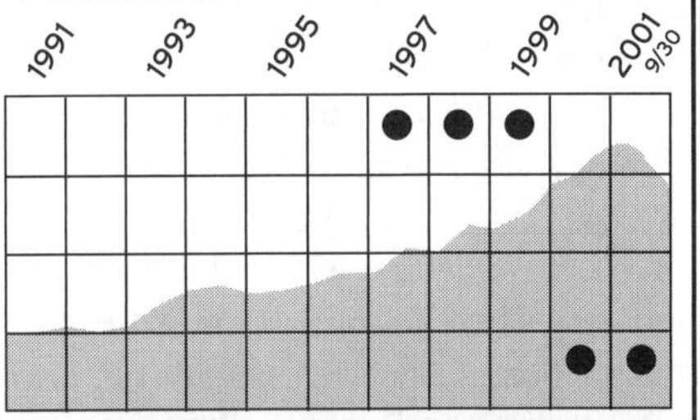

Risk

How often fund outperformed GICs	3 years in 3
How often fund lost money	1 year in 3
Worst year's rate of return	−32.19%

Reward-to-Risk Relationship

Sharpe Ratio Quartile Rankings

3-Year	1
5-Year	N/A

Morningstar Rating

★★★

Efficiency/MER

Management expense/$100

$2.91

- ● above average
- ○ average
- ○ below average

Style

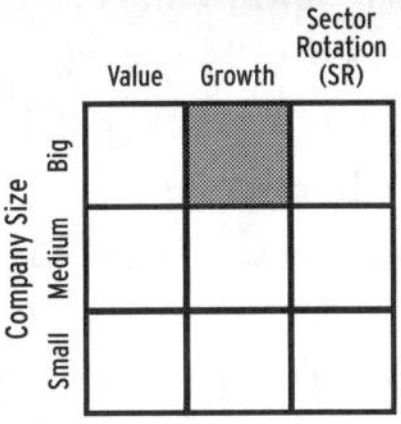

Complementary Fund:
Mac Cundill Value Series B

Similar Fund:
Great-West Life International Eq(P) A

In October 2000, the name of this fund was changed from Atlas International Large-Cap Fund.

Manager David Marvin of Delaware-based Marvin & Palmer Associates uses a three-step investment process to create his portfolios. First, he uses a proprietary relative strength screening model to analyze regions, countries, sectors, currencies, and stocks. He then uses fundamental analysis to validate the screening output, and finally, he constructs the portfolios using the results from steps one and two.

Marvin's top-down, macro approach has proven an effective one. Select International Growth has been a first-quartile performer over two and three years and has averaged 10.2% a year over four years, the second best result in our Morningstar database. International investing has not been a warm and fuzzy experience for Canadians over the past few years; the average international equity fund has averaged only 3.8% a year over the same four-year period.

His mandate is large-cap companies (capitalization greater than U.S.$350 million) anywhere outside North America. Marvin has a 67% exposure to European stocks, 23% to Japanese equities, and 6% to Hong Kong and other Asian countries. He notes that Japanese and European central banks have been slow to stimulate their economies and as a result, corporate earnings have been disappointing. However, Marvin believes that global economies appear to have bottomed out and economic activity—and the prospects for world equity markets—will start to improve.

New

RRSP

CLARICA MVP ASIAN PACIFIC NON-RSP EQUITY

Management Team/Knight, Bain, Seath & Holbrook

Consistency

Performance Trend

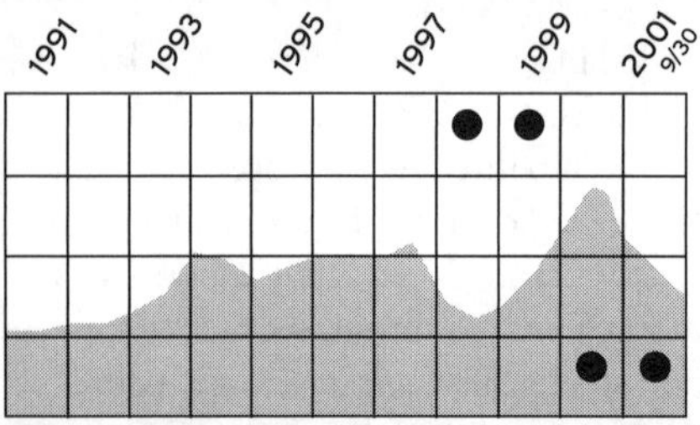

Risk

How often fund outperformed GICs	1 year in 2
How often fund lost money	1 year in 2
Worst year's rate of return	–52.64%

Reward-to-Risk Relationship

Sharpe Ratio Quartile Rankings

3-Year	2
5-Year	N/A

Morningstar Rating

★★★

Efficiency/MER

Management expense/$100

$2.84

○ above average
● average
○ below average

Style

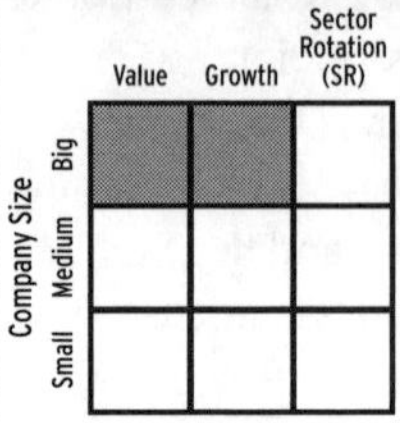

Complementary Fund:
AGF European Equity Class

Similar Fund:
Fidelity Japanese Growth

Clarica Mutual Funds have been very astute in the choice of external managers for their extensive fund line. Knight, Bain, Seath & Holbrook (KBSH), manager of Clarica MVP Asian Pacific Non-RSP Equity Fund, is relatively unknown to the average Canadian investor, but has an excellent reputation within the investment industry. Their key philosophy is fundamental financial analysis, resulting in disciplined security selection. KBSH uses computer models for "scenario" projections in equity valuations, but doesn't focus on technical market data.

The fund has less than 25 securities, with meaningful positions in their top holdings. For example, the largest individual security is Hong Kong-based Johnson Elec. Holdings, which represents 5.8% of the total portfolio. The top 15 holdings represent over 70% of the total portfolio assets.

The managers have a hefty 57% exposure to the Japanese market, which explains the recent under performance of the fund. Over the past 12 months, the fund plummeted by 45% versus only (!) 29% for the average fund in the category. Despite these substandard numbers, the prospects for the fund and the region remain promising. The earnings disappointments that have plagued most North American companies have not been as prevalent in the Far East, and managers feel that valuations are at very low levels. The much-anticipated rebound in global economies should benefit Asian firms with strong fundamentals and an orientation to global growth.

There is an RRSP eligible version of this fund available.

New

RRSP

STRATEGICNOVA ASIA-PACIFIC FUND
Ian Beattie (2000)/WorldInvest Ltd.

Consistency

Performance Trend

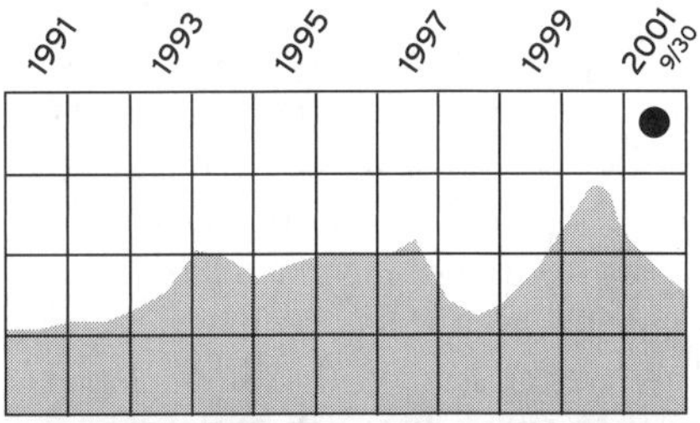

Risk

How often fund outperformed GICs	4 years in 4
How often fund lost money	1 year in 4
Worst year's rate of return	–40.97%

Reward-to-Risk Relationship
Sharpe Ratio Quartile Rankings

3-Year	N/A
5-Year	N/A

Morningstar Rating

N/A

Efficiency/MER

Management expense/$100

$2.95

● above average
○ average
○ below average

Style

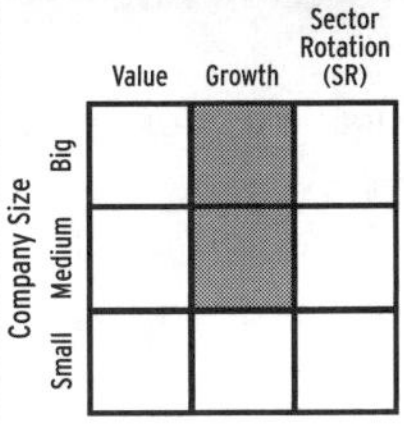

Complementary Fund:
HSBC European

Similar Fund:
Altamira Japanese Opportunity

Manager Ian Beattie has hit a home run with this fund. In a category where the average fund has lost 20.5% over the past 12 months, his StrategicNova Asia-Pacific Fund posted a rather startling 28.9% gain over the same time period. Over five years, the fund has averaged 9.8% a year versus a 5.7% annual loss for the average Asia ex-Japan fund.

As a manager who focuses on stocks trading at deep discounts to their intrinsic value, Beattie has avoided technology issues as well as the large, blue chip names that are standard issue for most funds specializing in this region. His blended top-down and bottom-up approach involves both an analysis of the structural changes that are making some markets investor friendly and fundamental, company-specific research. The result is a portfolio that is heavily weighted to Hong Kong investments. Although Hong Kong and China still represent over 55% of fund assets, Beattie has been taking profits in these markets, particularly in China. He likes the underowned countries like the Philippines, Indonesia, and Thailand, where valuations are still low.

2001 RRSP

ALTAMIRA JAPANESE OPPORTUNITY FUND

Mark Grammer (1997)/Altamira Investment Services

Consistency

Performance Trend

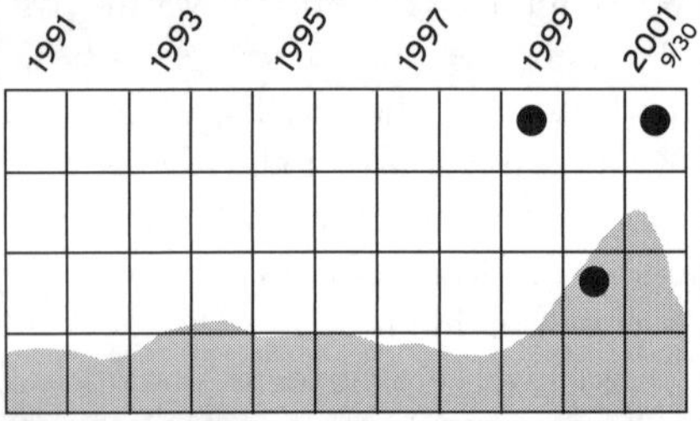

Risk

How often fund outperformed GICs	1 year in 2
How often fund lost money	4 years in 4
Worst year's rate of return	−38.52%

Reward-to-Risk Relationship
Sharpe Ratio Quartile Rankings

3-Year	1
5-Year	N/A

Morningstar Rating

N/A

Efficiency/MER

Management expense/$100
$2.51

○ above average
○ average
● below average

Style

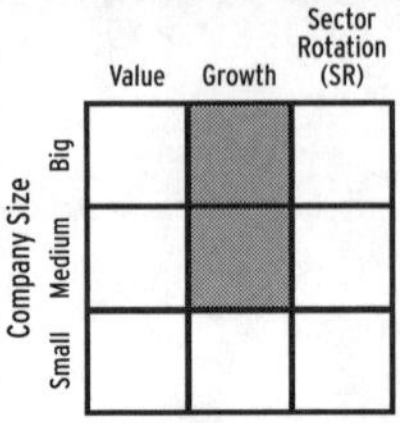

Complementary Fund:
HSBC European

Similar Fund:
Fidelity Japanese Growth

Managers of Japanese equity mutual funds remind us of that fellow in Greek mythology who was forever destined to push a rock up a hill. Our Morningstar database indicates that the Soloman Japan Equity Index has been up a rousing 1.2% a year over the past 10 years. The Altamira Japanese Opportunity Fund has been in existence since 1994 and annual returns have averaged a mere 0.3%. Still, Japan represents a healthy 15% of global markets and many of the world's premier companies are Japanese. As a result, investors with a global outlook have to consider Japanese investments for their portfolios.

Mark Grammer has been manager of this fund since 1997 and is therefore responsible for the 15.3% annual compound rate of return over the past three years. He hit a home run in 1999 with an exceptional 123% return, but the Japanese markets soured in 2000 and 2001, and the fund has dropped 34.4% over the past 12 months. The Japanese banking system's structural problems continue to weigh on financial markets, but Grammer feels that medium- and long-term prospects are good. Over the short term, the global slowdown has negative implications for Japanese GDP growth, prompting him to take a more defensive stance. He likes JR West and Nintendo, and has had success with Honda and Toyota.

There is a RRSP eligible version of this fund available.

New

RRSP

FIDELITY JAPANESE GROWTH FUND
Jay Talbot (1998)/Fidelity Management & Research Co.

Consistency

Performance Trend

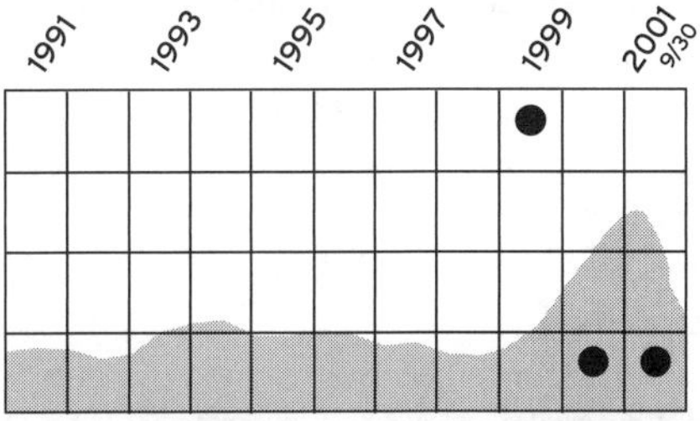

Risk

How often fund outperformed GICs	3 years in 3
How often fund lost money	4 years in 4
Worst year's rate of return	−46.69%

Reward-to-Risk Relationship
Sharpe Ratio Quartile Rankings

3-Year	1
5-Year	N/A

Morningstar Rating

N/A

Efficiency/MER

Management expense/$100

$2.67

- ○ above average
- ● average
- ○ below average

Style

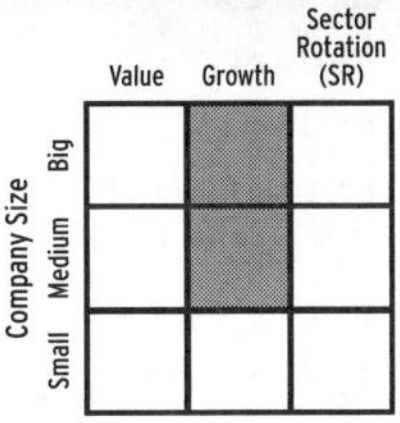

Complementary Fund:
HSBC European

Similar Fund:
Altamira Japanese Opportunity

We know that picking a fund with an annual compound rate of return of 2.5% since inception may seem a bit strange. Well, welcome to the world of Japanese equities, where the nightmare never seems to end. The Japanese economy has the worst 10-year growth rate of any major economy since World War II: the national debt of U.S.$8.6 trillion is the industrial world's worst, and interest rates are effectively zero.

In this environment, an annual compound rate of return of 16.4% over three years is impressive. Manager Jay Talbot employs the traditional Fidelity blended style of bottom-up fundamental research, but he is not blind to the macroeconomic issues that are so important in Japan. He feels that, notwithstanding the current malaise overhanging global markets, Japanese stocks are very attractive on a risk/return basis over the long term. Short term, the fund's overweighting to technology stocks will hurt performance relative to the index. However, Talbot's view is that the market is being driven by sentiment (which, unfortunately, is negative) and that Japanese stocks will benefit when world economies start to recover. We agree. Japanese firms continue to produce cutting edge products and technologies, and those with an export orientation will profit greatly. Hopefully investors will too.

There is an RRSP eligible version of this fund available.

New

RRSP

AGF EUROPEAN GROWTH CLASS-INTL GROUP FUND

John Arnold (1994), Rory Flynn (1994)/AGF International Advisors Co. Ltd.

Consistency

Performance Trend

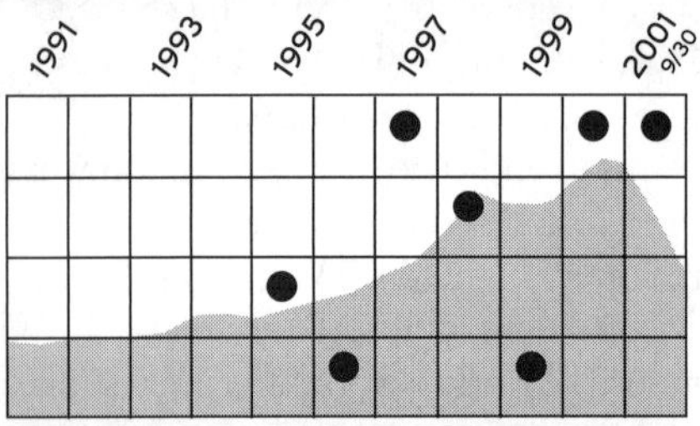

Risk

How often fund outperformed GICs	5 years in 6
How often fund lost money	0 years in 6
Worst year's rate of return	−9.17%

Reward-to-Risk Relationship
Sharpe Ratio Quartile Rankings

3-Year	1
5-Year	1

Morningstar Rating

★★★★★

Efficiency/MER

Management expense/$100

$2.79

○ above average
● average
○ below average

Style

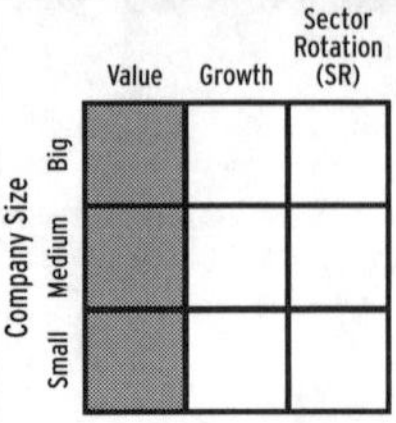

Complementary Fund:
Altamira Japanese Opportunity

Similar Fund:
Spectrum European Growth

Despite the "Growth" moniker, the AGF European Growth Class Fund is actually managed with a value mandate. The concentrated portfolio of only 40 to 50 securities exhibits most of the characteristics of value selections. The P/E and P/B values are less than those of the MSCI Europe Index, while the dividend yields are higher than the Index.

The fund underperformed its peers in 1999, which is not an unusual result for a value fund in a growth happy investment environment. Both recent and long-term performance has been impressive, however. The fund has been a first-quartile performer over one, three, and five years. The 14.3% five-year annual compound rate of return is almost a full 5% above the average European fund, which returned 9.6% over the same time period.

Fund managers John Arnold and Rory Flynn are currently overweighted in Continental European financial stocks and U.K. consumer issues. They feel that pension reform, company consolidation, and demographics favour the financial sector, while "robust" U.K. economic prospects are good news for consumer stocks. They continue to avoid technology, media, and telecommunications stocks. Even though Arnold and Flynn believe that a 30% decline in a company's share price from its 18-month peak is part of their "buy" process, the valuations in those sectors are still too high. The top holding is the U.K.-based MFI Furniture Group, with Societe Generale SA and Allied Domecq PLC rounding out the top three.

There is an RRSP eligible version of this fund available.

2001 RRSP

HSBC EUROPEAN FUND

Management Team/HSBC Asset Management (Europe) Ltd.

Consistency

Performance Trend

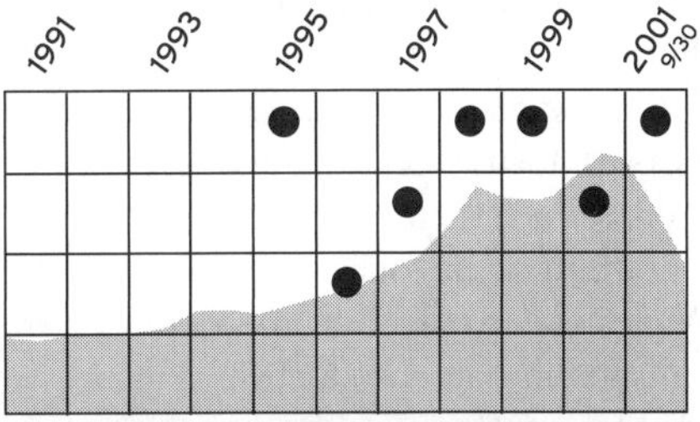

Risk

How often fund outperformed GICs	5 years in 5
How often fund lost money	1 year in 5
Worst year's rate of return	−22.72%

Reward-to-Risk Relationship

Sharpe Ratio Quartile Rankings

3-Year	1
5-Year	1

Morningstar Rating

★★★★★

Efficiency/MER

Management expense/$100

$2.28

○ above average
○ average
● below average

Style

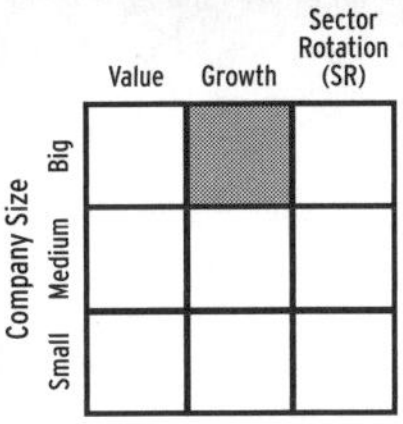

Complementary Fund:
Altamira Japanese Opportunity

Similar Fund:
Spectrum European Growth

The market analysts at HSBC aren't optimistic about the near-term prospects for European economies. This view is unusual in the investment management industry, where everyone seems to sport rose-coloured glasses where their own markets are concerned. The HSBC team feels that Europe will continue to exhibit slower growth, which is reflected in that region's lower stock markets and lower corporate earnings expectations. As a result, HSBC is focusing on defensive sectors and has underweighted the portfolio's exposure to Germany. On the other hand, France is overweighted based on a belief that the country will have one of the highest growth rates in the European region. The largest country allocation is to U.K. stocks, which represent 25.4% of total fund assets.

HSBC European Fund has been a first-quartile performer over three and five years, and has gained 14.8% a year since inception (1994). Performance has been average over the past 12 months, however; the fund fell 21.5% versus a 20.5% decline for the average fund in the category.

The fund remains fully invested. Cash represents only 8.4% of fund assets compared with 25.9% for the average European mutual fund. If the equity markets outperform both bonds and cash over the next 12 months, as the HSBC gurus expect, then this more aggressive stance will benefit the fund.

New

RRSP

SPECTRUM EUROPEAN GROWTH FUND
Edoardo Mercandante (1997)/Mercury Asset Management Canada Ltd.

Consistency

Performance Trend

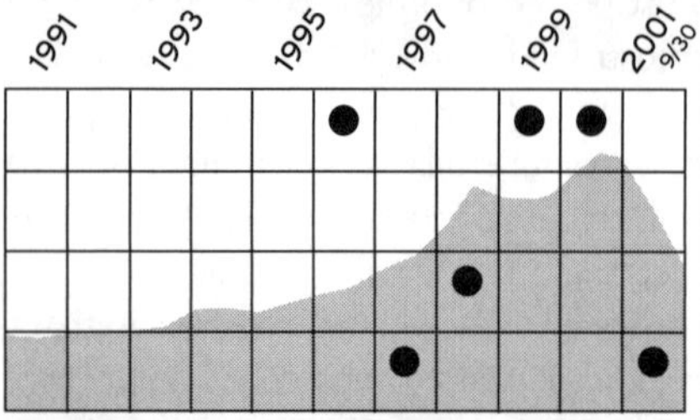

Risk

How often fund outperformed GICs	4 years in 5
How often fund lost money	0 years in 5
Worst year's rate of return	−35.51%

Reward-to-Risk Relationship
Sharpe Ratio Quartile Rankings

3-Year	1
5-Year	1

Morningstar Rating

★★★★

Efficiency/MER

Management expense/$100

$2.93

● above average
○ average
○ below average

Style

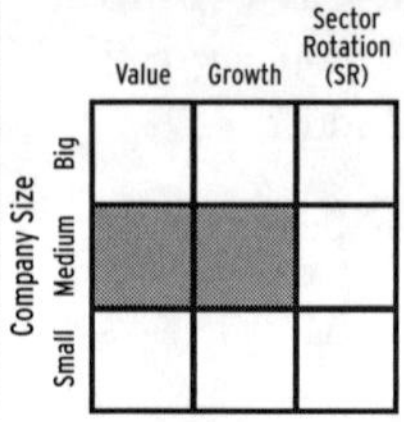

Complementary Fund:
Altamira Japanese Opportunity

Similar Fund:
HSBC European

Manager Edoardo Mercandante is a bottom-up stock picker with a difference. Awarded the "Best Regional Equity Fund" at the 2000 Canadian Mutual Fund Awards, Spectrum European Growth focuses on themes or sector trends. Each theme can represent only one-third of the total portfolio. Mercandante currently likes demography, outsourcing, and productivity enhancement as areas to provide attractive long-term investment opportunities.

The fund's mandate is to invest in companies with a market capitalization of less than U.S.$4 billion that operate in the mature economies of Europe. There are no country or regional restraints. This directive makes the fund fairly unique, as most European equity mutual funds available to Canadian investors specialize in large-cap issues. The small-cap sector of the market is the most inefficient and it is here that astute stock picking can add much value.

Mercandante's largest holding is a 3.1% exposure to Denmark-based Group 4 Falck A/S. The fourth largest holding, Vestas Wind Systems AS, has a Canadian connection: it built the massive 117-metre-tall wind turbine that looms over the Toronto waterfront.

New

RRSP

AGF EMERGING MARKETS VALUE FUND

Charles Brandes, Jeff Busby (1994)/ Brandes Investment Partners

Consistency

Performance Trend

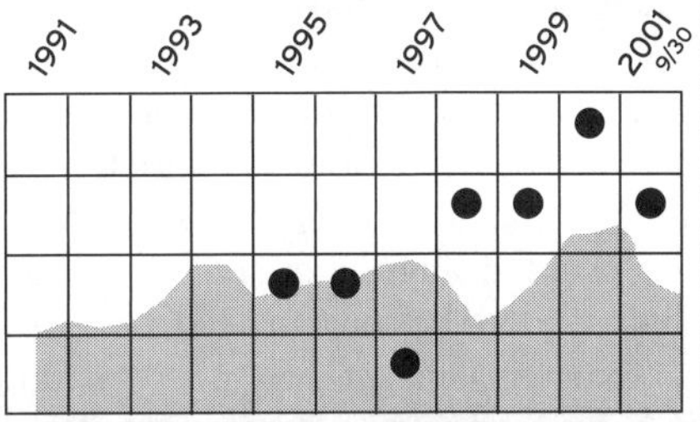

Risk

How often fund outperformed GICs	1 year in 2
How often fund lost money	4 years in 4
Worst year's rate of return	–51.56%

Reward-to-Risk Relationship

Sharpe Ratio Quartile Rankings

3-Year	1
5-Year	1

Morningstar Rating

★★★★

Efficiency/MER

Management expense/$100

$3.18

- ● above average
- ○ average
- ○ below average

Style

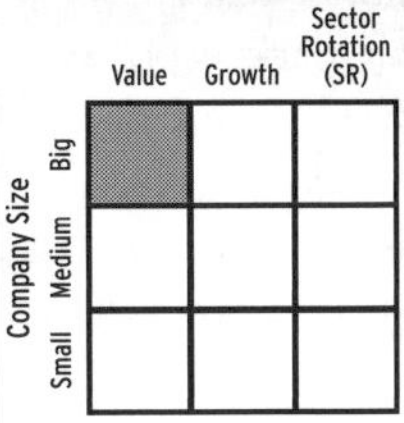

Complementary Fund:
Fidelity Japanese Growth

Similar Fund:
TD Latin American Growth

"Emerging Markets" and "Value" are two terms that aren't usually used in the same sentence. In the case of the AGF Emerging Markets Value Fund, the managers at Brandes Investment Partners have successfully married the two to create a Top Fund choice for 2002. Brandes and Busby are traditional bottom-up value stock pickers using an approach that can trace its roots back to the late 1930s and the late Benjamin Graham, the father of value investing.

Emerging markets have been a black hole for many investors. Events that moderately effect the more mature world markets usually have more serious consequences for emerging markets, and last year was no exception to this tendency. The technology meltdown had a disproportionate effect on emerging economies that were relying heavily on job growth, infrastructure spin-offs and tax revenues from the sector. Fortunately for the Brandes managers, "Technology" is another term rarely used in the same sentence as "Value"; they avoided the huge declines that most emerging markets funds experienced.

The AGF Emerging Markets Value Fund has returned an average annual compound rate of 11.5% over the past three years, despite a 5% loss over the past twelve months. In contrast, the average emerging markets fund is down 24% over the past year and has slipped by 0.5% annually over the past three years. The Pacific Rim represents 37% of the fund assets, Latin America 35%, Emerging Europe 19%, and the Middle East and Africa, 9%.

1999, 2000, 2001 RRSP

CI EMERGING MARKETS FUND

Nandu Narayanan (1997)/Trident Investment Management

Consistency

Performance Trend

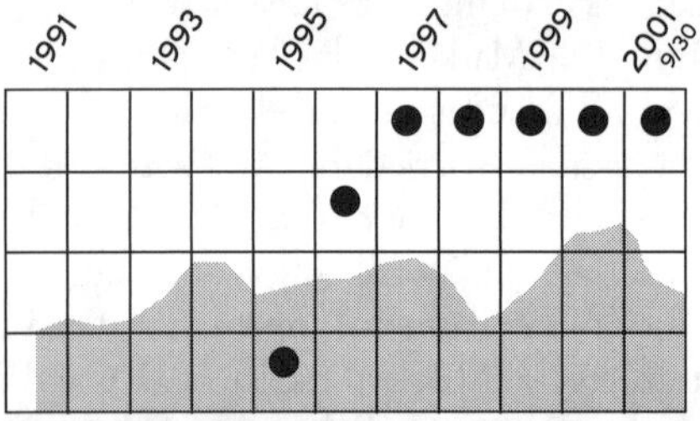

Risk

How often fund outperformed GICs	5 years in 5
How often fund lost money	4 years in 5
Worst year's rate of return	−28.76%

Reward-to-Risk Relationship

Sharpe Ratio Quartile Rankings

3-Year	1
5-Year	1

Morningstar Rating

★★★★★

Efficiency/MER

Management expense/$100

$2.84

○ above average
● average
○ below average

Style

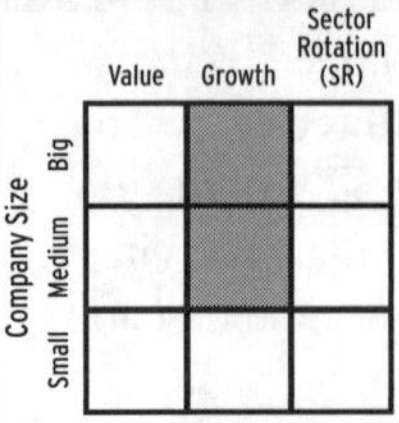

Complementary Fund:
Strategic Nova Asia-Pacific

Similar Fund:
AGF Emerging Markets Value

Nandu Narayanan's CI Emerging Markets Fund has been the top-performing emerging markets fund over the past five years. Unfortunately, this honour only translates into a compounded annual rate of return of 5.2%. However, since the average fund in the category lost 4.3% a year over the same period, Dr. Narayanan should indeed be congratulated.

Emerging markets have not been kind to investors. There are many compelling arguments for their inclusion in a diversified portfolio, but real world experience hasn't been as convincing. Dr Narayanan, however, *is* convinced that there are excellent investment opportunities for his fund. In his view, the underlying factors that make emerging markets attractive are still there: a large labour force with low wage rates, huge consumer demand from a slowly emerging middle class, and largely unexploited natural resources. Worldwide, the continued shift from "new economy" to "old economy" companies will benefit emerging markets as their competitive advantages will become increasingly compelling. His largest country allocation is Mexico, followed by Brazil and South Africa. Dr. Narayanan feels that Mexico will benefit from higher oil prices and the tendency of U.S. firms to use Mexican factories as low cost alternatives to American production facilities.

Dr. Narayanan believes that, apart from Europe, emerging markets possess the most attractive long-term investment opportunities available today. For beleaguered investors, this is good news at last.

An RRSP eligible version of this fund is available.

2001 RRSP

TD LATIN AMERICAN GROWTH FUND

Andy Skov (1997), Michael Perl/Morgan Stanley Investment Management Inc.

Consistency

Performance Trend

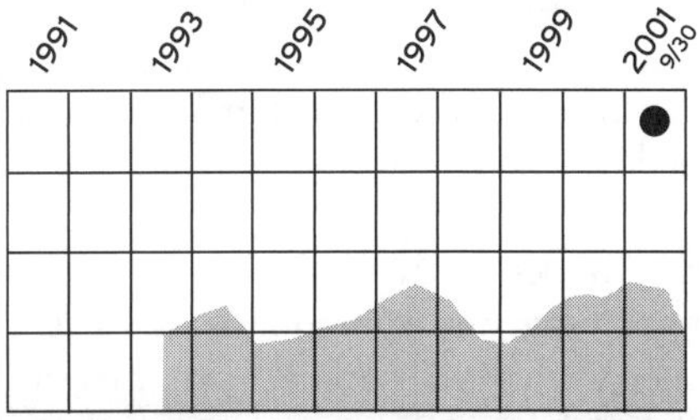

Risk

How often fund outperformed GICs	3 years in 3
How often fund lost money	3 years in 3
Worst year's rate of return	−41.2%

Reward-to-Risk Relationship
Sharpe Ratio Quartile Rankings

3-Year	N/A
5-Year	N/A

Morningstar Rating

N/A

Efficiency/MER

Management expense/$100

$2.80

○ above average
● average
○ below average

Style

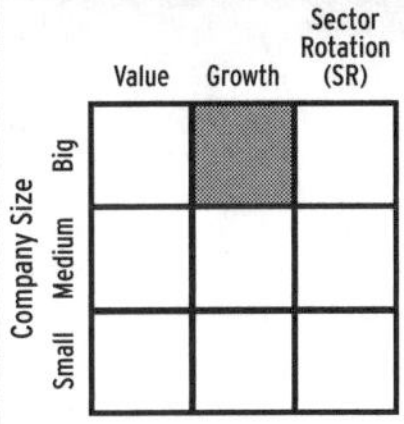

Complementary Fund:
Fidelity Japanese Growth

Similar Fund:
AGF Emerging Markets Value

TD Latin American Growth Fund has been the top performing fund in its category over the last three and five years. Unfortunately, this result doesn't translate into stellar numbers. The fund has gained an average of 4.2% annually over three years and 5.3% annually over five years. Such are the joys of Latin American investing.

Morgan Stanley has been a major force in international investment research and has created many of the indexes used as international markets benchmarks. Its expertise in Latin America and other emerging markets is particularly impressive.

The biggest economies by far in the region are Brazil and Mexico, so it's not surprising that both countries compose over 80% of the portfolio. The largest individual holding is in the Mexican telecommunications giant, Telefonos de Mexico SA. There are over 75 stock positions in the portfolio, which is much higher than average for Latin American funds, providing a level of diversification that is rare in the category.

The health of Latin American markets is largely dependent on the state of global economies. Managers Robert Meyer and Michael Perl feel that valuations are attractive and fundamentals are improving in the region, setting the stage for the fund to do well when the markets see signs of any global economic recovery.

New

RRSP

CI SIGNATURE CANADIAN RESOURCE FUND

Robert Lyon (1999)/C.I. Mutual Funds Inc.

Consistency

Performance Trend

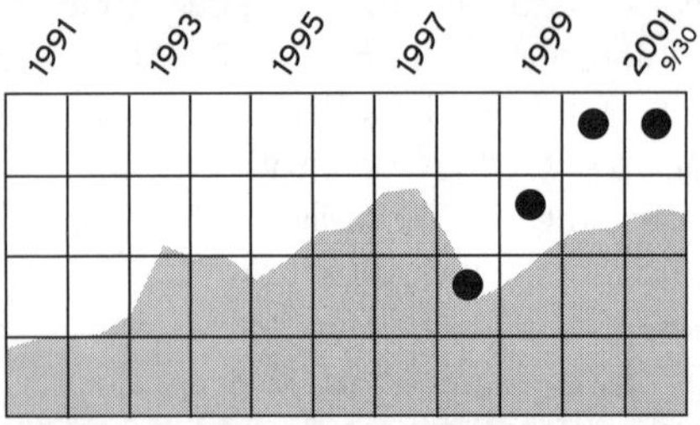

Risk

How often fund outperformed GICs	2 years in 2
How often fund lost money	1 year in 2
Worst year's rate of return	–49.7%

Reward-to-Risk Relationship

Sharpe Ratio Quartile Rankings

3-Year	1
5-Year	N/A

Morningstar Rating

★★★★★

Efficiency/MER

Management expense/$100

$2.59

- ○ above average
- ● average
- ○ below average

Style

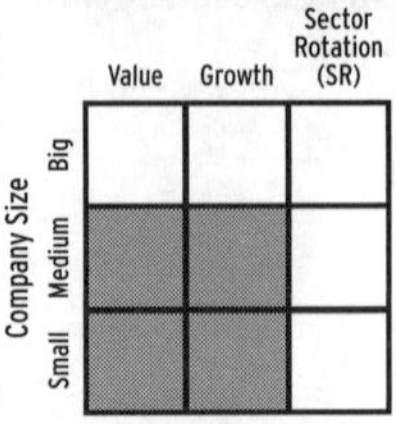

Complementary Fund:
Talvest Global Health Care

Similar Fund:
Royal Energy

The managers at the Signature Group pride themselves on being stock pickers. To their way of thinking, investors need to ignore all the confusing market signals and just focus on what opportunities there are in the market today.

A good example of this theory is the negative sentiment for the oil and gas sector: Despite the common wisdom that energy prices will decline, fund manager Robert Lyon believes some companies will still perform relatively well. He cites Suncor Energy, one of his top equity holdings, as proof. Lyon also feels that much of the action in the sector is moving to offshore drilling sites. That's why he has CHC Helicopters, a transportation company specializing in offshore rig servicing, in his top 10 holdings.

CI Signature Canadian Resource Fund gained 31.0% over the past 12 months and has an annual compound rate of return of 13.5% over the past 3 years. By comparison, the average fund in the Canadian resource category rose 12% and 3.6% over the past year and past three years respectively.

2001 RRSP

DOMINION EQUITY RESOURCE FUND
Dean Prodan (1998)/Crescent Capital Corp.

Consistency

Performance Trend

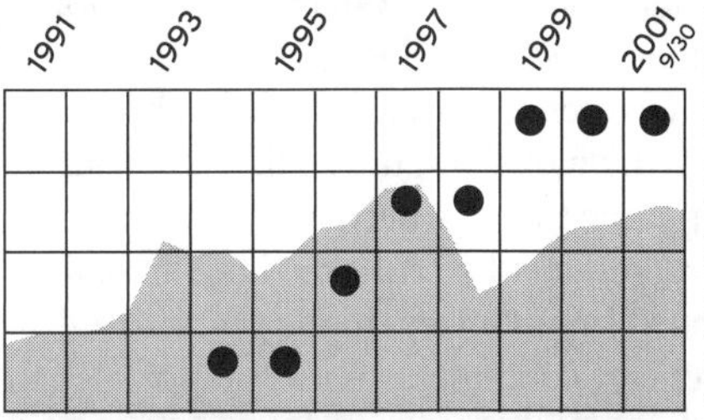

Risk

How often fund outperformed GICs	5 years in 6
How often fund lost money	4 years in 6
Worst year's rate of return	−41.86%

Reward-to-Risk Relationship
Sharpe Ratio Quartile Rankings

3-Year	1
5-Year	1

Morningstar Rating

★★★★★

Efficiency/MER

Management expense/$100

$2.09

- ○ above average
- ○ average
- ● below average

Style

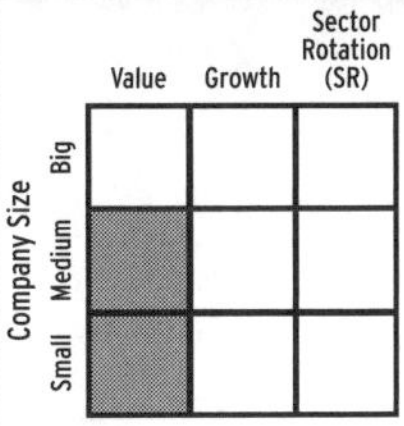

Complementary Fund:
Talvest Global Health Care

Similar Fund:
CI Signature Canadian Resource

Last year we picked the Dominion Equity Resource Fund as a Top Fund and commented that it would be a good choice for aggressive investors hoping to "hit a home run in oil and gas." We think a 44.8% return over the past 12 months probably counts as a home run year. In fact, this fund has posted an annual compound rate of return of 31.5% a year over the past three years and 16.7% a year over the past decade.

Calgary-based manager Dean Prodan's approach is based on four principles. First, he does bottom-up analysis with a focus on small- to mid-cap companies in the Canadian oil and gas sectors. Secondly, he has direct contact with the management of the companies he invests in, which is a "cornerstone" of his decision making process. Third, he constantly uses his oil and gas contacts and relationships to keep track of industry trends and developments. Finally, he is always prepared to act quickly when circumstances change.

Despite recent weakness in natural gas prices, Prodan remains bullish on the sector. He has, however, reduced his exposure to those smaller producers that might be adversely affected by lower prices and has invested in some of the larger players, such as Anderson Exploration, Talisman Energy, and Rio Alto Exploration. Prodan also likes the oil and gas service sector, which will benefit from the increased drilling activity that Western Canada is experiencing.

2001 RRSP

FIDELITY FOCUS NATURAL RESOURCES FUND

Scott Offen (1997)/Fidelity Investments Canada Ltd.

Consistency

Performance Trend

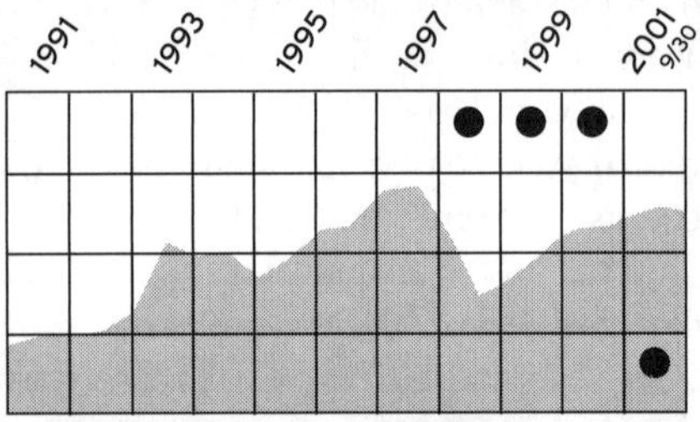

Risk

How often fund outperformed GICs	2 years in 2
How often fund lost money	1 year in 2
Worst year's rate of return	−20.26%

Reward-to-Risk Relationship

Sharpe Ratio Quartile Rankings

3-Year	2
5-Year	N/A

Morningstar Rating

★★★★

Efficiency/MER

Management expense/$100

$2.67

- ○ above average
- ● average
- ○ below average

Style

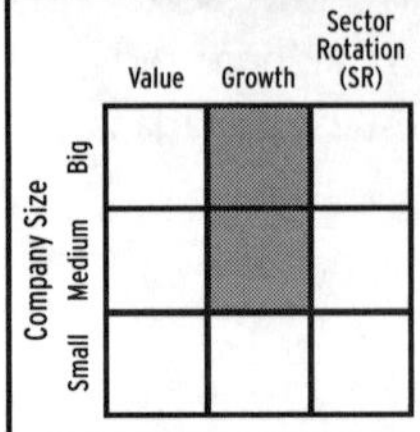

Complementary Fund:
Talvest Global Health Care

Similar Fund:
CI Signature Canadian Resource

Fidelity has a broad definition of natural resources. It includes agriculture and precious metals as part of the mandate for the Focus Natural Resources Fund. However, manager Scott Offen has stuck to traditional resource holdings when putting together his portfolio. Oil and gas represent 48% of the total holdings; the next largest sectors in the portfolio are energy equipment and services at 15% of the portfolio, and metals and mining at 11%.

Offen has been manager of this fund since inception (1997) and has posted first-quartile returns over two and three years. His performance has slipped over the past 12 months as the largely U.S.-based blue chip energy stocks in his portfolio underperformed many of the small- to mid-cap companies in the market. The average fund in the natural resources category rose 12.1% over the past year, while Fidelity Focus Natural Resources gained only 5.5% over the same period.

Offen remains overweighted to forest and paper products and metals and minerals. He's cautious about the prospects for the energy sector over the short term and is underweight oil and gas. The largest holding in the 117-securities portfolio is Chevron, followed by Exxon and BP. The top 10 holdings represent 44% of the total fund assets.

2000 RRSP

ROYAL ENERGY FUND

Gordon Zive (1994)/RBC Global Investment Management Inc.

Consistency

Performance Trend

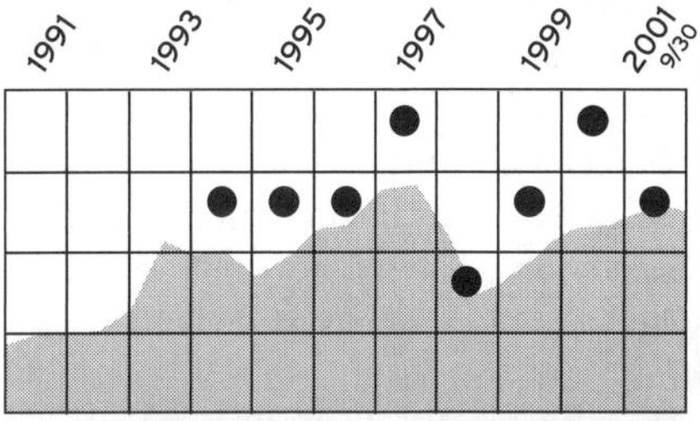

Risk

How often fund outperformed GICs	5 years in 7
How often fund lost money	3 years in 7
Worst year's rate of return	−40.37%

Reward-to-Risk Relationship
Sharpe Ratio Quartile Rankings

3-Year	2
5-Year	1

Morningstar Rating

★★★★★

Efficiency/MER

Management expense/$100

$2.36

○ above average
○ average
● below average

Style

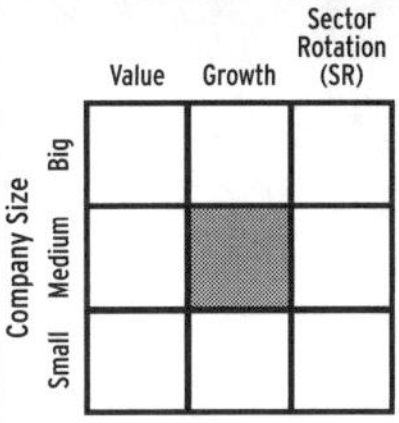

Complementary Fund:
Talvest Global Health Care

Similar Fund:
CI Signature Canadian Resource

Manager Gordon Zive's mandate is to invest in Canadian companies involved either directly or indirectly in the exploration, development, production, or distribution of petroleum-based products. His portfolio consists of only 31 names and the top 10 holdings represent over 60% of total assets. The names are familiar to Canadians: Petro-Canada, Talisman, Alberta Energy, Suncor, etc.

Mergers and acquisitions activity in the oil patch is staring to heat up, and new companies have been added and old companies removed. For example, Ketch Energy and Kick Energy are new names to the portfolio; they are the result of the takeover of Post Energy. Gulf Canada was removed after it was taken over by Conoco. Anderson Energy, another holding in the portfolio, is also in play.

His sector allocation is well diversified among senior, intermediate, and junior producers; integrated oils; and service companies. Zive expects that the demand for Canadian resources will pick up when global economies start to improve, and notes that even the lame duck Canadian dollar has been strengthening as investors anticipate higher resources prices.

1998, 1999, 2000 RRSP

UNIVERSAL CANADIAN RESOURCE FUND

Fred Sturm (1978)/Mackenzie Financial Corp.

Consistency

Performance Trend

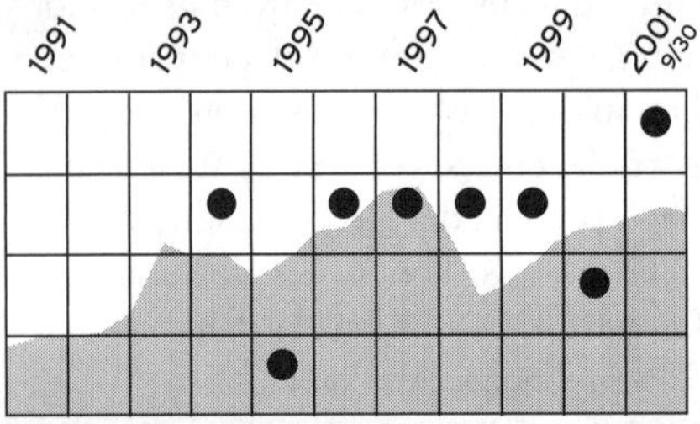

Risk

How often fund outperformed GICs	5 years in 6
How often fund lost money	4 years in 6
Worst year's rate of return	–48.72%

Reward-to-Risk Relationship

Sharpe Ratio Quartile Rankings

3-Year	1
5-Year	1

Morningstar Rating

★★★★

Efficiency/MER

Management expense/$100

$2.51

○ above average
○ average
● below average

Style

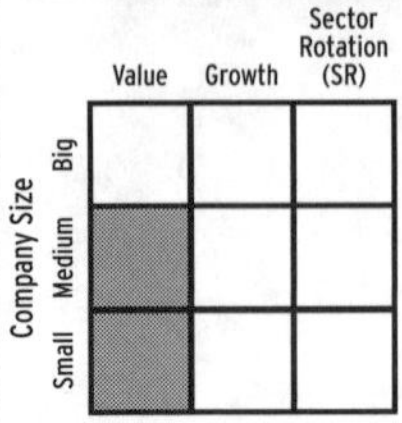

Complementary Fund:
Talvest Global Health Care

Similar Fund:
CI Signature Canadian Resource

Veteran stock picker Fred Sturm can look back on 1998 as an important low for the resource sector and for his fund. Universal Canadian Resource lost 28.7% that year when the collapse of the Asian markets unfortunately coincided with new resource capacity built for an expected Asian boom. The subsequent love affair with technology stocks made "old economy" investments unfashionable and valuations cheap. However, the resource sector is back in fashion despite a global slow-down.

Sturm's approach stresses diversification and discipline. In his portfolio, 39% of the holdings are in the oil and gas sector, 21% are in precious metals mining stocks, and 13% are in paper and forest products issues. His largest holding is a 4.8% weighting to Hurricane Hydrocarbons, which is a Kazakhstan-based oil firm. In fact, three of the top ten holdings are not based in Canada.

Universal Canadian resource has an excellent long-term record, with a 12.4% annual average compound rate of return over 10 years. Of course, investors should be aware that volatility of returns goes hand in hand with any sector mutual fund. This fund gained 41% in 1996, but gave it all back over the next two years with losses of 10.2% and 28.7%.

1998 RRSP

UNIVERSAL PRECIOUS METALS FUND

Fred Sturm (1994)/Mackenzie Financial Corp.

Consistency

Performance Trend

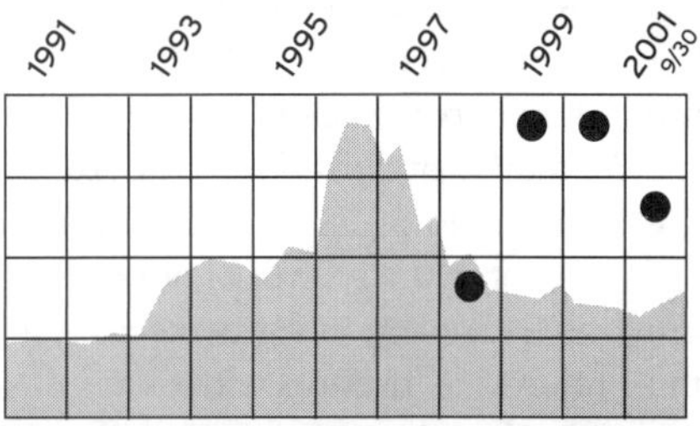

Risk

How often fund outperformed GICs	2 years in 4
How often fund lost money	2 years in 4
Worst year's rate of return	−47.51%

Reward-to-Risk Relationship

Sharpe Ratio Quartile Rankings

3-Year	1
5-Year	N/A

Morningstar Rating

N/A

Efficiency/MER

Management expense/$100

$2.55

○ above average
● average
○ below average

Style

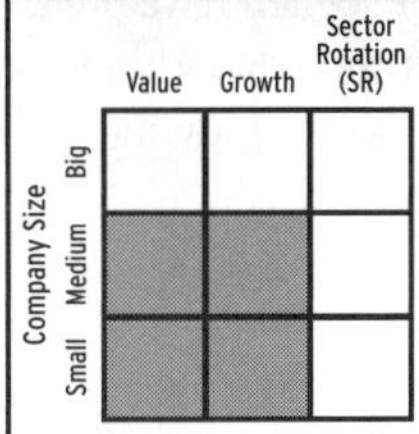

Complementary Fund:
Talvest Global Science & Tech

Similar Fund:
Mac Universal Canadian Resource

Our data shows that assets invested in precious metals funds represent less than 0.001% of the almost $562 billion that Canadians have put into mutual funds. Only the Latin American and country-specific sectors have fewer investor dollars. Yet in our experience, this category always comes up in backyard conversations and everyone seems to have an opinion.

Fred Sturm's Universal Precious Metals Fund has been the top performing precious metals fund over the past five years. This may seem like faint praise, as the average annual rate over that five-year period was –6.3%. However, the average precious metals fund has lost an average of –15.4% over the same time period.

Sturm believes that a long-term reversal in the price of gold has occurred. Prospects of a lower U.S. dollar, excess demand, a scarcity of new discoveries, and renewed industry mergers and acquisition activities are all positive for the precious metals markets. Sturm has a diversified portfolio of gold producers, gold exploration stocks, and diamond exploration companies. Senior companies with significant international operations, such as Barrick Gold, are represented in the fund, as well as some of the smaller, more junior players. Gold bullion can also be held, but there are no such holdings in the portfolio at this time.

2001 RRSP

AIM GLOBAL TECHNOLOGY FUND

Bill Keithler (1999), Michelle Espelien/AIM Capital Management

Consistency

Performance Trend

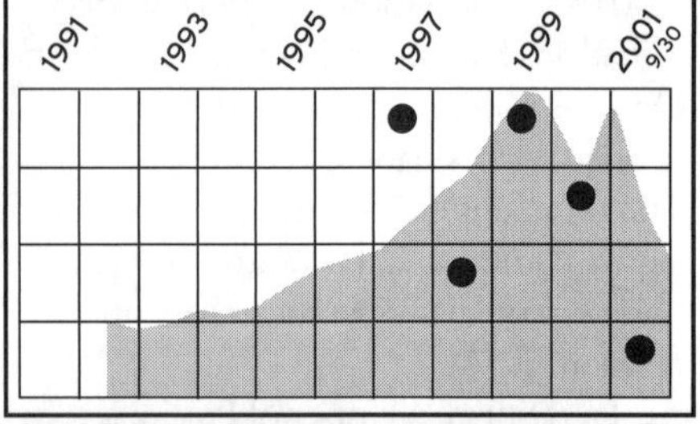

Risk

How often fund outperformed GICs	3 years in 3
How often fund lost money	1 year in 3
Worst year's rate of return	−74.91%

Reward-to-Risk Relationship

Sharpe Ratio Quartile Rankings

3-Year	2
5-Year	N/A

Morningstar Rating

★★★★

Efficiency/MER

Management expense/$100

$2.98

- ● above average
- ○ average
- ○ below average

Style

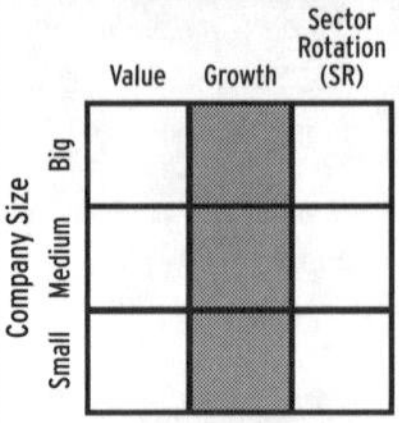

Complementary Fund:
Talvest Global Health Care

Similar Fund:
Talvest Global Science & Tech

The meltdown in the science and technology sector over the past 18 months has left investors poorer and in some cases, hopping mad. They've left the sector—most of them permanently.

We think that decision is a mistake. Technological advances will continue to be a huge factor in the growth of our economy and technology investments will continue to provide investors with excellent gains over time. Surviving a market event like the recent tech wreck depends on three key factors: having realistic expectations about risk and return, diversifying among different companies and sectors, and possessing a willingness to invest for the long term.

AIM Global Technology Fund is a case in point. The fund has returned 17.85% a year over the past three years and 24.3% a year from its inception (November 1996). These are wonderful numbers. There are 110 holdings in the portfolio and it is well diversified by sector. Most of the fund investments are U.S.-based firms, but interestingly, the top three holdings include Flextronics International Ltd. (Singapore), SmartForce PLC (U.K.), and Celestica Inc. (Canada). The top 10 holdings constitute only 20% of the fund's total assets.

In response to the fund's 56.8% plunge over the past year, managers Bill Keithler and Michelle Espelien have built up their cash positions and have added some more defensive, slower growing technology issues.

2000, 2001 RRSP

ALTAMIRA SCIENCE & TECHNOLOGY FUND

Ian Ainsworth (1995)/Altamira Investment Services

Consistency

Performance Trend

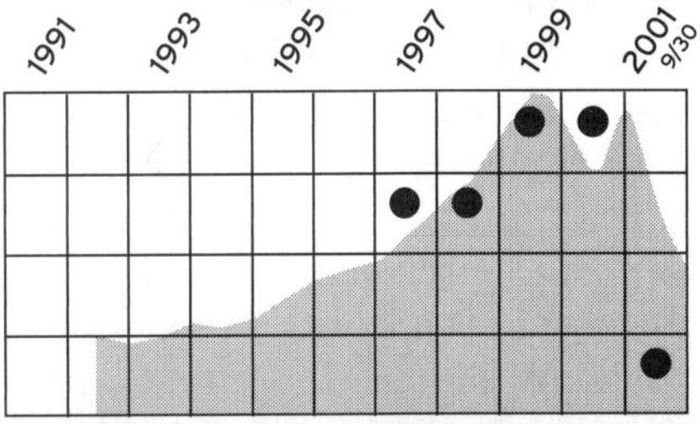

Risk

How often fund outperformed GICs	4 years in 4
How often fund lost money	1 year in 4
Worst year's rate of return	−77.01%

Reward-to-Risk Relationship

Sharpe Ratio Quartile Rankings

3-Year	1
5-Year	N/A

Morningstar Rating

★★★★

Efficiency/MER

Management expense/$100

$2.48

○ above average
○ average
● below average

Style

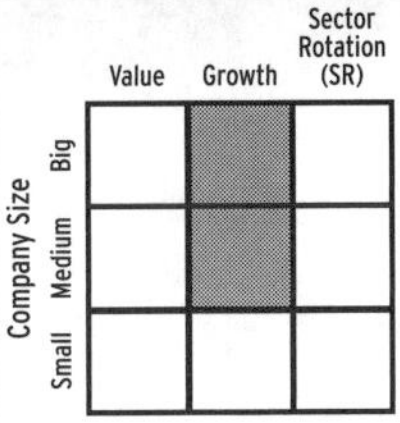

Complementary Fund:
Talvest Global Health Care

Similar Fund:
Talvest Global Science & Tech

According to our Morningstar database, someone with the foresight to invest $1,000 in this fund at the end of August 1995 would have seen that investment grow to over $4,193 by the end of June 2001. An investor putting $1,000 into this fund at the end of August 2000 would have received $377 at the end of June 2001. Timing is everything.

We liked this fund two years ago, we liked it last year, and we still like it. Manager Ian Ainsworth has been at the helm since inception and the breadth of his technology sector knowledge impresses us. Having said that, we won't comment on the fact that Nortel is still the largest holding in the portfolio.

Ainsworth feels that the near-term fundamentals in the sector continue to be weak, although he expects many investors to "perceive this time as a buying opportunity." He's not optimistic that the large carriers and equipment manufacturers won't see further declines, but he does like the prospects for some of the smaller companies in the sector. Ainsworth is therefore adding some small-cap names to the fund. At the other end of the size spectrum, Microsoft still represents 3.0% of the fund. Ainsworth believes that whatever the actual details of the eventual agreement between the company and the U.S. government, the lawsuit's final resolution will be positive for the industry.

There is a RRSP eligible version of this fund available.

New

RRSP

TALVEST GLOBAL HEALTH CARE FUND

Edward Owens (1996)/Wellington Management Co.

Consistency

Performance Trend

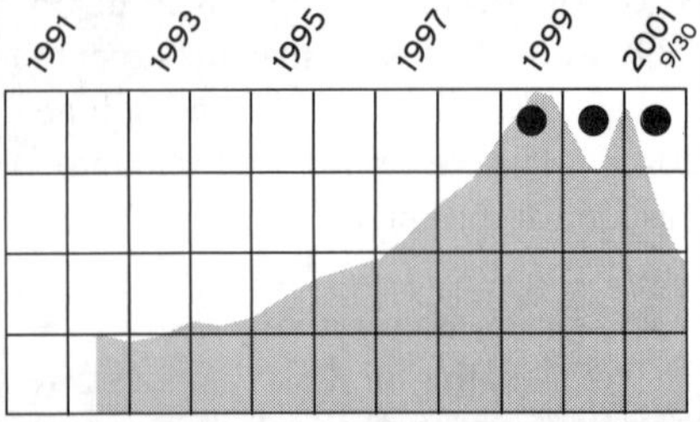

Risk

How often fund outperformed GICs	4 years in 4
How often fund lost money	0 years in 4
Worst year's rate of return	5.55%

Reward-to-Risk Relationship

Sharpe Ratio Quartile Rankings

3-Year	N/A
5-Year	N/A

Morningstar Rating

N/A

Efficiency/MER

Management expense/$100

$2.50

- ○ above average
- ○ average
- ● below average

Style

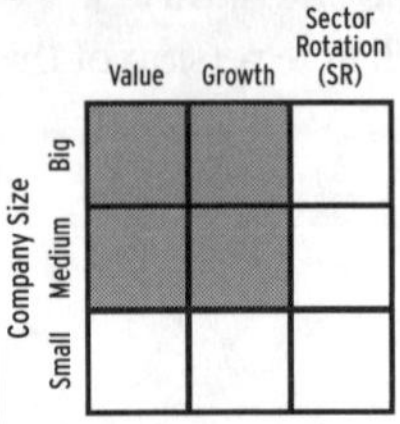

Complementary Fund:
AIM Global Technology

Similar Fund:
TD Health Sciences

One-year gain: 35.8%. Gain over three years: 47.0%. No, these aren't typos. Edward Owens, manager of the Talvest Global Health Care Fund, has posted these stellar returns for two reasons: (1) he is a bottom-up value manager in a sector that is usually populated with growth-oriented managers and (2) he and his company are simply very good at what they do. Wellington Management Co. is a specialist in the health care field and has over U.S.$11 billion in health care investment assets worldwide.

Owens's approach is to seek out companies with strong earnings, good growth potential, and attractive prices. He is currently underweighted to the volatile biotechnology and pharmaceutical sectors and will remain so until the biotech correction eases. He likes medical supply distributors and medical products, as the valuations are more to his liking. The largest holding in the 93-security portfolio is a 3.5% exposure to Pharmacia Corp.

Health care funds are unfortunately lumped together with the telecommunications- and internet-focused funds that have dragged down the science and technology sector over the past two years. The performance history of this fund confirms that the areas obviously have little in common.

There is an RRSP eligible version of this fund available.

2000, 2001 RRSP

TALVEST GLOBAL SCIENCE & TECHNOLOGY FUND

Stephen Kahn (1996)/TAL Global Asset Management Inc.

Consistency

Performance Trend

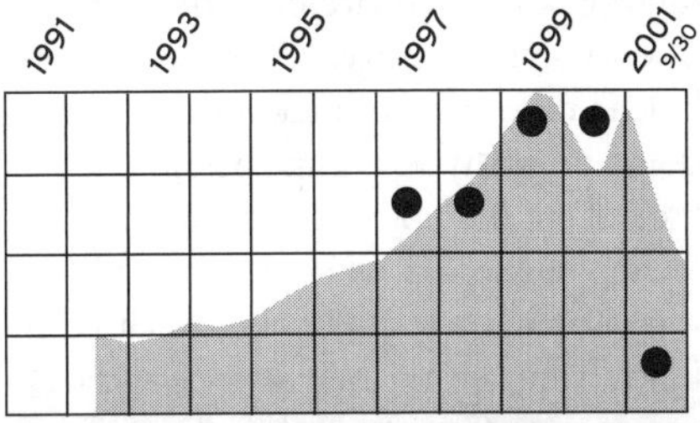

Risk

How often fund outperformed GICs	**3 years in 3**
How often fund lost money	**1 year in 3**
Worst year's rate of return	**−77.83%**

Reward-to-Risk Relationship

Sharpe Ratio Quartile Rankings

3-Year	**1**
5-Year	**N/A**

Morningstar Rating

★★★★

Efficiency/MER

Management expense/$100

$2.25

- ○ above average
- ○ average
- ● below average

Style

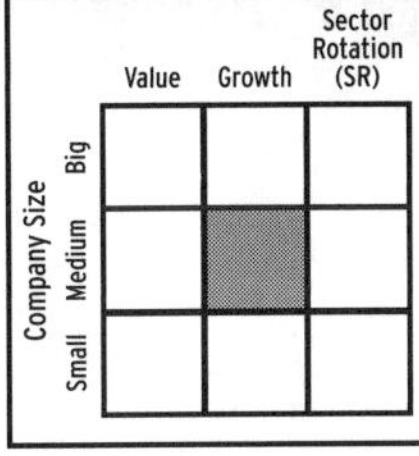

Complementary Fund:
Royal Energy

Similar Fund:
AIM Global Technology

Ouch! A 61.2% one-year loss hurts. Even with 12 years as a technology stock expert under his belt, manager Stephen Kahn couldn't have seen that result coming. Yet he remains optimistic about the prospects for the sector generally and his fund in particular. While acknowledging that the short-term prognosis is not good, Kahn is still bullish in the long term. He expects the U.S. economy to stabilize in late 2001 and technology stocks to subsequently rally.

Until then, he's in a defensive mode. Cash balances are higher than normal and maximum individual stock positions are limited to 3% of fund assets. When the tech sector bottoms out, Kahn will deploy his cash into stocks that he feels will benefit first from a recovery. His focus will be on companies that specialize in Internet infrastructure, wireless communication, and software applications.

This fund, as mentioned above, fell 61.2% in the past 12 months. Notwithstanding that loss, however, investors with a healthy appetite for risk who were early to get into this fund have done very well indeed. Since the inception date of October 1996, the fund has returned an average of 25.7% a year.

There is an RRSP eligible version of this fund available.

New

RRSP

TD HEALTH SCIENCES FUND

Kris Jenner (inception)/T. Rowe Price Associates, Inc.

Consistency

Performance Trend

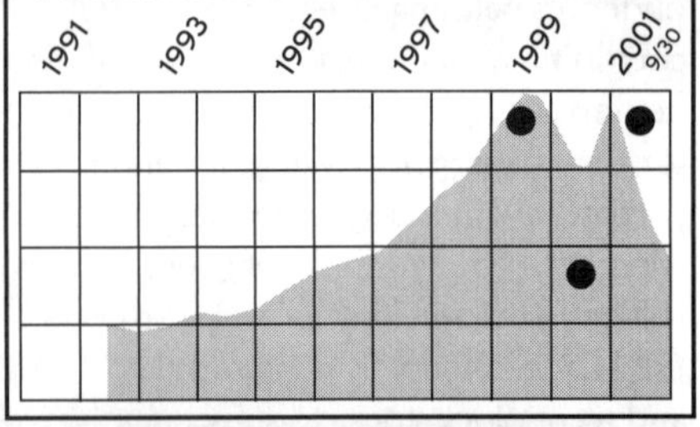

Risk

How often fund outperformed GICs	3 years in 3
How often fund lost money	1 year in 3
Worst year's rate of return	−21.88%

Reward-to-Risk Relationship
Sharpe Ratio Quartile Rankings

3-Year	N/A
5-Year	N/A

Morningstar Rating

N/A

Efficiency/MER

Management expense/$100

$2.74

- ○ above average
- ● average
- ○ below average

Style

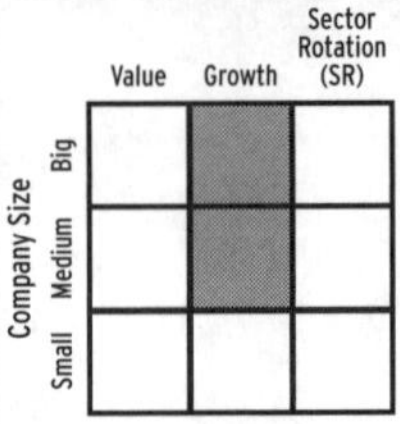

Complementary Fund:
Dominion Equity Resource

Similar Fund:
Talvest Global Health Care

In the past, we've recommended that investors in health care/health science funds ignore the quartile rankings of their investments. Health care companies have little in common with telecommunications and software companies, and yet they all are members of the science and technology sector. Of course, our advice was given in early 2000 when health care funds were lagging their science and technology counterparts. Today, our advice is the same, but for the opposite reasons: health care funds have been a relatively bright spot in the recently very dark science and technology sector.

Demographics make health care funds very attractive. Aging populations, new drug and medicine discoveries, and higher health care spending are all positives for the sector.

The fund has averaged 16.5% a year over the past three years, despite only gaining 0.6% over the past twelve months. By contrast, the average science and technology fund was off 39.9% over the same one-year period.

There is an RRSP eligible version of this fund available.

2001 RRSP

BEUTEL GOODMAN INCOME FUND

Bruce Corneil (1995), David Gregoris (1993)/Beutel Goodman Managed Funds Inc.

Consistency

Performance Trend

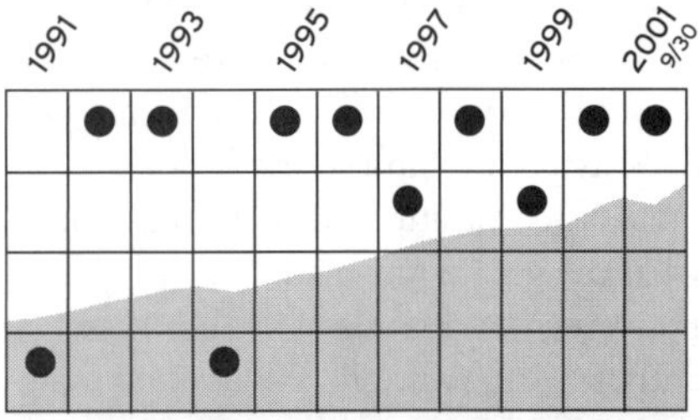

Risk

How often fund outperformed GICs	8 years in 8
How often fund lost money	2 years in 8
Worst year's rate of return	–10.02%

Reward-to-Risk Relationship

Sharpe Ratio Quartile Rankings

3-Year	1
5-Year	1

Morningstar Rating

★★★★

Efficiency/MER

Management expense/$100

$0.62

○ above average
○ average
● below average

Style

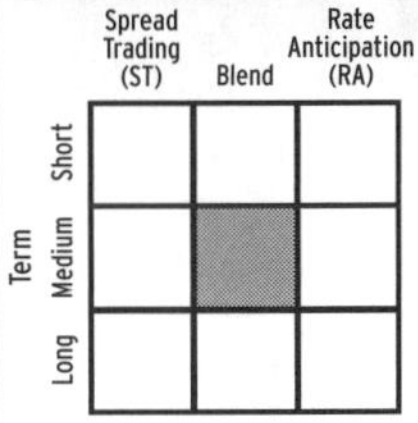

Complementary Fund:
TD Real Return Bond

Similar Fund:
McLean Budden Fixed Income

The Beutel Goodman people are firm believers in the active management of bond portfolios and the use of independent research to support investment decisions. The superior performance of their Income Fund seems to validate their philosophy.

The fund has been a first-quartile performer over one, two, three, five, and ten years. A management expense ratio that is a full 1.1% below that of the average Canadian bond fund certainly helps performance numbers, but the lower fees don't mean that the investor is being short-changed. The portfolio consists of a 26.8% exposure to corporate bonds and in the uncertain economic climate we're currently experiencing, credit analysis of these holdings has become an important issue. Luckily, fund investors can rely on excellent in-house equity research capabilities. 52% of the portfolio consists of AAA bonds, the highest quality rating. 19% are AA bonds and the balance are A rated.

The portfolio has an average term to maturity of 9.57 years. This a little longer than average and reflects the managers' view that the Bank of Canada and the Federal Reserve will continue to lower short-term interest rates. As mentioned previously, the fund is actively managed and 78.5% of the portfolio is turned over annually.

New

RRSP

GREAT-WEST LIFE INCOME (M) B FUND

Neil Lovatt (1996)/Mackenzie Financial Corp.

Consistency

Performance Trend

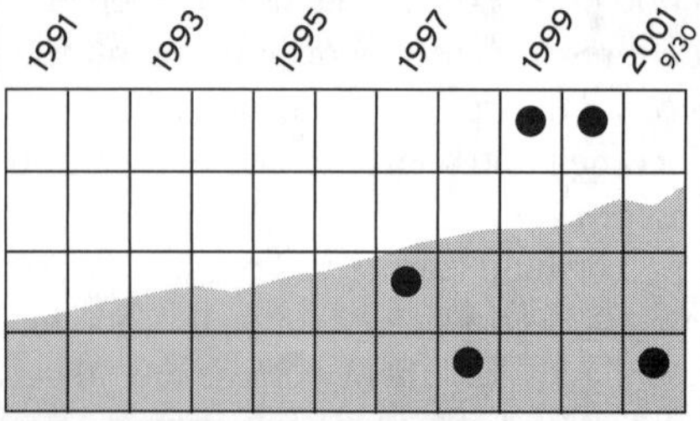

Risk

How often fund outperformed GICs	2 years in 4
How often fund lost money	0 years in 4
Worst year's rate of return	−2.46%

Reward-to-Risk Relationship

Sharpe Ratio Quartile Rankings

3-Year	1
5-Year	2

Morningstar Rating

★★★★

Efficiency/MER

Management expense/$100

$2.09

- ● above average
- ○ average
- ○ below average

Style

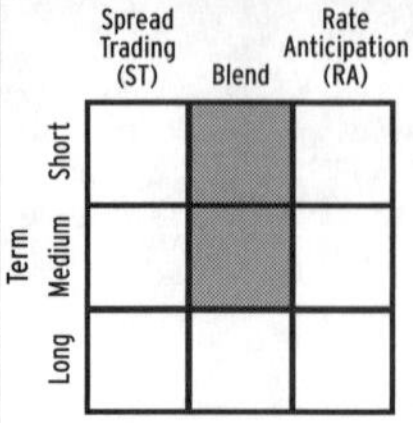

Complementary Fund:
TD Real Return Bond

Similar Fund:
Elliott & Page Monthly

Our favourite saying is that to grow the largest tomato in the garden, all you have to do is paint a cantaloupe red! Well, we've found a cantaloupe here: Great-West Life's Income (M) Fund is categorized as a bond fund by the IFSC, the industry committee that determines into what category a fund should be placed. However, our analysis of the fund assets and of Great-West Life's marketing materials reveal it to be a balanced fund.

The asset mix is 55% Canadian bonds, 30% Canadian stocks, 10% foreign stocks, and 5% cash. Clearly, this is not a bond fund in the traditional sense. Performance has been first-quartile over one, three, and five years. We compared these numbers with those of the average balanced fund and still found them impressive. The average balanced fund has returned –2.9%, 3.4%, and 7.7% over one, three, and five years respectively. Great-West Life Income (B) gained 9.2%, 5.9%, and 8.0% over those same time frames.

Manager Neil Lovatt is actually a Mackenzie Financial money manager. Great-West Life has a broad line of segregated funds managed by both in-house and external managers, and the "M" in the name of some of its funds indicates a Mackenzie manager.

1997, 1998, 1999, 2000, 2001 RRSP

MCLEAN BUDDEN FIXED INCOME FUND

Management Team/McLean Budden Ltd.

Consistency

Performance Trend

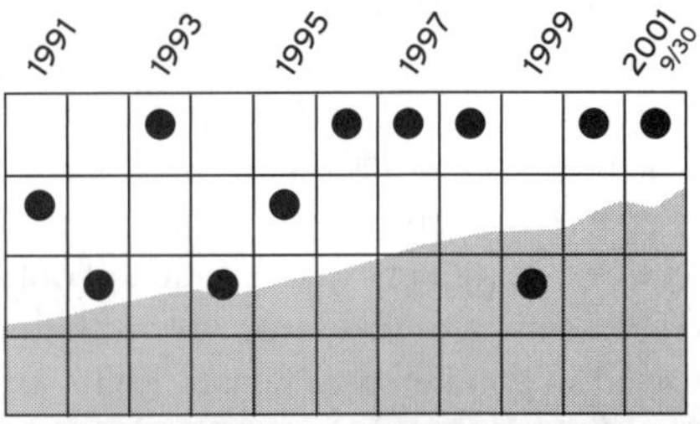

Risk

How often fund outperformed GICs	7 years in 8
How often fund lost money	2 years in 8
Worst year's rate of return	−8.29%

Reward-to-Risk Relationship

Sharpe Ratio Quartile Rankings

3-Year	1
5-Year	1

Morningstar Rating

★★★★

Efficiency/MER

Management expense/$100

$0.69

- ○ above average
- ○ average
- ● below average

Style

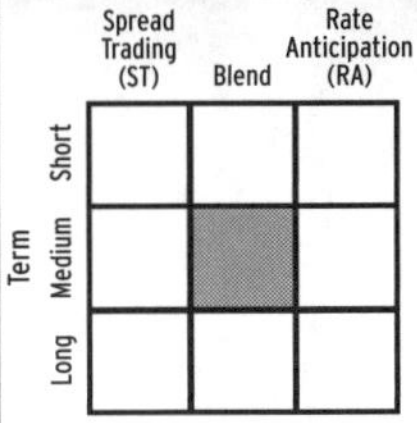

Complementary Fund:
TD Real Return Bond

Similar Fund:
Beutel Goodman Income

McLean Budden credits its investment discipline for the success of its funds, including the Fixed Income Fund. McLean Budden doesn't make the "big bets," it just tries to add value. It's a pretty elementary concept, but the company has been very successful with it.

This fund has been a first-quartile performer over one, two, three, five, and ten years. It has returned 6.5% over the past 12 months, which is higher than both the average fund in the category and the benchmark Scotia Capital Markets Universe Bond Index. Longer term, the fund has risen an average of 7.5% a year over five years and 9.0% a year over ten years.

The portfolio is overweighted to the shorter end of the maturity spectrum. The management team feels the inflationary impact of aggressive central bank easing will hurt long-term bonds. The prices of corporate issues have benefited from investors looking to enhance investment yields in the short-term market. This environment helped the McLean Budden Fixed Income Fund, which is overweighted to high quality corporate bonds and debentures.

1996, 1997, 1998, 1999, 2000, 2001 RRSP

PHILLIPS, HAGER & NORTH BOND FUND

Scott Lamont (1990)/Phillips, Hager & North Investment Management

Consistency

Performance Trend

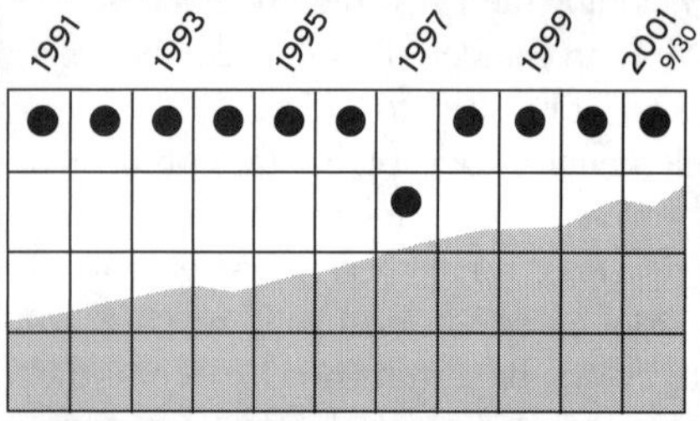

Risk

How often fund outperformed GICs	8 years in 8
How often fund lost money	2 years in 8
Worst year's rate of return	–6.07%

Reward-to-Risk Relationship

Sharpe Ratio Quartile Rankings

3-Year	1
5-Year	1

Morningstar Rating

★★★★★

Efficiency/MER

Management expense/$100

$0.57

- ○ above average
- ○ average
- ● below average

Style

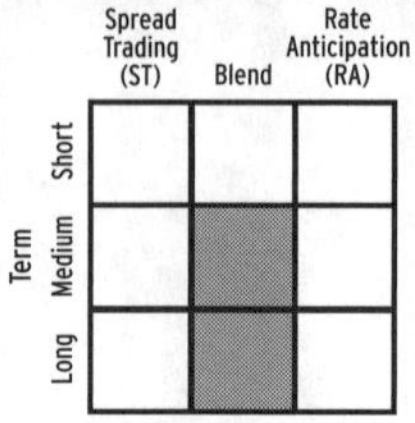

Complementary Fund:
Elliott & Page Monthly

Similar Fund:
Perigee Index Plus Bond

PH&N Bond has been a first-quartile performer in thirteen of the past fifteen calendar years. Tellingly, it has never been the top performing bond fund in any one year. In fact, its best performance by rank was third place in 1989 and 1987. We value its consistency and we value its low fees. A management expense ratio of only 0.58% compares very favourably with the Canadian bond fund average of 1.839%.

Manager Scott Lamont's expectation is for modestly lower interest rates as slow economic growth and a lack of "pricing power" lead to lower inflation. He's well aware, however, of the inflationary ramifications of further aggressive central bank easing. As a result, Lamont will continue to use multiple interest rate anticipation and spread trading strategies to help preserve investor capital.

The portfolio has a 47% weighting to Government of Canada bonds, a 29% corporate bond weighting, and the balance is in provincial bonds, foreign bonds, and mortgages. These weightings are slightly more conservative than those of the average bond fund. However, the average term to maturity of 10.6 years is slightly higher than the average and reflects the PH&N view that interest rates and inflation are headed for even lower lows.

2001 RRSP

PERIGEE INDEX PLUS BOND FUND

Management Team (inception)/Perigee Investment Counsel Inc.

Consistency

Performance Trend

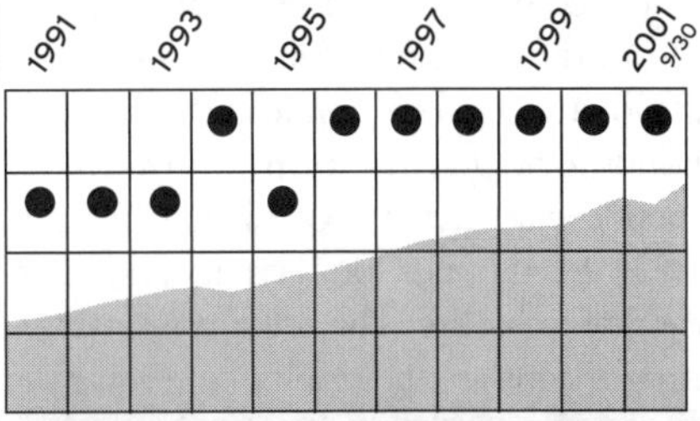

Risk

How often fund outperformed GICs	7 years in 8
How often fund lost money	2 years in 8
Worst year's rate of return	–6.07%

Reward-to-Risk Relationship

Sharpe Ratio Quartile Rankings

3-Year	1
5-Year	1

Morningstar Rating

★★★★

Efficiency/MER

Management expense/$100

$0.75

○ above average
○ average
● below average

Style

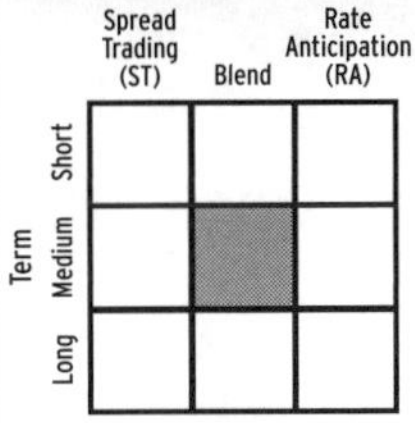

Complementary Fund:
TD Real Return Bond

Similar Fund:
PH&N Bond

The "Index Plus" part of this fund's name refers to Perigee's management approach here. It uses what is called a "constrained duration bond process" to match the portfolio's interest rate sensitivity to the benchmark's (in this case, the Scotia Capital Markets Universe Bond Index). To earn their management fees, which are a very low 0.75%, the Perigee managers add value and enhance returns through interest rate anticipation and trading activities.

For example, the current portfolio is overweighted to both provincial and corporate bonds. In addition, the maturity structure of the portfolio is overweighted at both the short and long end of the spectrum. Both of these strategies reflect Perigee's view that the economy will start to rebound during the second half of 2001 and into 2002. If this scenario unfolds, the higher yielding provincial and corporate issues will benefit.

The fund has been a first-quartile performer over three, five, and ten years, averaging 3.9%, 7.0%, and 8.9% a year respectively.

CANADIAN BOND

New

RRSP

SCEPTRE BOND FUND

Richard Knowles (2000)/Sceptre Investment Counsel Ltd.

Consistency

Performance Trend

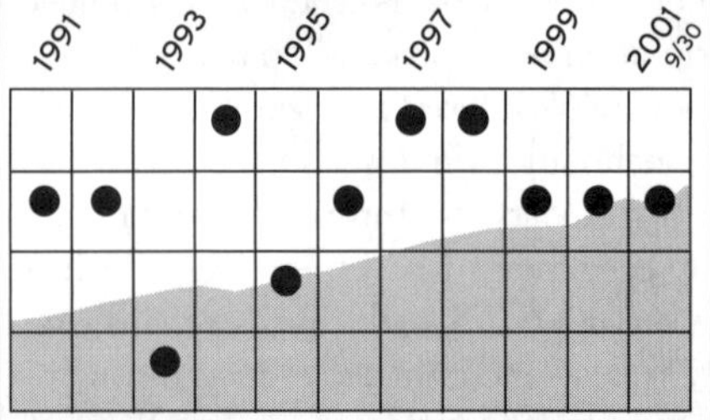

Risk

How often fund outperformed GICs	7 years in 8
How often fund lost money	2 years in 8
Worst year's rate of return	−6.24%

Reward-to-Risk Relationship

Sharpe Ratio Quartile Rankings

3-Year	2
5-Year	1

Morningstar Rating

★★★★

Efficiency/MER

Management expense/$100

$0.94

○ above average
○ average
● below average

Style

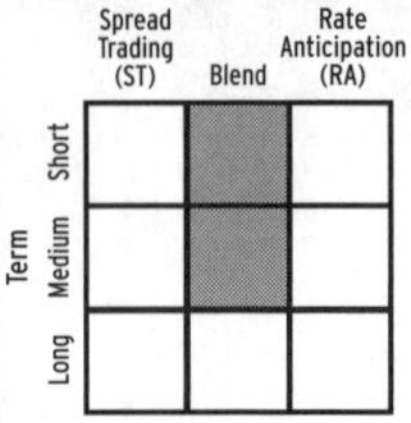

Complementary Fund:
TD Real Return Bond

Similar Fund:
Perigee Index Plus Bond

Manager Richard Knowles utilizes a three-pronged approach to manage this fund. Knowles, who joined Sceptre from Jones Heward Investment Management in 2000, invests in corporate and municipal bonds for yield enhancement, government securities for asset mix flexibility, and foreign bonds for currency and interest rate exposure. The actual asset mix proportions are the result of interest rate movements, inflation, economic developments, and credit ratings. The current mix is 44% corporate bonds, 27% Government of Canada bonds, and 24% provincial issues.

The fund has averaged 7.5% a year over the past five years and 8.8% over fifteen years. The average Canadian bond fund gained 6.1% and 8.2% respectively over the same time periods.

The average term to maturity is 8.4 years, which is slightly less than the category average. A management expense ratio of only 0.95% is much lower than average and is a key reason why this fund has been such a consistently superior performer.

1999, 2000, 2001 RRSP

TD CANADIAN BOND FUND

Satish Rai (1988), Paul Gardner (1998)/TD Asset Management Inc.

Consistency

Performance Trend

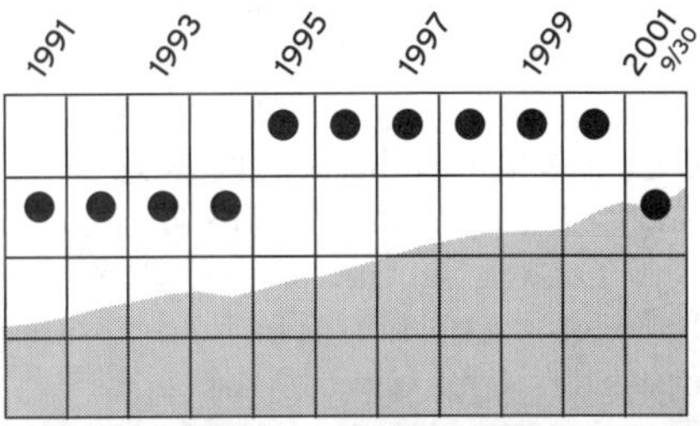

Risk

How often fund outperformed GICs	7 years in 8
How often fund lost money	2 years in 8
Worst year's rate of return	–7.95%

Reward-to-Risk Relationship
Sharpe Ratio Quartile Rankings

3-Year	1
5-Year	1

Morningstar Rating

★★★★★

Efficiency/MER

Management expense/$100

$1.00

○ above average
○ average
● below average

Style

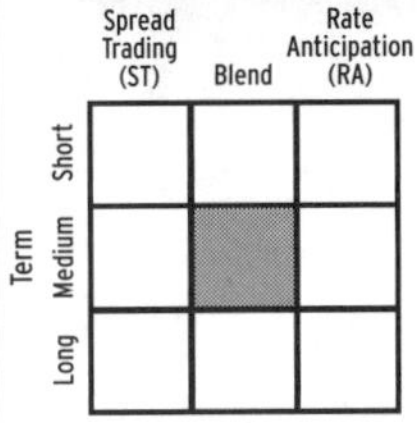

Complementary Fund:
Elliott & Page Monthly

Similar Fund:
PH&N Bond

TD Canadian Bond Fund is managed more like an equity fund than a bond fund. The fund has two full-time analysts who do fundamental analysis, consult with their equity management colleagues and even visit companies for some up-close-and-personal due diligence. A 62% weighting to corporate issues means that Rai and his team have to take the process very seriously. Proof of their expertise is that they've never had a bond default. This feat is even more impressive given that Rai generally holds his bonds to maturity and tries to keep portfolio turnover as near to zero as possible.

The average term to maturity of the fund assets is 12.1 years. By comparison, the average Canadian bond fund's term to maturity is only 9.0 years. Normally, longer-term bonds are vulnerable to inflationary pressures in the economy. Rai, however, has a 10% weighting to real return bonds, which are Government of Canada issues that are indexed to inflation and are therefore immune to the effects of inflation.

The TD Canadian Bond Fund has averaged 9.5% annually over the past 10 years versus 7.9% for the average Canadian bond fund. Over the past 12 months, investors earned 6.0% compared with 4.3% for the average fund.

2001 RRSP

TD CANADIAN GOVERNMENT BOND INDEX FUND

Kevin LeBlanc (1993)/TD Quantitative Capital, Lori MacKay (1995)/TD Mutual Funds

Consistency

Performance Trend

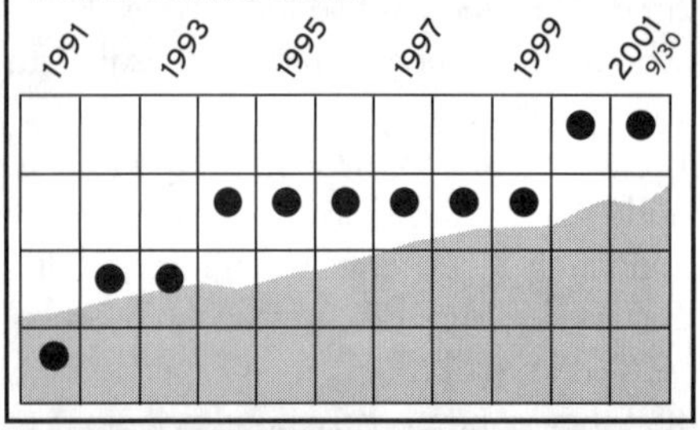

Risk

How often fund outperformed GICs	7 years in 8
How often fund lost money	2 years in 8
Worst year's rate of return	−7.24%

Reward-to-Risk Relationship

Sharpe Ratio Quartile Rankings

3-Year	1
5-Year	1

Morningstar Rating

★★★★

Efficiency/MER

Management expense/$100

$0.86

- ○ above average
- ○ average
- ● below average

Style

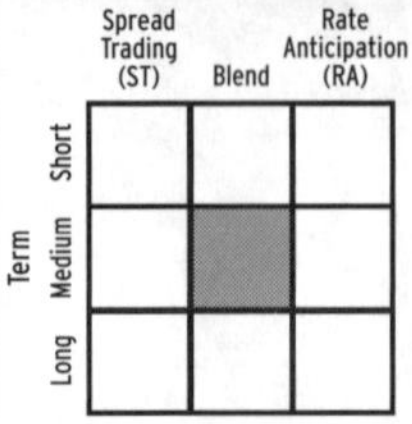

Complementary Fund:
TD Real Return Bond

Similar Fund:
Perigee Index Plus Bond

This is an excellent fund for investors who believe two things: (1) active management of an asset class—especially bonds—doesn't add value and (2) paying management fees averaging 1.84% a year for an asset class that has historically yielded single-digit returns doesn't make sense.

TD Canadian Government Bond Index fits the bill here. The fund passively tracks the Scotia Capital Markets All Governments Universe Bond Index; there is no active trading, nor is any attempt made to adjust the term structure or asset mix of the portfolio. As a result, there are no research or transaction costs and the management expense ratio is a rock-bottom 0.86% a year. The bonds in the portfolio are all government issues and the default risk is almost zero. It isn't zero because 1.7% of the assets are municipal bonds and while civic bankruptcies are rare, they're not unknown.

The fund has averaged 6.8% a year over the past five years and 4.9% in the past twelve months. There aren't many bells and whistles to this fund—what you see is what you get. However, what you get is a low-cost, low-maintenance portfolio of government guaranteed bonds that makes an excellent core holding in a conservative portfolio.

New

RRSP

TD REAL RETURN BOND FUND

Satish Rai (1994), Paul Gardner/TD Asset Management Inc.

Consistency

Performance Trend

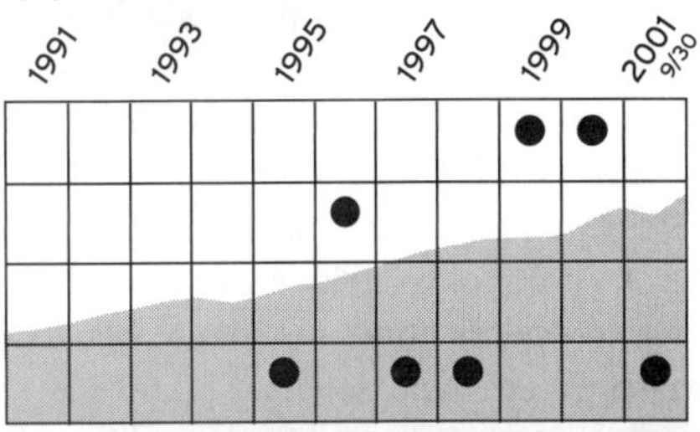

Risk

How often fund outperformed GICs	4 years in 6
How often fund lost money	0 years in 6
Worst year's rate of return	−0.23%

Reward-to-Risk Relationship

Sharpe Ratio Quartile Rankings

3-Year	1
5-Year	2

Morningstar Rating

★★★★

Efficiency/MER

Management expense/$100

$1.63

○ above average
○ average
● below average

Style

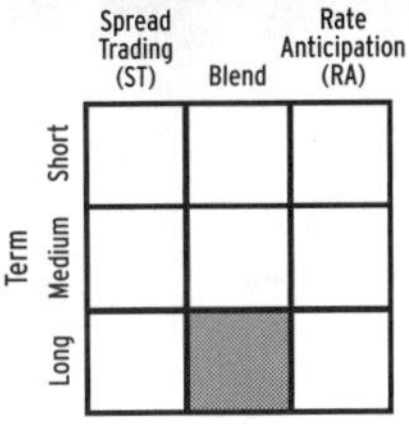

Complementary Fund:
Sceptre Bond

Similar Fund:
TD Monthly Income

Inflation is a bond's worst enemy. Inflation erodes the value of the future cash flows that a bond promises to repay, and bond markets get punished when there are inflationary pressures in the economy. "Real return" bonds are a solution to this problem. The principal on real return bonds increases by the change in inflation, as measured by the Consumer Price Index (CPI), and the existing interest rate is applied to this increased amount. This action causes the interest payment to increase over time. At maturity, the principal is repaid at the inflated amount. As a result, an investor has complete inflation protection, as long as the investor's inflation rate equals the CPI.

The TD Real Return Bond Fund invests solely in real return bonds—three of them, in fact! The bonds all have long maturities of 20 years and more. The current issues pay 3.55% plus the rate of inflation, but the actual portfolio has performed much better than that. The fund has returned 9.6% over one year, 7.1% a year over three years, and 9.0% a year over five years.

It may appear that the battle against inflation has been won in Canada, but higher energy prices and government deficit concerns should act as a reminder that inflation is always a threat. This fund is an excellent choice for investors who want the income and guarantees that bonds offer, but also inflation protection.

2001 RRSP

ALTAMIRA SHORT-TERM CANADIAN INCOME

Edward Jong (1997)/Altamira Management Ltd.

Consistency

Performance Trend

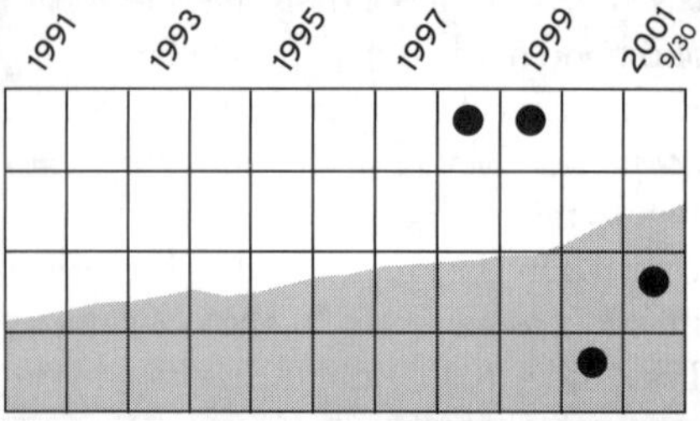

Risk

How often fund outperformed GICs	1 year in 3
How often fund lost money	0 years in 3
Worst year's rate of return	4.29%

Reward-to-Risk Relationship

Sharpe Ratio Quartile Rankings

3-Year	1
5-Year	N/A

Morningstar Rating

★★★★★

Efficiency/MER

Management expense/$100

$0.60

- ○ above average
- ○ average
- ● below average

Style

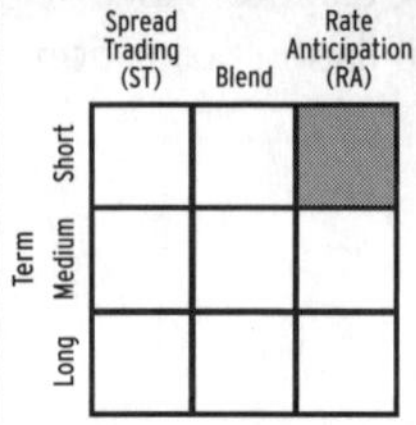

Complementary Fund:
TD Real Return Bond

Similar Fund:
HSBC Mortgage

The formula for a successful short-term bond fund is straightforward: Provide consistent returns and charge low fees. Manager Edward Jong provides investors with both and that's why his is a Top Fund for the second year in a row.

The standard deviation of returns, a key measure of volatility, is the second lowest of all the funds in the category. The management expense ratio of 0.60% is the lowest of any actively managed fund in the category. Low expenses always translate into higher returns in the short-term bond category where investment management skills aren't a key determinant of success. Indeed, this fund has delivered an annual compounded rate of return of 5.4% a year over the past three years, the second best in the category.

There are only five securities in the portfolio: three Government of Canada T-bills and two provincial floating rate notes. Distributions are made monthly and the fund is therefore appropriate for risk-averse investors with a need for consistent and regular income.

New

RRSP

TD MONTHLY INCOME FUND

Doug Warwick, Gregory Kocik/TD Asset Management Inc.

Consistency

Performance Trend

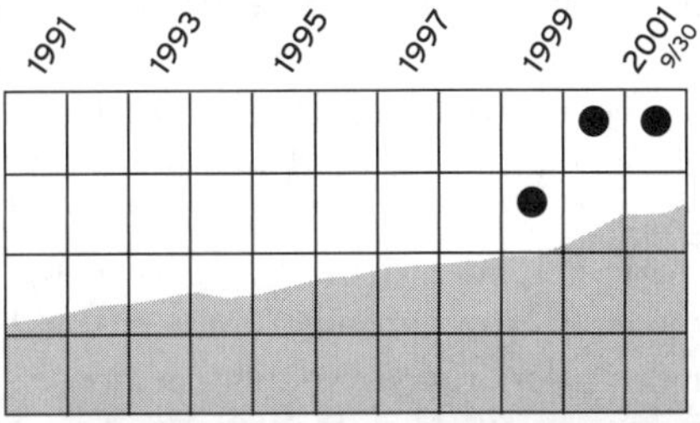

Risk

How often fund outperformed GICs	1 year in 2
How often fund lost money	0 years in 2
Worst year's rate of return	1.33%

Reward-to-Risk Relationship

Sharpe Ratio Quartile Rankings

3-Year	1
5-Year	N/A

Morningstar Rating

★★★★

Efficiency/MER

Management expense/$100

$1.26

○ above average
○ average
● below average

Style

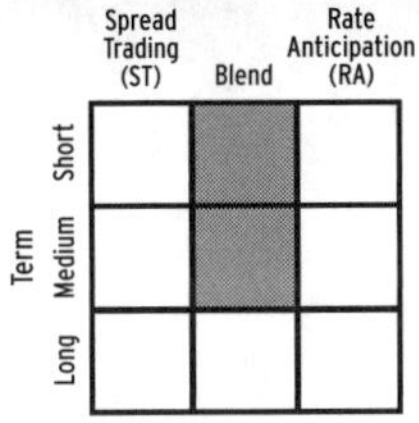

Complementary Fund:
Sceptre Bond

Similar Fund:
Great-West Life Income

We suspect that this is one of those funds that will move to a new fund category in the near future. Call it a balanced fund or a high income balanced fund, but don't call it a short-term bond fund. An asset allocation of 50% corporate bonds, 45% common and preferred shares, and 5% cash is probably not what the traditional short-term bond investor has in mind when looking for a fund.

This is still an excellent fund, however. Managers Doug Warwick and Gregory Kocik have to balance the goal of providing consistent income for investors with the secondary objective of generating capital growth. The result is a mix of common shares, preferred shares, income trusts, and short/midterm bonds. For example, the top ten holdings consist of four banks, three income trusts, and three corporate bonds. A full 65% of the bonds in the portfolio have maturities of one to five years; 30% are five- to ten-year issues.

The fund has been a first-quartile performer over the past three years, posting an average annual compound rate of return of 5.4%. A gain of 8.6% over the past 12 months is tops in the category.

1997, 1998, 1999, 2000, 2001 RRSP

HSBC MORTGAGE FUND

Jim Gilliland (1992)/HSBC Asset Management (Canada) Ltd.

Consistency

Performance Trend

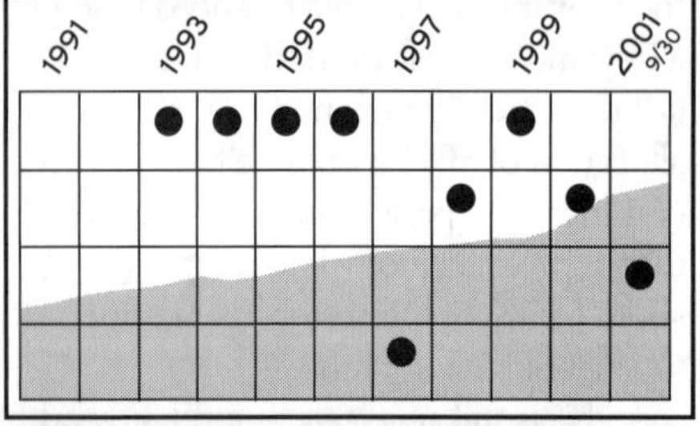

Risk

How often fund outperformed GICs	4 years in 8
How often fund lost money	0 years in 8
Worst year's rate of return	0.99%

Reward-to-Risk Relationship

Sharpe Ratio Quartile Rankings

3-Year	1
5-Year	2

Morningstar Rating

★★★

Efficiency/MER

Management expense/$100

$1.55

○ above average
○ average
● below average

Style

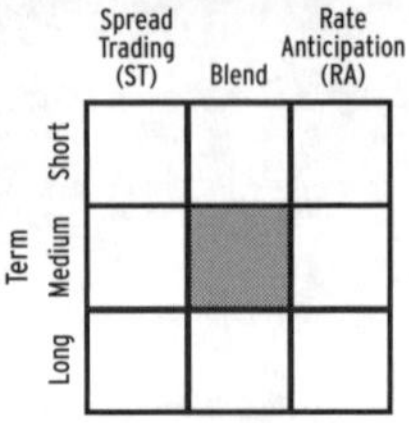

Complementary Fund:
TD Real Return Bond

Similar Fund:
Altamira Short Term Canadian Income

This is the sixth appearance for the HSBC Mortgage Fund in *Top Funds*. We are impressed that the fund has provided investors with superior returns without having to resort to investing in higher yielding commercial and industrial mortgages. This fund's mandate is to invest primarily in residential mortgages issued by the HSBC parent bank. Commercial and industrial mortgages typically have longer terms, and therefore higher interest rates, than their residential counterparts.

Low management expenses also help. Our Morningstar database reveals that the HSBC Mortgage Fund's MER of 1.55% is the fourth lowest of any mortgage fund offered in Canada. The average mortgage fund MER is 1.86%.

Investors in this fund earned 6.9% over the past 12 months. The annual rate of return has averaged 5.0% over three years and 5.7% over five years.

2001 RRSP

SCOTIA CANAM U.S.$ INCOME FUND
Management Team (inception)/ Scotia Cassels Investment Counsel Ltd.

Consistency
Performance Trend

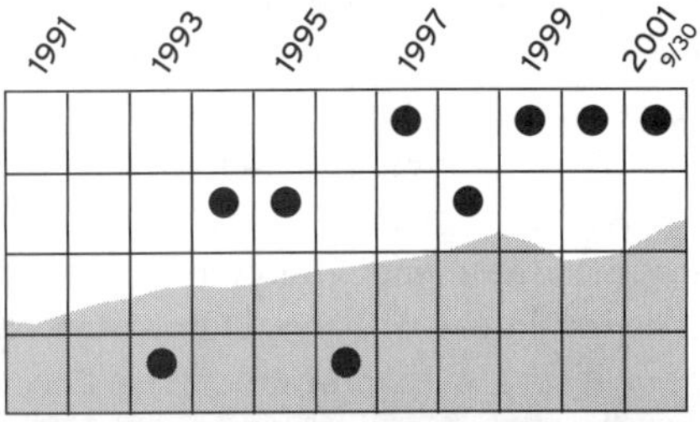

Risk

How often fund outperformed GICs	6 years in 8
How often fund lost money	1 year in 8
Worst year's rate of return	−8.38%

Reward-to-Risk Relationship
Sharpe Ratio Quartile Rankings

3-Year	1
5-Year	1

Morningstar Rating
★★★★★

Efficiency/MER
Management expense/$100

$1.71

○ above average
○ average
● below average

Style

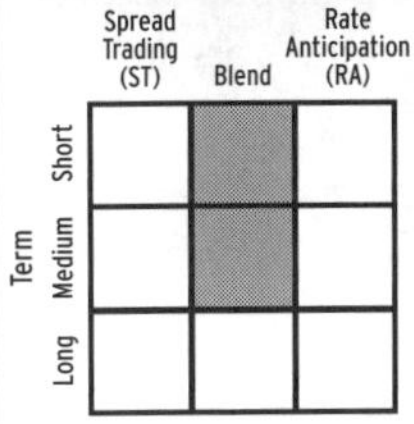

Complementary Fund:
N/A

Similar Fund:
N/A

Conservative Canadian investors who are becoming increasingly skeptical about the prospects for the Canadian dollar should consider this fund. Although denominated in U.S. dollars, the fund's holdings consist of bonds and Treasury bills issued by Canadian federal, provincial, and municipal governments; Canadian corporations; and "supranational entities." The latter indicates international agencies and organizations, such as the World Bank; supranational entities are 100% eligible as Canadian investments for RRSP purposes. In fact, there is no actual foreign content in this foreign bond fund.

A full 95% of the bonds are short- to midterm issues, so the interest rate risk is relatively low. Almost two-thirds of the bonds are corporate and provincial issues, which offer higher yields with minimal added risk. The fund rose 12.7% over the past twelve months and has average 7.5% annually over the past five years. By comparison, the average foreign bond fund rose 0.6% over one year and 2.7% annually over five years.

2001 RRSP

AIM CANADIAN BALANCED FUND

Clas Olsson (1997), Jason Holtzer (1999), Bob Alley (1997)/AIM Capital Management

Consistency

Performance Trend

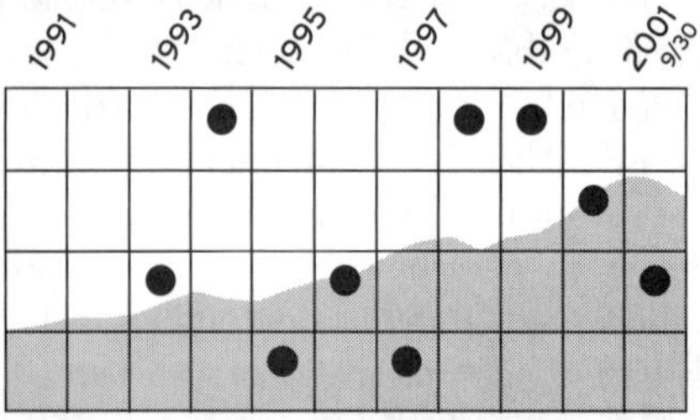

Risk

How often fund outperformed GICs	5 years in 8
How often fund lost money	0 years in 8
Worst year's rate of return	−17.07%

Reward-to-Risk Relationship

Sharpe Ratio Quartile Rankings

3-Year	1
5-Year	1

Morningstar Rating

★★★★★

Efficiency/MER

Management expense/$100

$2.46

○ above average
● average
○ below average

Style

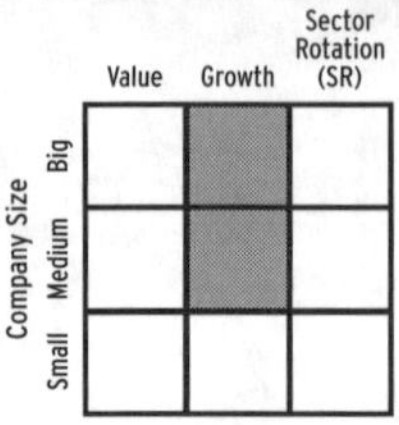

Complementary Fund:
Mac Ind Income Class A

Similar Fund:
Fidelity Canadian Asset Allocation

The balanced fund category is a very broad one. At one end of the spectrum, there are funds with over 60% of assets in bonds and money market investments. Astra 125, a Quebec-based fund, has a 90% bond exposure. Conversely, many funds have less than 10% of assets in fixed income investments. Our point is that the traditional view of balanced funds as nicely diversified, low-risk investments isn't necessarily true across the board.

The AIM Canadian Balanced Fund resides on the more aggressive end of the spectrum. The fund currently has a 38% bonds–62% equities asset allocation, which is in line with its investment policy. The equities are blue chip names with a growth bias. The result is a fund that has many of the characteristics of a pure equity fund—double-digit returns and moderate price volatility. The fund was named "Best Canadian Balanced Fund" at the 2000 Canadian Mutual Fund Awards.

The fund has gained an impressive 11.7% a year over the past five years, which is fifth best in the Canadian Balanced category. However, the fund has lost 10.4% over the past 12 months, which confirms our view that this fund is more appropriate for investors with a higher risk tolerance.

The portfolio is a well diversified mix of almost 180 securities. The largest holding is Canadian Pacific Ltd., but it represents only 2.1% of the fund's assets.

2001 RRSP

CLARINGTON CANADIAN BALANCED FUND

Peter Marshall (1996)/Seamark Asset Management Ltd.

Consistency

Performance Trend

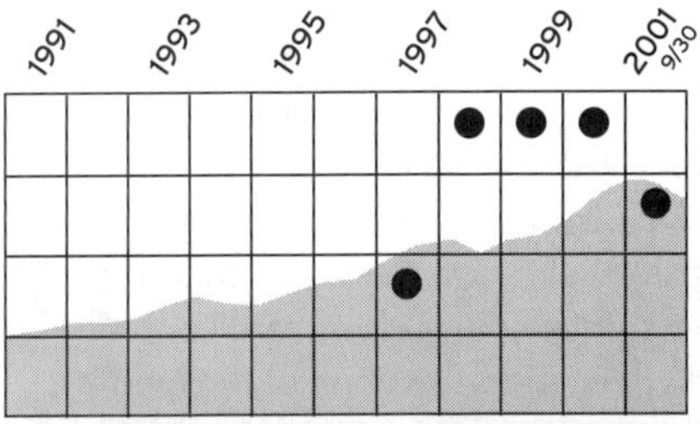

Risk

How often fund outperformed GICs	4 years in 4
How often fund lost money	0 years in 4
Worst year's rate of return	−6.8%

Reward-to-Risk Relationship

Sharpe Ratio Quartile Rankings

3-Year	1
5-Year	1

Morningstar Rating

★★★★★

Efficiency/MER

Management expense/$100

$2.90

● above average
○ average
○ below average

Style

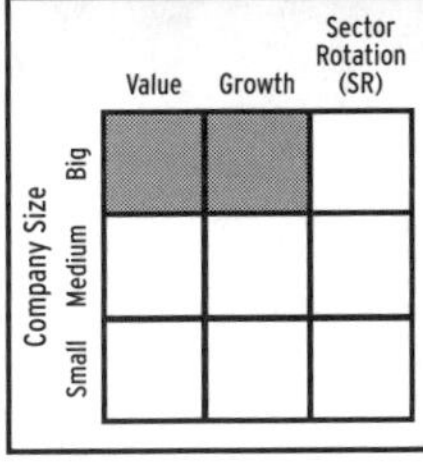

Complementary Fund:
Mac Ind Income Class A

Similar Fund:
TD Balanced Growth

Fund manager and Seamark Asset Management Ltd. founder Peter Marshall can't see the forest for the trees. He's not really interested in the market's long-term trends or the macroeconomic factors and influences that many investment experts feel are the key to investment success. Marshall is a classic bottom-up fundamental manager who chooses his equity and fixed income investments on the basis of superior quality and long-term investment merit.

Marshall's balanced funds are balanced: a 45% weighting to bonds and cash is above average for the category and reflects his view that asset mix plays an important role in determining long-term performance. The actual asset class mix is determined by Marshall's view of whether bonds and/or stocks are fairly valued or not. If he sees no opportunities in either bonds or stocks, then he'll simply build his cash positions until "windows of opportunity" occur.

Clarington Canadian Balanced has been a first-quartile performer over the past three years. The fund has enjoyed an annual compound rate of return of 8.9%, which handily beats the 3.6% annual return of the average Canadian balanced fund.

2001 RRSP

HSBC CANADIAN BALANCED FUND

Stephen MacInnes (1989)/HSBC Asset Management (Canada) Ltd.

Consistency

Performance Trend

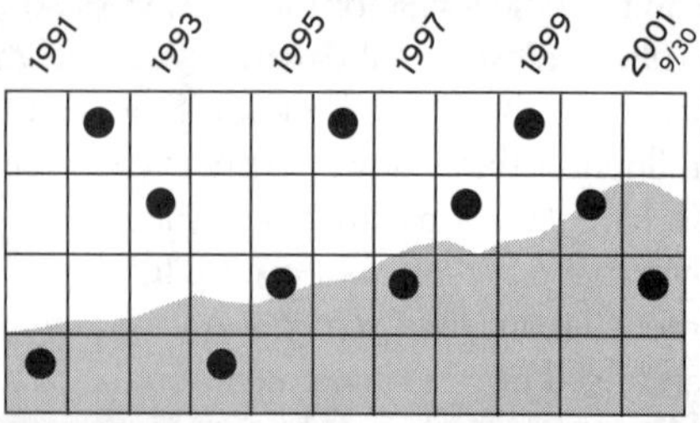

Risk

How often fund outperformed GICs	8 years in 9
How often fund lost money	1 year in 9
Worst year's rate of return	−13.94%

Reward-to-Risk Relationship

Sharpe Ratio Quartile Rankings

3-Year	2
5-Year	2

Morningstar Rating

★★★★

Efficiency/MER

Management expense/$100

$1.87

- ○ above average
- ○ average
- ● below average

Style

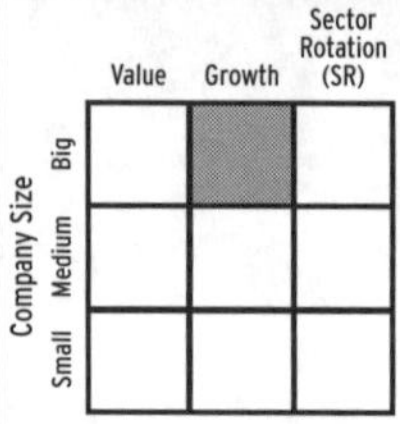

Complementary Fund:
Mac Ind Income Class A

Similar Fund:
Standard Life Balanced

Stephen MacInnes is a bottom-up manager with a focus on individual security selection. The equity portion of his HSBC Canadian Balanced Fund is currently overweighted to the financial services and industrial products sectors. Five of the top ten holdings are banks or insurance companies, although the largest individual security holding is Bombardier.

The asset allocation of the fund is a conservative 60% equity/40% bond mix. Unfortunately, an environment that rewards short-term returns has encouraged some fund managers to increase their equity weightings at the expense of their bond holdings. MacInnes seems to have resisted that impulse: 65% of the bonds in the portfolio are mid- to long-term issues, which is slightly higher than the average balanced mutual fund, to take advantage of anticipated further declines in interest rates.

The fund has actually performed poorly over the last 12 months with a loss of 8.0%. By contrast, the average Canadian balanced fund fell only 2.9%. Over the long term, however, HSBC Canadian Balanced has been a superior fund. Over 10 years, the fund has averaged 10.6% annually, a first-quartile result. The three-year annual return is a first-quartile 5.7%.

New

RRSP

INDUSTRIAL INCOME CLASS "A" FUND

Bill Procter (1992), Tim Gleeson (1992)/Mackenzie Financial Corp.

Consistency

Performance Trend

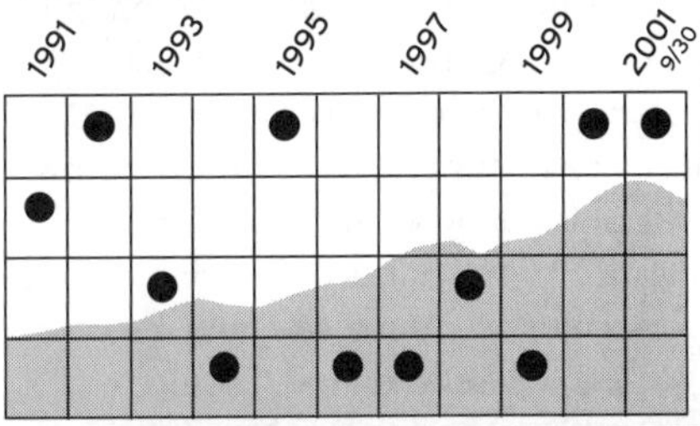

Risk

How often fund outperformed GICs	6 years in 9
How often fund lost money	1 year in 9
Worst year's rate of return	–8.91%

Reward-to-Risk Relationship

Sharpe Ratio Quartile Rankings

3-Year	1
5-Year	1

Morningstar Rating

★★★★★

Efficiency/MER

Management expense/$100

$1.92

○ above average
○ average
● below average

Style

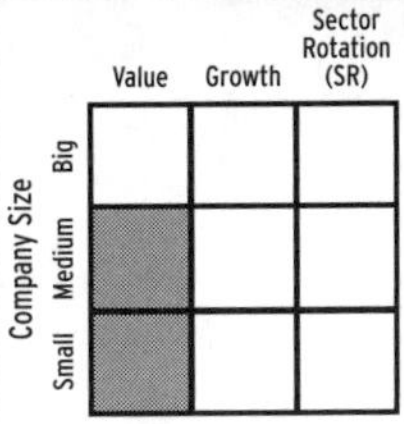

Complementary Fund:
AIM Canadian Balanced

Similar Fund:
Trimark Income Growth

Managers Procter and Gleeson have combined their strengths to create something of an anomaly these days: a conservative balanced fund. The equity component can account for a maximum of only 40% of fund assets; many balanced funds have higher equity limits. Some, in fact, have no restrictions. However, the unsettled markets over the past two years have made this type of fund a refuge for many disappointed investors.

The descriptor "conservative" refers to stability and the performance of this fund has been remarkably consistent. Industrial Income Class "A" gained 9.4% over the past twelve months, 8.6% annually over two years, 8.7% over five years, and 9.1% over fifteen years. Bank stocks and large conglomerates make up the core of the equity component, while Government of Canada bonds and high quality corporate issues compose the fixed income portion. The largest equity holding is Riocan REIT, a real estate investment trust, followed by Power Corp and Brascan. The equity holdings currently are at the 40% portfolio limit and since they usually represent only 35% of the total, we can therefore deduce that Tim Gleeson, who has asset allocation responsibilities for the fund, is bullish about the prospects for Canadian equities.

1998, 1999, 2000, 2001 RRSP

MCLEAN BUDDEN BALANCED GROWTH FUND

Management Team (inception)/McLean Budden Ltd.

Consistency

Performance Trend

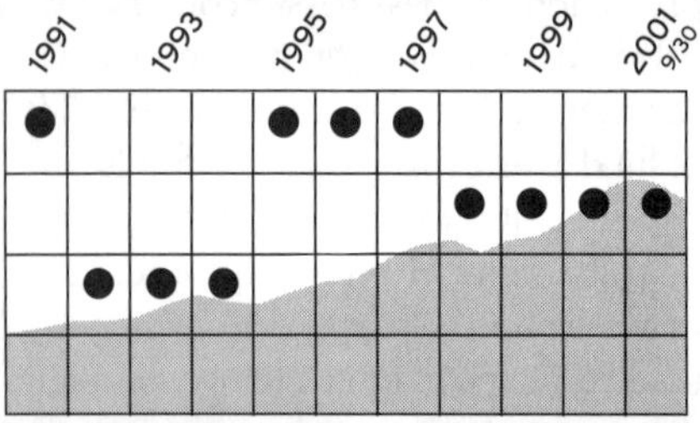

Risk

How often fund outperformed GICs	8 years in 9
How often fund lost money	1 year in 9
Worst year's rate of return	−8.8%

Reward-to-Risk Relationship

Sharpe Ratio Quartile Rankings

3-Year	1
5-Year	1

Morningstar Rating

★★★★

Efficiency/MER

Management expense/$100

$1.00

- ○ above average
- ○ average
- ● below average

Style

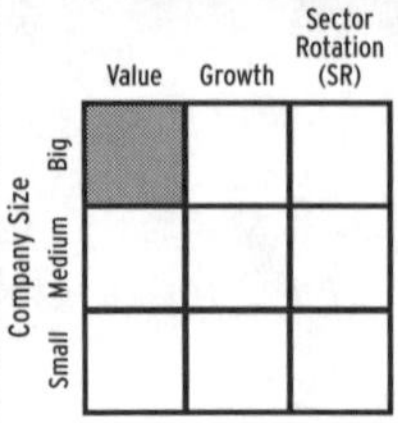

Complementary Fund:
Mac Ind. Income Class A

Similar Fund:
TD Balanced Growth

McLean Budden's investment philosophy is to add value through security selection in its equity portfolios and to emphasize income generation in its bond holdings by making moderate adjustments to both term-to-maturity and sector allocations. The philosophy seems to be working; Balanced Growth has been a first-quartile performer over three, five, and ten years.

A true balanced fund, Balanced Growth's asset allocation targets between 45% to 65% in equities. The current equity exposure is 56%, with 32% in Canadian stocks and 24% in foreign stocks. Roughly half of the foreign stocks are U.S. issues. The largest equity holding in the well-diversified portfolio with 200 securities is a 2.3% weighting to Nortel.

The management expense ratio of 1.00% is a full 1.43% below the average MER for Canadian balanced funds. A larger-than-average minimum investment of $10,000 helps to create some economies of scale, enabling McLean Budden to charge lower fees.

1999, 2000, 2001 RRSP

STANDARD LIFE BALANCED FUND

Management Team (inception)/Standard Life Portfolio Management Ltd.

Consistency

Performance Trend

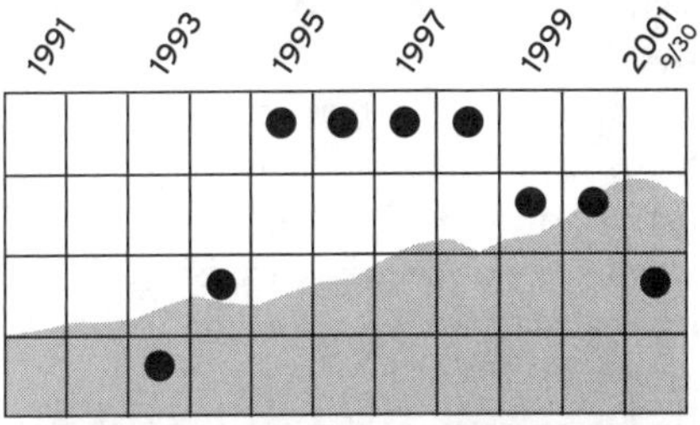

Risk

How often fund outperformed GICs	7 years in 7
How often fund lost money	1 year in 7
Worst year's rate of return	−13.02%

Reward-to-Risk Relationship

Sharpe Ratio Quartile Rankings

3-Year	3
5-Year	2

Morningstar Rating

★★★★

Efficiency/MER

Management expense/$100

$2.00

○ above average
○ average
● below average

Style

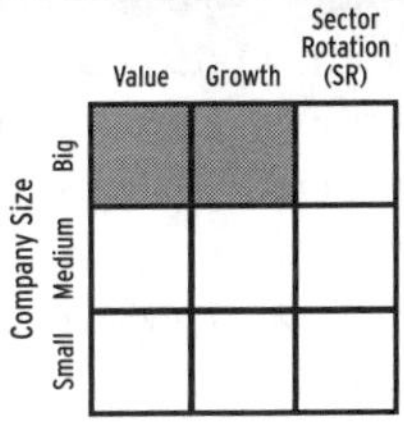

Complementary Fund:
Mac Ind Income Class A

Similar Fund:
HSBC Canadian Balanced

The motto here is "live by the sword and die by the sword." A 23.5% equity weighting to Nortel Networks helped propel Standard Life Balanced to a sparkling 20.1% return for the 12-month period ending June 30, 2000. Unfortunately, that weighting is also the reason why the fund fell 6.9% over the next 12 months and why it was a third-quartile performer over that period. Longer term however, the fund has been a consistent second-quartile performer.

The managers here have adopted a defensive stance for the fund this year. Cash balances are higher than normal and the fund is overweight in both energy and financial stocks, and is underweight in technology. Nortel continues to be the largest individual equity holding, although it now represents only 2.0% of total fund assets.

The fixed income component of the portfolio represents almost 43% of fund assets and is actively managed. Standard Life feels that midterm bonds (five to ten years) provide superior risk adjusted returns and it has therefore made them the core of the fixed income holdings. Cash and longer-term bonds are traded around these core holdings, based on Standard Life's expectations of interest rates three to six months down the road.

2001 RRSP

TD BALANCED GROWTH FUND

Mary Hallward (1993), Lewis Jackson/McLean Budden Ltd.

Consistency

Performance Trend

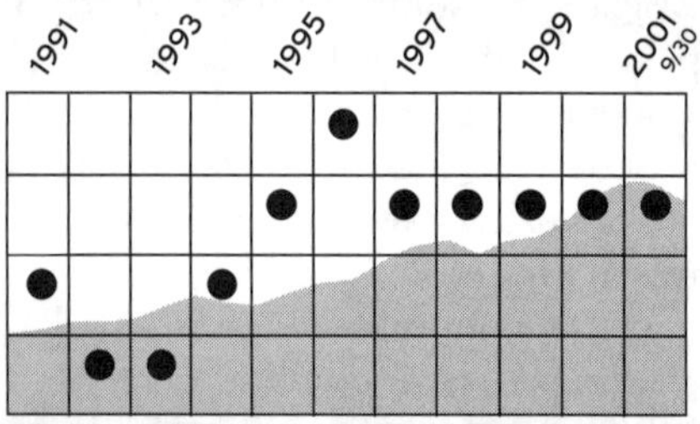

Risk

How often fund outperformed GICs	8 years in 9
How often fund lost money	1 year in 9
Worst year's rate of return	−9.38%

Reward-to-Risk Relationship

Sharpe Ratio Quartile Rankings

3-Year	1
5-Year	1

Morningstar Rating

★★★★

Efficiency/MER

Management expense/$100

$2.11

○ above average
● average
○ below average

Style

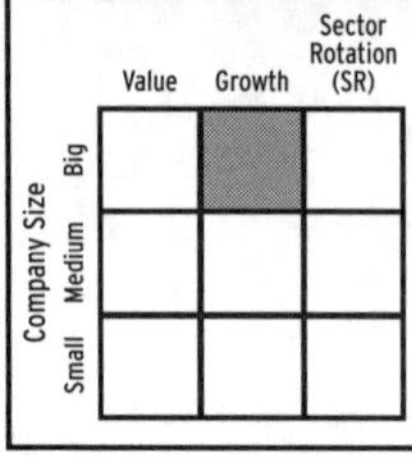

Complementary Fund:
Mac Ind. Income Class A

Similar Fund:
McLean Budden Balanced Growth

Two very capable fund managers from McLean Budden manage this fund. In fact, these two folks also run McLean Budden's own Balanced Growth Fund, which is also a Top Fund this year. Both funds have similar holdings and similar performance. TD's version has lagged by about 1.0% a year; not surprising when the management expense ratio of the fund is 1.12% higher than McLean Budden's in-house counterpart (2.12% versus 1.0%). In defense of the bank's higher MER, the minimum investment is only $1,000 compared with $10,000 for McLean Budden Balanced Growth. The TD Balanced Growth Fund is also a little more accessible to the average Canadian. It can be obtained at any TD Canada Trust branch as well as through independent financial planners, brokers, and mutual fund sales organizations.

The asset allocation is 33.7% Canadian bonds, 32.8% Canadian stocks, 22.6% foreign equities, and 10.9% cash, which is very similar to the average balanced fund allocation. What is *not* similar to the average balanced fund—or to any equity fund for that matter—is the admission by the managers that they have increased their Nortel holdings. In fact, it's the largest equity holding in the portfolio as Hallward and Jackson now feel that Nortel's valuations are attractive enough to warrant investing again.

It's this type of investment decision making that has made this fund so successful. An average annual rate of return of 10.4% over five years and 9.6% over ten years should satisfy anyone looking for a one-decision fund that is available almost anywhere.

1996, 1997, 1998 RRSP

TRIMARK INCOME GROWTH FUND

Patrick Farmer (1993), Vince Hart (1997), Rex Chong (1997)/AIM Funds Mgmt Inc.

Consistency

Performance Trend

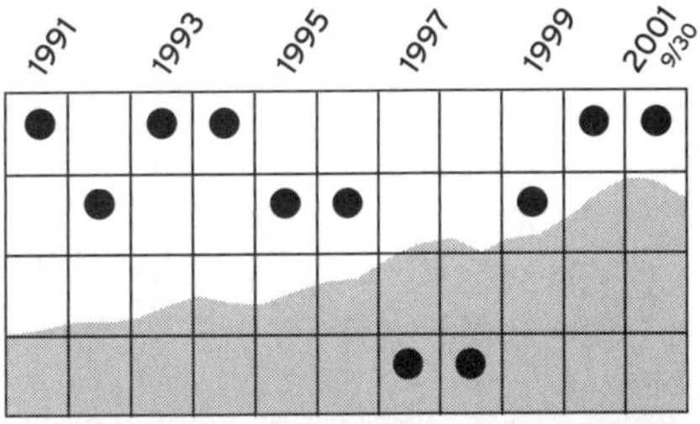

Risk

How often fund outperformed GICs	6 years in 9
How often fund lost money	1 year in 9
Worst year's rate of return	−13.63%

Reward-to-Risk Relationship

Sharpe Ratio Quartile Rankings

3-Year	1
5-Year	1

Morningstar Rating

★★★★★

Efficiency/MER

Management expense/$100

$1.66

○ above average
○ average
● below average

Style

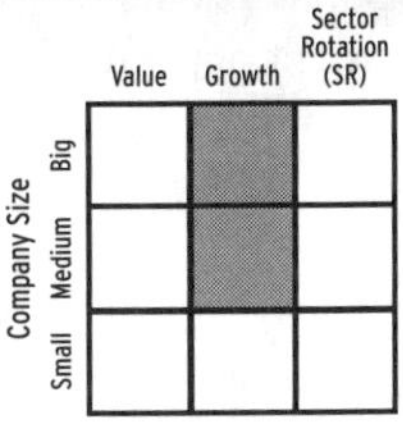

Complementary Fund:
HSBC Canadian Balanced

Similar Fund:
Clarington Canadian Balanced

It's good to see an old friend return to Top Fund status. The Trimark Income Growth Fund was a Top Fund selection in 1996, 1997, and 1998 and is back this year.

The fund is managed in the traditional Trimark fashion: a bottom-up investment style with a blended growth/value orientation. The asset allocation is also traditional. The mix is 29% bonds, 35% Canadian equities, 22% foreign equities, and the balance is mortgage-backed securities, income trusts and cash. There are over 160 holdings in the well-diversified portfolio. The largest equity position, Trizec Hahn Corp., represents only 1.8% of the total assets in the fund.

The fund gained an impressive 18.4% over the past 12 months and has averaged 10.98% a year over the past 10 years. There are two management expense ratios applicable to this fund. Front-end or zero-commission investors pay a 1.66% management expense ratio. Investors investing under the deferred sales charge option pay a higher 2.44%, which helps subsidize the 4.9% commission that the fund salesperson receives from Trimark.

New

RRSP

ELLIOTT & PAGE MONTHLY HIGH INCOME FUND

Management Team/Elliott & Page Ltd.

Consistency

Performance Trend

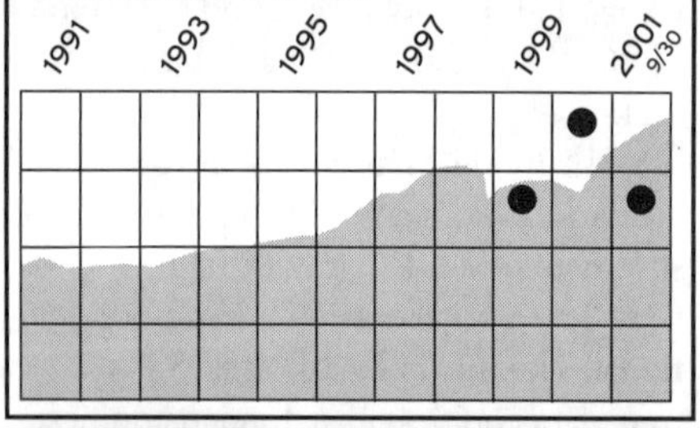

Risk

How often fund outperformed GICs	1 year in 2
How often fund lost money	1 year in 2
Worst year's rate of return	–12.5%

Reward-to-Risk Relationship
Sharpe Ratio Quartile Rankings

3-Year	1
5-Year	N/A

Morningstar Rating

N/A

Efficiency/MER

Management expense/$100

$2.43

- ○ above average
- ● average
- ○ below average

Style

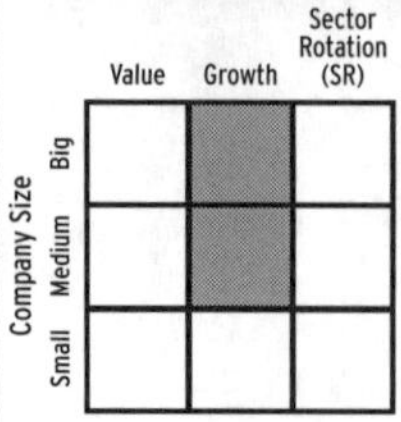

Complementary Fund:
Sceptre Bond

Similar Fund:
Altamira Short Term Canadian Income

Investors with a need for regular monthly income will find this a fund that fits the bill. The fund has 52% of its assets invested in a diversified mix of income trusts, with the balance allocated to bonds, equities, and cash. Income trusts generate tax-deferred income and usually have a payout rate that is higher than GICs or term deposits, with moderately low risk. They aren't completely risk-free, however. Oil and gas income trust returns have proven volatile and investors run the risk of asset depletion (i.e., the trust runs out of oil to sell if new wells aren't developed). REITs (real estate investment trusts) have more stable income streams, but the yields are lower. Other income trusts invest in coal, iron ore, pipelines, etc.

Elliott & Page Monthly High Income has gained 26% over the past 12 months and has posted a 10.9% annual compound rate of return over three years. By comparison, the average high income balanced fund rose by 18.5% over the past year and by 6.5% a year over three years.

Elliott & Page's bond and value equity managers manage the fund jointly. The largest equity holdings are TransCanada PipeLines, Bank of Nova Scotia, and CIBC. The managers continue to keep the fund in defensive mode; they believe that a continued slow-down in the U.S. economy will hurt corporate profits, so they will look for investment opportunities that exhibit stable earnings and cash flows.

2000, 2001 RRSP

FIDELITY CANADIAN ASSET ALLOCATION FUND

Dick Habermann (1994), Ford O'Neil (1994), Alan Radlo (1994)/Fidelity M & R Co.

Consistency

Performance Trend

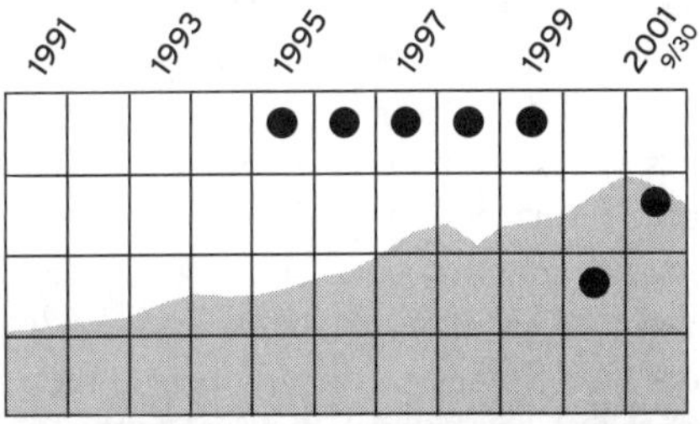

Risk

How often fund outperformed GICs	5 years in 6
How often fund lost money	0 years in 6
Worst year's rate of return	−9.47%

Reward-to-Risk Relationship

Sharpe Ratio Quartile Rankings

3-Year	1
5-Year	1

Morningstar Rating

★★★★★

Efficiency/MER

Management expense/$100

$2.49

- ○ above average
- ● average
- ○ below average

Style

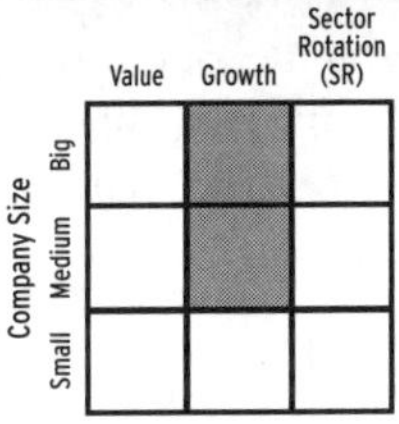

Complementary Fund:
Mac Ind Income Class A

Similar Fund:
Standard Life Balanced

The old joke that a camel is a horse designed by a committee doesn't apply here: Each of the three co-managers of Fidelity Canadian Asset Allocation Fund bring a different skill to the table and the result is a fund that has been a Top Fund choice for three years in a row.

Dick Habermann has overall asset allocation responsibilities, while Alan Radlo and Ford O'Neil take care of the stocks and bonds respectively. Radlo and O'Neil have excellent credentials; both have responsibilities for other Fidelity funds and have been Top Fund managers in past years (Radlo is manager of Fidelity True North Fund, a Top Fund this year). The fund has over 260 holdings, so three managers isn't overkill. Remarkably, two years ago there were over 400 securities in the portfolio.

The current asset allocation is 51% Canadian equities, 34% bonds, 9% cash, and the balance is in foreign equities. Since the neutral asset mix for this fund is 65% equities, 30% fixed income and 5% cash, one can deduce, correctly, that Habermann and his team are still cautious about the prospects for Canadian equities. Although a bit more optimistic about bonds, they feel that bond prices will come under pressure when interest rates start to stabilize. Consequently, cash balances are slightly overweighted.

1998, 1999, 2000, 2001 RRSP

AGF AMERICAN TACTICAL ASSET ALLOCATION FUND

Management Team (1996)/Barclays Global Investors

Consistency

Performance Trend

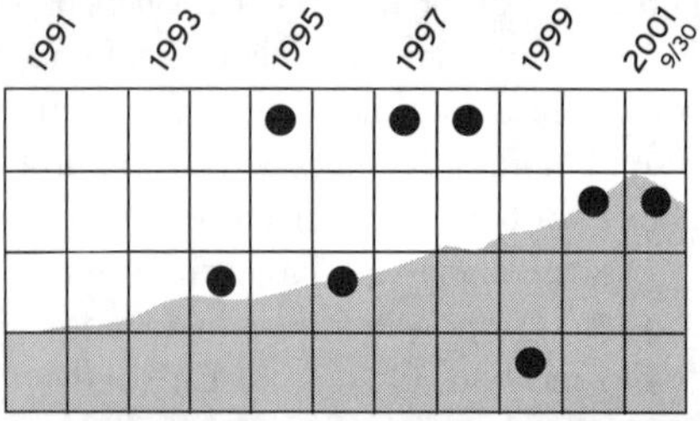

Risk

How often fund outperformed GICs	**7 years in 10**
How often fund lost money	**0 years in 10**
Worst year's rate of return	**–12.75%**

Reward-to-Risk Relationship
Sharpe Ratio Quartile Rankings

3-Year	**2**
5-Year	**1**

Morningstar Rating

★★★★★

Efficiency/MER

Management expense/$100

$3.00

● above average
○ average
○ below average

Style

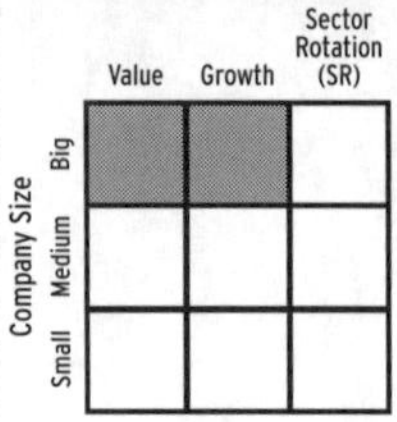

Complementary Fund:
CI International Balanced

Similar Fund:
Fidelity Global Asset Allocation

The debate over whether the tactical asset allocation approach to investment management is better or worse than the strategic approach doesn't matter much to investors in the AGF American Tactical Asset Allocation Fund. They have seen the fund return an average 12.0% compounded annually over the past five years and 13.3% over the past ten years. Both results are first-quartile numbers in the Global Balanced & Asset Allocation category. In comparison, returns for the average fund in the category are only 6.0% and 9.5% respectively over the same period.

This entry also has appeal for index fund lovers. Its only active management is the decision making process used to create the asset mix. The stock component is represented by the S&P 500 Index, the bond component mirrors the Lehman Brothers Long Bond Index, and cash is held in 90-day U.S. T-bills. The current asset allocation is 70% equities, 30% bonds, and 0% cash, which is slightly less aggressive than the mix in early 2001. The 3.0% MER will disappoint investors familiar with the comparatively low MERs that most index funds charge. There are higher MERs out there, however, and the value added component provided by the tactical asset allocation process is arguably worth 3.0% annually.

The AGF American Tactical Asset Allocation Fund has exhibited only moderate price volatility over the past five years and is therefore a solid investment choice for the risk averse investor.

2001 RRSP

CI INTERNATIONAL BALANCED FUND

Bill Sterling (1994)/ C.I. Global Advisors LLP

Consistency

Performance Trend

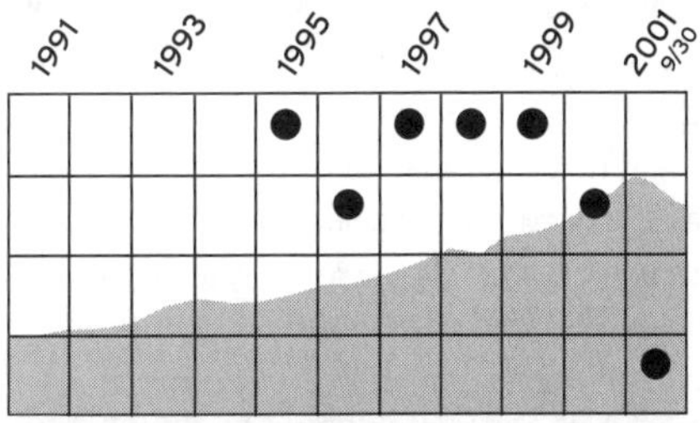

Risk

How often fund outperformed GICs	5 years in 6
How often fund lost money	0 years in 6
Worst year's rate of return	-25.04%

Reward-to-Risk Relationship

Sharpe Ratio Quartile Rankings

3-Year	3
5-Year	2

Morningstar Rating

★★★★

Efficiency/MER

Management expense/$100

$2.50

○ above average
● average
○ below average

Style

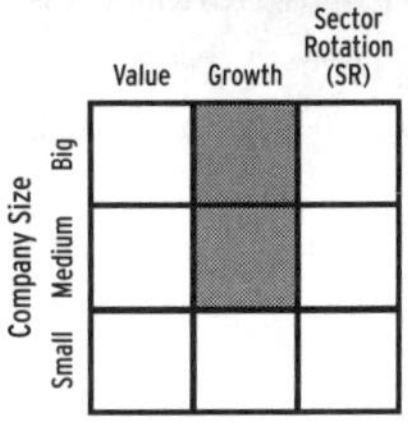

Complementary Fund:
AGF American Tactical Allocation

Similar Fund:
Investors Growth Plus Portfolio

Manager Bill Sterling has the world as his oyster. He has no restrictions on his asset allocation decisions and can invest when and where he wants anywhere in the world.

CI International Balanced Fund has been a first-quartile performer over three and five years, although the its growth equity focus hurt returns over the past year. The fund lost 16.1% over the past 12 months, compared with only a 9.2% decline for the average fund in the category.

Sterling's current view is that stocks will outperform cash and bonds over the short term and he has positioned the portfolio accordingly. In April the fund had a 26% bond weighting and a 23.2% cash weighting. Three months later, the bond allocation had shrunk to 21.5% and cash position was only 21.4%. The average term to maturity of the bond holdings was also shortened. Sterling feels that, although further monetary easing is likely, many investors are already pricing an economic recovery by the end of the year and therefore the shorter end of the maturity spectrum will benefit.

He is also increasing his exposure to both Japan and emerging markets. Both sectors are undervalued and Sterling is very bullish on prospects in those markets. He also thinks there are some segments of the communication sector that offer opportunities for astute investors.

There is an RRSP eligible version of this fund available.

1999, 2000, 2001 RRSP

FIDELITY GLOBAL ASSET ALLOCATION FUND

Dick Habermann (1996), Charles Morrison (1997), John Chow (1998)/Fidelity M & R Co.

Consistency

Performance Trend

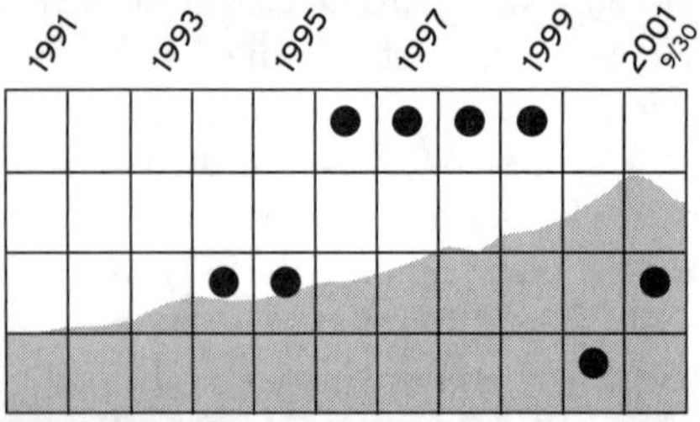

Risk

How often fund outperformed GICs	5 years in 5
How often fund lost money	2 years in 5
Worst year's rate of return	−20.93%

Reward-to-Risk Relationship

Sharpe Ratio Quartile Rankings

3-Year	2
5-Year	1

Morningstar Rating

★★★★

Efficiency/MER

Management expense/$100

$2.53

○ above average
● average
○ below average

Style

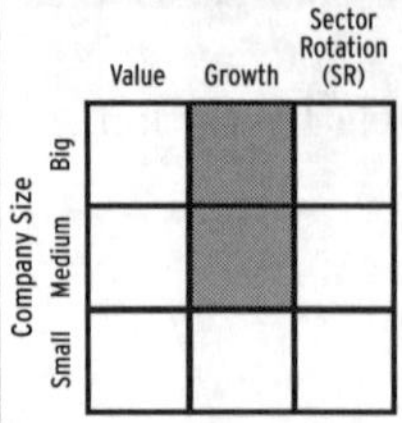

Complementary Fund:
CI International Balanced

Similar Fund:
AGF American Tactical Allocation

Worldwide research capability is one of Fidelity's strengths and, in our view, its main competitive advantage. This fund is an example of what can be achieved when this capability is fully utilized.

The management approach is to assign each subportfolio to a dedicated manager, who is overseen by a lead manager. The lead manager has overall asset allocation responsibility. The asset allocation decision is determined by a combination of fundamental bottom-up research and computer modelling, which helps determine optimal asset weightings.

The fund benchmark is a blend of the MSCI World Index, Lehman Bros. Aggregate Bond Index and Lehman Bros. Three-Month T-bill Index. The neutral weightings are 70%, 25%, and 5% respectively. By contrast, the current portfolio has a 74% equity, 22% bonds, and 5% cash asset allocation. These weightings reflect Habermann's optimistic outlook for world equity markets, which resulted in a reduction in the fund's bond exposure and a liquidation of cash positions. He is overweighted in Europe and Japan and underweighted in the U.S. market, although the U.S. still represents over 67% of fund assets.

Fidelity Global Asset Allocation has been a first-quartile performer over the past 5 years, although the past 12 months have been challenging for the fund: it declined 14.5%. We, however, believe that the fund will remain a superior fund in years to come.

There is an RRSP eligible version of this fund available.

New

RRSP

INVESTORS GROWTH PLUS PORTFOLIO FUND
Bob Darling (1989)/Investors Group

Consistency

Performance Trend

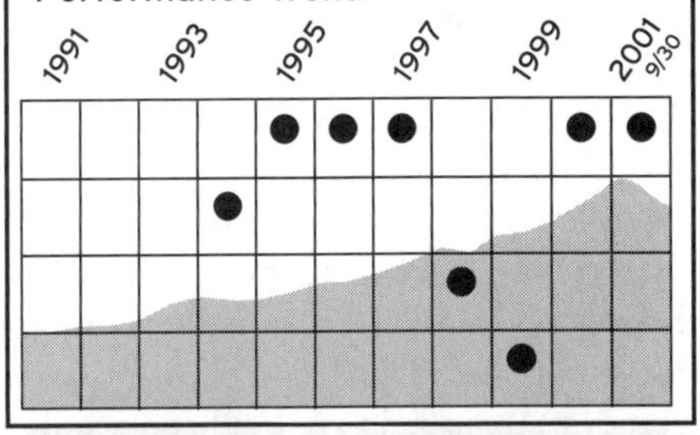

Risk

How often fund outperformed GICs	7 years in 10
How often fund lost money	0 years in 10
Worst year's rate of return	−3.33%

Reward-to-Risk Relationship
Sharpe Ratio Quartile Rankings

3-Year	1
5-Year	1

Morningstar Rating

★★★★★

Efficiency/MER

Management expense/$100

$2.80

- ○ above average
- ● average
- ○ below average

Style

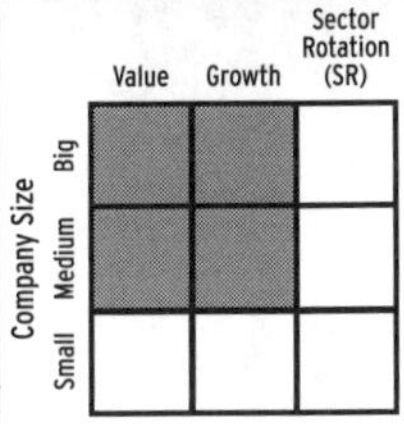

Complementary Fund:
AGF American Tactical Allocation

Similar Fund:
CI International Balanced

Managers of global balanced and asset allocation funds have the opportunity to browse all the markets of the world. The asset allocation that results here is a complex blend of security selection decisions, market and economic forecasting, and efficient frontier analysis within the constraints dictated by the mandate of the fund. Bob Darling does things a little differently by focusing on the asset allocation himself, leaving the security selection to others. Investors Group Growth Plus Portfolio consists of six other Investors Group mutual funds and the performance of this fund seems to indicate that Darling's approach is working.

One of the component funds, Investors U.S. Large-Cap Value, is a Top Fund this year and another, Investors Real Property, gained 8.0% over the past 12 months. These two funds, which make up 25% of the total, were the main reasons behind Growth Plus Portfolio's gaining 5.6% over the past twelve months. The other four funds are average performers as stand-alone investments, but when combined into a diversified portfolio, the results speak for themselves: Growth Portfolio has been a first-quartile performer over one, two, three, and five years, with a level of volatility that is much lower than the average fund in the category.

CANADIAN MONEY MARKET

2001 RRSP

ALTAMIRA T-BILL FUND
Edward Jong (1997)/Altamira Management Ltd.

Consistency

Performance Trend

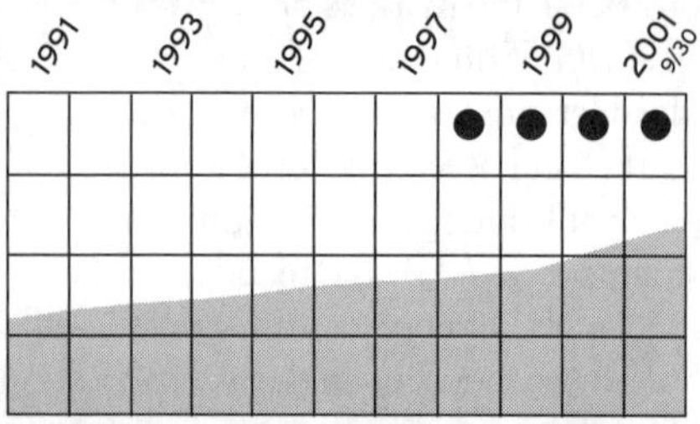

Risk

How often fund outperformed GICs	0 years in 3
How often fund lost money	0 years in 3
Worst year's rate of return	3.38%

Reward-to-Risk Relationship
Sharpe Ratio Quartile Rankings

3-Year	1
5-Year	N/A

Morningstar Rating

★★★★★

Efficiency/MER

Management expense/$100

$0.38

○ above average
○ average
● below average

Style

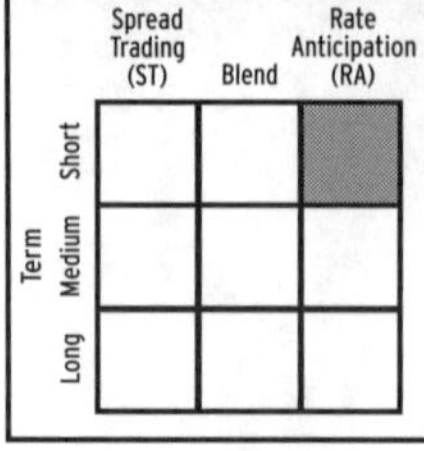

Complementary Fund:
N/A

Similar Fund:
N/A

This fund has a rock-bottom management expense ratio of only 0.38%. By contrast, the average Canadian money market management expense ratio is 1.08%. Thus, Altamira T-Bill Fund starts out with a big advantage.

Manager Edward Jong doesn't let his fund run on autopilot, however. The fund has a good blend of federal and provincial treasury bills and the blend of maturities is actively managed to reflect his view on interest rates. Currently, Jong anticipates further rate cuts by both the U.S. Federal Reserve and the Bank of Canada and has kept the portfolio very close to its benchmark duration of 90 days.

1999, 2000, 2001 RRSP

BISSETT MONEY MARKET CLASS F FUND
Guy LeBlanc/Bissett Investment Management

Consistency

Performance Trend

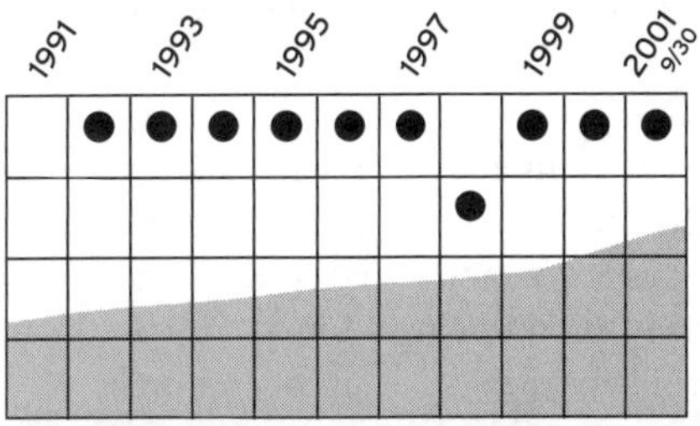

Risk

How often fund outperformed GICs	0 years in 9
How often fund lost money	0 years in 9
Worst year's rate of return	3.21%

Reward-to-Risk Relationship
Sharpe Ratio Quartile Rankings

3-Year	2
5-Year	1

Morningstar Rating

★★★★★

Efficiency/MER

Management expense/$100

$0.54

○ above average
○ average
● below average

Style

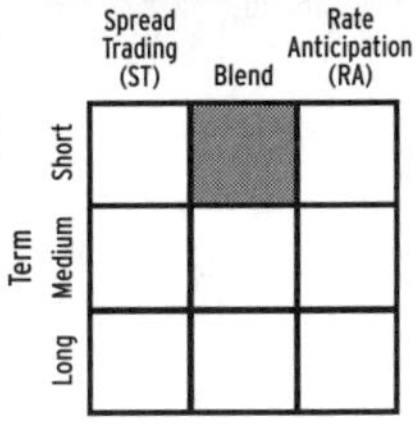

Complementary Fund:
N/A

Similar Fund:
N/A

The "Class F" refers to units of the fund that were available to Bissett Money Market investors prior to the Franklin Templeton purchase of Bissett & Associates. Investors paid no commissions and no trailer fees were paid out to advisors, and the resulting management expense ratio was only 0.50% a year. "F" units are still available, but it is most likely that only investors with "fee for service" arrangements with their advisors will be able to invest in them. The regular "A" units have a management expense ratio of 1.0%, which will seriously effect the return advantage that the fund enjoys. Curiously, Templeton's Treasury Bill Fund has only a 0.80% management expense ratio. Since two money market funds offered by the same company really doesn't make sense, we anticipate that a merger of these two is likely.

The portfolio consists of both government and corporate money market securities. The corporate holdings are a diversified mix of blue chip names, such as Merrill Lynch, General Electric, and Bank of Montreal, while the government securities are from federal, provincial, and municipal issues. The result is a portfolio with superior returns, but with only marginally more risk than a 100% Government of Canada T-bill portfolio.

New

RRSP

PHILLIPS, HAGER & NORTH CDN MONEY MARKET FUND

Lynn Delahey (1987)/Phillips, Hager & North Investment Management

Consistency

Performance Trend

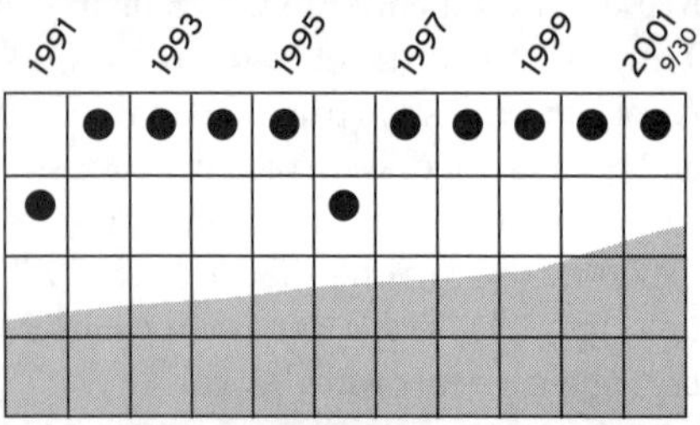

Risk

How often fund outperformed GICs	0 years in 10
How often fund lost money	0 years in 10
Worst year's rate of return	2.8%

Reward-to-Risk Relationship

Sharpe Ratio Quartile Rankings

3-Year	1
5-Year	1

Morningstar Rating

★★★★★

Efficiency/MER

Management expense/$100

$0.47

○ above average
○ average
● below average

Style

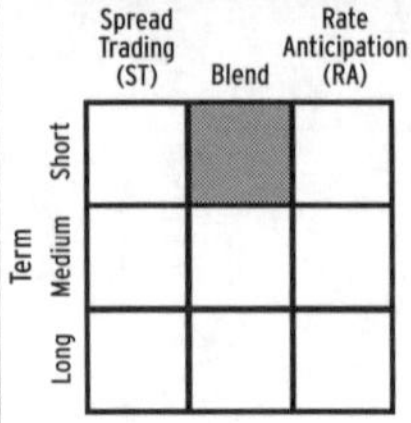

Complementary Fund:
N/A

Similar Fund:
N/A

With over 71% of the fund assets invested in higher-yielding corporate notes, manager Lynn Delahey could be accused of ignoring the principle of capital conservation for the pursuit of higher returns. But that's nonsense, of course. Delahey's portfolio has an average term to maturity of only 43 days, which is shorter than most money market funds. The portfolio contains over 45 different corporate names, and all are the *crème de la crème* of Canadian business: names include RBC, CIBC, Bell Canada, Ford Credit, Colgate Palmolive, etc. The actual portfolio risk is very low and investors pick up higher interest rates.

Over the past 12 months, the fund returned 5.07% to investors. The average Canadian money market fund gained 4.43% over the same time period. The 0.48% management expense ratio is, like that of all PH&N funds, very reasonable.

2000, 2001 RRSP

PERIGEE T-PLUS FUND
Management Team (inception)/Perigee Investment Counsel Inc.

Consistency

Performance Trend

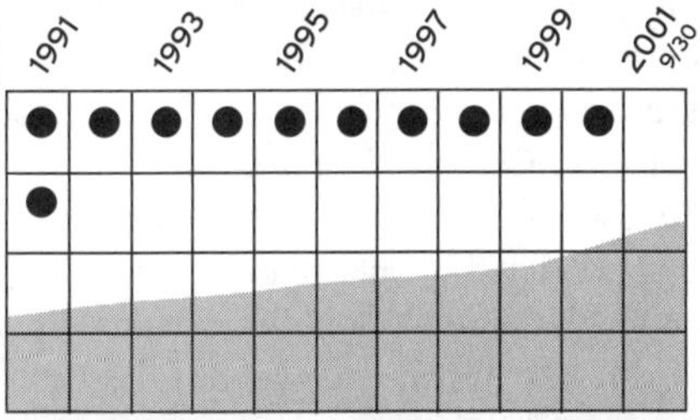

Risk

How often fund outperformed GICs	1 year in 10
How often fund lost money	0 years in 10
Worst year's rate of return	3.15%

Reward-to-Risk Relationship
Sharpe Ratio Quartile Rankings

3-Year	1
5-Year	1

Morningstar Rating

★★★★★

Efficiency/MER

Management expense/$100

$0.47

○ above average
○ average
● below average

Style

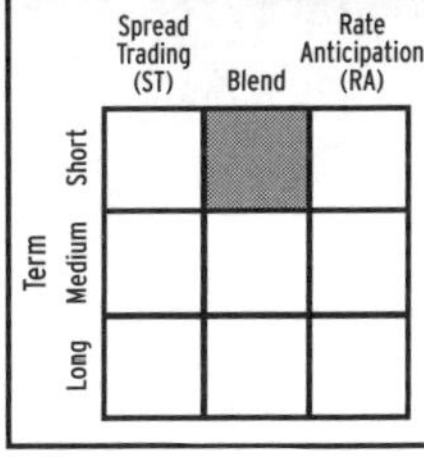

Complementary Fund:
N/A

Similar Fund:
N/A

How different can money market funds be? All of them basically invest in short-term Government of Canada treasury bills, with varying degrees of exposure to higher yielding provincial and corporate notes. However, as in every asset class, investors should wring out every penny possible.

The management team at Perigee has attempted to wring out the pennies for its clients by employing a barbell strategy during the first part of the year. This approach involves investing in maturities at both ends of the permitted range and generating returns higher than the benchmark. The barbell was unwound when the spread between three- and six-month securities narrowed. The Perigee managers were also active traders with the portfolio in anticipation of Bank of Canada interest rate cuts.

One place Perigee doesn't try to wring pennies is out of investors' pockets. The T-Plus Fund's management expense ratio of 0.47% is much lower than average for the category. Most of the money market funds with lower MERs have minimum investments much higher than the $2,500 that this fund requires.

1999, 2000, 2001 RRSP

CI U.S. MONEY MARKET FUND

Wally Kusters (1995)/C.I. Mutual Funds Inc.

Consistency

Performance Trend

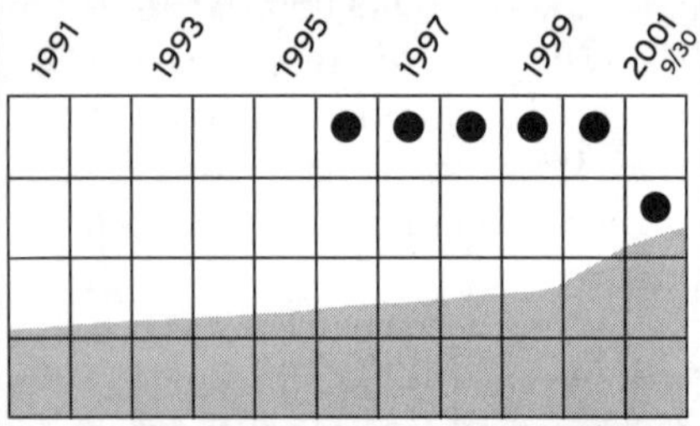

Risk

How often fund outperformed GICs	1 year in 5
How often fund lost money	0 years in 5
Worst year's rate of return	4.08%

Reward-to-Risk Relationship

Sharpe Ratio Quartile Rankings

3-Year	1
5-Year	1

Morningstar Rating

N/A

Efficiency/MER

Management expense/$100

$0.89

○ above average
○ average
● below average

Style

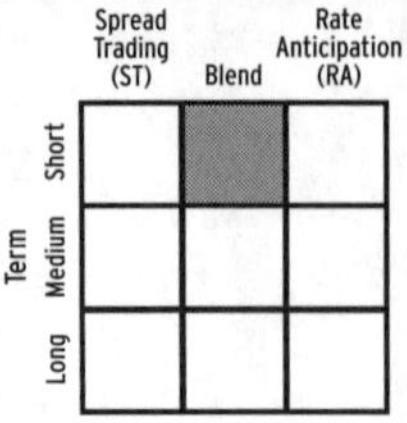

Complementary Fund:
N/A

Similar Fund:
N/A

A low management expense ratio of 0.89% and a nicely diversified portfolio of U.S. dollar denominated money market instruments has made this fund a Top Fund for four years in a row. The portfolio consists primarily of high-quality corporate issues. The fund has rates of return that are slightly higher than average and although the notes don't have the credit quality of government guaranteed issues, the risk of capital loss is minimal.

Manager Wally Kusters also tries to add value through interest rate anticipation trading strategies, although in our view, any incremental returns that result from actively trading a money market portfolio are minimal.

1998, 1999, 2000, 2001 RRSP

PHILLIPS, HAGER & NORTH U.S.$ MONEY MARKET FUND
Lynn Delahey (1990)/Phillips, Hager & North Investment Management

Consistency

Performance Trend

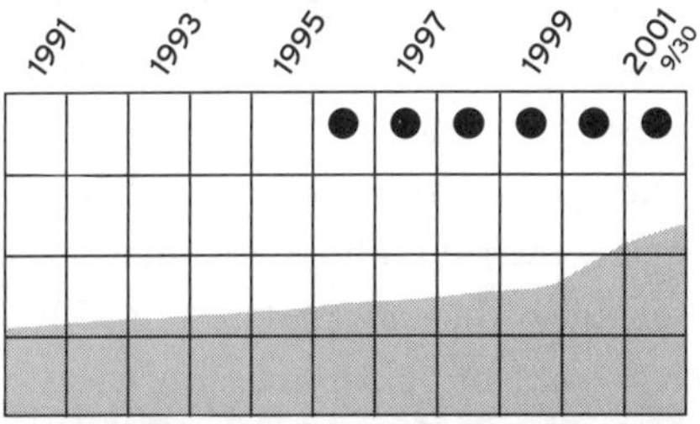

Risk

How often fund outperformed GICs	1 year in 10
How often fund lost money	0 years in 10
Worst year's rate of return	2.63%

Reward-to-Risk Relationship
Sharpe Ratio Quartile Rankings

3-Year	1
5-Year	1

Morningstar Rating

N/A

Efficiency/MER

Management expense/$100

$0.55

○ above average
○ average
● below average

Style

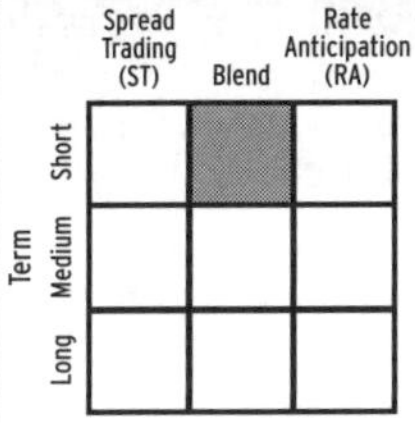

Complementary Fund:
N/A

Similar Fund:
N/A

This fund has a management expense ratio of only 0.55% versus 1.16% for the average foreign money market fund. This difference is an insurmountable obstacle for PH&N's competitors to overcome in a category where the average fund has averaged only 5.49% annually over the past 15 years.

There are only nine securities in this fund. Over 70% of the portfolio consists of U.S. dollar denominated Government of Canada T-bills. The next largest position is a 11.2% weighting to Export Development Corp. short-term notes, and the balance is a mix of corporate and provincial issues, which provides higher yields. However, given the MER advantage this fund enjoys, manager Lynn Delaney could probably just mail it in and still be top of the pack.

Top Funds Fund Company of the Year: How We Choose It

The main criterion in determining the Company of the Year winner is the number of individual company funds that appear in our "100 Top Funds" list. But, it's not quite that simple, of course. Today, fund managers and fund companies manage investment assets on a contract basis for other firms. For example, Altamira Management Ltd. has a superb reputation for its line of no-load mutual funds that are sold directly to investors, usually over the phone or online. The company, however, also manages a family of funds that are part of the M.R.S. Keystone asset allocation program, which is sold on a commission basis by financial planners and mutual fund salespeople. To confuse things even further, M.R.S. is owned by Mackenzie Financial, which is in turn now owned by Investors Group. MAXXUM Financial Services, which sells the Scudder MAXXUM fund family in Canada is also owned by the parent company of Investors Group. Mackenzie announced recently that the MAXXUM family was being brought under the Mackenzie umbrella and that most of the MAXXUM fund managers will be leaving to "pursue other opportunities." Adding to the confusion is the fact that MAXXUM's no-load Janus and Scudder funds won't be part of the Mackenzie family, but will continue to be marketed as separate entities.

We don't treat Mackenzie, MAXXUM, and Investors Group as one fund company. We feel investors should be able to transfer freely between all the funds in a family and the inability to do so disqualifies a fund from inclusion in the totals. On the other hand, Mackenzie allows full transferability between their Cundill, Ivy, Industrial, Mackenzie, and Universal funds and as a result, all of these groups are included in our Fund Company of the Year determination. If the MAXXUM funds gain full transferability status within the Mackenzie family, which we suspect will happen, then we will include the MAXXUM funds in our Mackenzie numbers.

It's hard to keep track of the all the players without a program. We have a hard time keeping tabs on all the changes and we suspect Canadian investors do too.

And so, with no further ado, this year's Fund Company of the Year is...

TD Asset Management Inc.

For the first time in four years, we have a new Fund Company of the Year. TD Asset Management Inc. toppled AGF Funds Inc. from the top ranking that AGF has either shared or held outright since 1999. TD Asset Management had eight Top Funds this year:

1. TD Balanced Growth Fund
2. TD Canadian Bond Fund
3. TD Canadian Government Bond Index Fund
4. TD Health Sciences Fund
5. TD Latin American Growth Fund
6. TD Monthly Income Fund
7. TD Real Return Bond Fund
8. TD U.S. Index Fund

The TD Asset Management funds have always appeared on our Top Funds radar screen and the firm's arrival at the top this year is not a surprise to us. The fund family consists of over 50 actively managed funds, with excellent diversification by asset class, sector, and style. TD also has 12 index funds, as well as a comprehensive managed asset program and 2 low-cost exchange traded fund offerings. In our opinion, TD's strength is its superb index and bonds funds. It is a pioneer in index funds and has been selling them to Canadians since the mid-'80s. The bond fund family has both indexed and actively managed funds, but both management styles have one thing in common: rock-bottom management expenses. And as one of our "Research News" sidebars reveals, low costs translate to high returns in the world of bond funds.

Most of the funds are managed in-house, but TD's external managers have excellent reputations. Canadian investors have probably heard of T. Rowe Price Associates, Inc., Morgan Stanley Dean Witter Investment Management Inc., JP Morgan Investment Management Inc., and Credit Suisse Asset Management Limited, but other less public names such as Montgomery Asset Management LLC, Schroders, McLean Budden Limited, Jarislowsky Fraser Limited, and Invesco are all well regarded within the investment management community.

Traditionally, TD funds have been available only through branches of the TD Bank and their subsidiaries. Although independent financial planners and mutual fund sales people could sell the funds, there was little financial incentive for them to do so. In 2001, TD created the "Advisor Series" of funds. These are selected TD funds that will be available in both front-end and deferred sales charge (DSC) and low load versions and should result in the TD fund family being more widely available to the Canadian investing public. There are also the "F-Series" funds, which pay no commissions or trailers and are intended for investors who have fee-based financial planners. The management expense ratios here are between 0.5% and 1.5% lower than their Advisor Series counterparts.

Honourable Mentions

C.I. Funds and Mackenzie Financial tied for second this year, with seven funds each on our "100 Top Funds" list.

C.I.'s seven funds are:

1. CI Emerging Markets Fund
2. CI Global Fund
3. CI Harbour Fund
4. CI International Balanced Fund
5. CI Signature Canadian Resource Fund
6. CI Signature Select Canadian Fund
7. CI U.S.$ Money Market Fund

Mackenzie's seven funds are:

1. Cundill Canadian Security Series B Fund
2. Cundill Value Series B Fund
3. Industrial Income Class A Fund
4. Ivy Canadian Fund
5. Universal Canadian Resource Fund
6. Universal Future Fund
7. Universal Precious Metals

Fidelity Investments and AGF Funds placed six funds in our Top 100. AIM Funds and Altamira Financial Services each had five funds on our list.

It is interesting to note that there are 40 different fund companies represented in our Top 100, three less than last year. The trend towards industry consolidation suggests that this number will continue to shrink in the years ahead.

5

Top Funds Investment Strategies

Depending on your investment style, your level of expertise, and the amount of time you feel you can afford to devote to managing your portfolio personally, several investment strategies may be of interest and of help.

The Dollar Cost Averaging Strategy

This is probably the best and simplest way for people to invest in mutual funds.

Ideally, every investor seeks to buy at a low price and sell at a higher price at a later date. The question is how to do that, given the fact that there are market fluctuations. Nobody seems to mind the upward trends; it's those slides that upset us so much. However, by using a simple strategy called "dollar cost averaging," even the downside fluctuations can actually work to your advantage! It's as close as one can get to infallible investing—and most people don't even know about it.

Psychologically, if you are committed to regular investments and if you are prepared to invest over the long term, then downward trends (which are bound to come along) are simply opportunities to buy additional shares at lower-than-usual prices. As always, of course, the upward trends will continue to be rewarding and satisfying.

> surfing
> ## the web
>
> A free Canadian site that is chock full of investor goodies, including 25 pages of financial humour! (Sample: Did you hear that the Post Office just recalled their latest stamps? They had pictures of stockbrokers on them and people couldn't figure out which side to spit on.) There are articles that address many different investment and financial planning issues, as well as links to other financial sites. The writers aren't cheerleaders for the investment industry and aren't afraid to speak their minds. Take a look.
>
> **www.independentfinancial.on.ca**

Let's see how it actually works by using the following three examples. We're going to invest $100 a month for nine years (that is, $10,800 will be invested).

Scenario 1

Because the unit prices constantly increase, the number of shares purchased each year actually declines, as the chart shows. For example, in Year 1, the unit price is $6 and therefore $1,200 per year ($100 per month) buys 200 units. By the end of Year 6, the unit price has increased to $8.50, and therefore $1,200 buys only 141 units. At the end of nine years, at $10 per unit, the value of the portfolio is $13,869—a 28% increase.

Scenario 1
Averaging in an Increasing Market

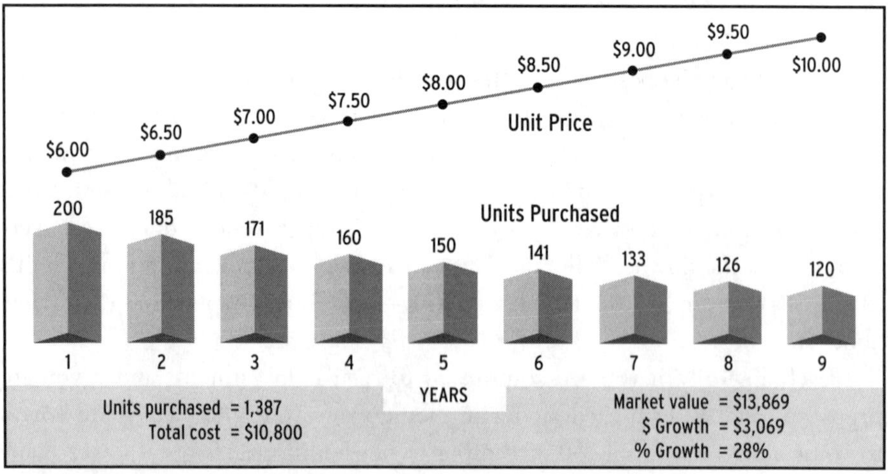

Scenario 2
Averaging in a Down and Up Market

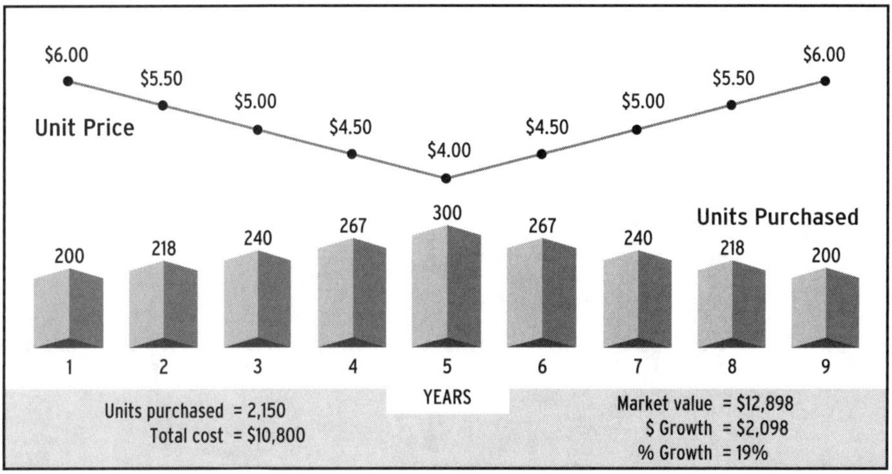

Scenario 2

Notice here that for the first five years, the unit price declines. Imagine how happy you'd be in that situation! But patience is rewarded. The result of lower unit prices is that a larger number of units are purchased while you continue to invest $100 per month. Note that in Scenario 2 the original purchase price and the final purchase price are the same ($6), so there is no market rise at all.

Nonetheless, 2,150 units have been acquired. And even at a $6 unit price at the end of nine years, the value of the portfolio is $12,898—a 19% increase. Significant growth in the value of your investment actually occurs in a declining and recovering market. You get the benefit of purchasing more mutual fund units when prices are at a reduced value.

Scenario 3

Here the unit price increases and decreases over time. Therefore, in some years more units are purchased than in others. This example is probably the most realistic in reflecting actual conditions. After nine years, the number of units purchased is greater than in Scenario 1—1,479 to be exact. At $10 per unit at the end of Year 9, the investment is worth $14,787—a 37% increase in value.

Scenario 3
Averaging in a Fluctuating Market

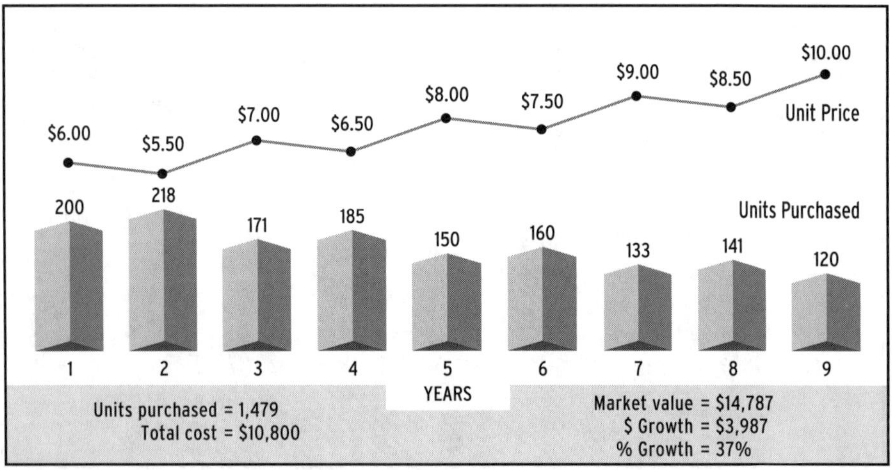

Dollar cost averaging can remove the psychological barrier to purchasing more shares when prices are low—and that's the very best time to buy. (Remember the goal: buy low, sell high.) It also removes the problem of timing from investment management. By investing regularly, you don't get hung up on timing, for you've now got a logical comprehensive investment strategy based on confidence in the long-term health of the Canadian and international economies.

It's true! For most people, dollar cost averaging is the best way to invest.

The Buy-and-Hold Strategy

This approach is similar to dollar cost averaging except that with this strategy, the investment may not be made as regularly. Assuming you've done your research or have taken the advice of a financial advisor, there's a strong argument for picking a fund, investing your money, and getting on with your life.

Templeton Growth Fund is a classic example of a buy-and-hold fund. A $10,000 investment in this fund in November 1954—with no subsequent contributions or withdrawals—was worth over $5.4 million on April 30, 1999. You could have been Rip Van Winkle, slept for 40 years, and still have done very well with Templeton Growth.

But even if your interest is to buy and hold, we're generally not comfortable ignoring the investment completely. So we suggest that you monitor it: look for changes in the fund's management or for changes to its investment philosophy and, of course, continue to be aware of its performance compared with other funds in its category.

The buy-and-hold strategy isn't as exciting as some of the others, but if you can find a true buy-and-hold fund, you'll be a happy investor.

The Bob-and-Weave Strategy

This approach is quite the opposite from the buy-and-hold and dollar cost averaging strategies. It's based on a belief that we, as individuals, can anticipate certain trends, developments, or events, and can "bob and weave," or switch among funds and asset categories to take advantage of them.

Most fund companies now allow you to switch from one of their funds to another—generally at no cost, although a fund's prospectus often provides a fee of up to 2%. Some of the no-load funds charge an administration fee each time you switch after a certain number of "free" switches.

Now, it's true that certain asset categories tend to do better at different times in the economic cycle. For example, when interest rates are falling, government bonds will tend to do well; when interest rates are low, equities will likely do well; and when rates are rising, a cash-type investment may perform best.

But we believe very strongly that you should hold a balanced portfolio. So we urge that the bob-and-weave approach not be taken too far. Sure, there could be strategic times to rebalance, but those who attempt to be "market timers" do not consistently come out on top. It's a risky strategy, one that we advise be used with caution—probably as part of ongoing discussions with your financial advisor.

The Asset Allocation Strategy

The asset allocation approach is a much more disciplined and more effective strategy than the bob-and-weave. With this strategy, the overall mix between fixed income and equities is determined by your age and aggressiveness as an investor (for more about asset allocation, see pages 38–41). Then the specific components of the portfolio are selected and "plugged in" to the overall framework.

Remember, the research shows very clearly that the overall mix between equities and fixed income is the single most important decision an investor will make. All other variables, including market timing, are of very little importance.

Of course, it will be necessary to rebalance your portfolio from time to time, particularly if one asset category has done extremely well in the past year. If it has, it may have grown to a larger-than-appropriate percentage of the portfolio.

research news

Is It Different This Time?

Sir John Templeton is famous for saying that the four most dangerous words in investing are, "This time it's different." However, some new research indicates that perhaps it *is* different this time. The study concludes that structural changes in the U.S. mutual fund market have had a role in creating the current valuations in the market and that these valuations are likely to continue.

Attractive tax incentives and a general lack of confidence in the U.S. Social Security System have resulted in a huge increase of self-managed retirement plans. A substantial portion of these retirement assets is in mutual funds. Systematic contribution plans and penalties for early withdrawals mean that mutual fund assets remain relatively stable and are unlikely to be withdrawn even when markets are weak.

In our view, these changes would also apply to the Canadian market. Our system has similar tax incentives and a similar lack of trust in the Old Age Security and Canada Pension Plan programs.

Michael Mosebach and Mohammad Najand, "Are the Structural Changes in Mutual Funds Investing Driving the U.S. Stock Market to Its Current Levels?" *Journal of Financial Research* 7, no.3 (Fall 1999).

Rebalancing Your Portfolio

Rebalancing is the process of adjusting a portfolio in order to maintain a target asset mix. The discipline of rebalancing serves to maintain the portfolio risk that is appropriate for you, by reducing overweighted positions.

In addition to managing portfolio risk, an effective rebalancing program will "force" a methodical and disciplined process of buying low and selling high. When your asset mix moves away from the target mix, it is very often due to one or two asset classes outperforming the others. In order to correct the portfolio, it is necessary to sell off some of the asset classes that have outperformed, and use the proceeds to buy the asset classes that have underperformed.

A recent research study tracked the market value of two portfolios from January 1, 1987 to December 1, 1996. Both portfolios began with $500,000

The Effects of Rebalancing

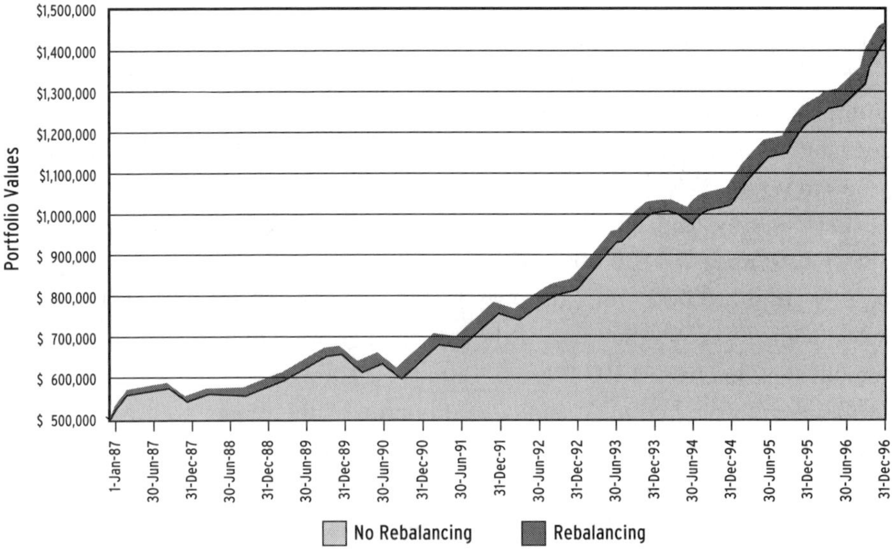

SOURCE: Assante Advisory Services

invested in the same asset mix, representative of a moderate risk tolerance. However, after the initial investment, one portfolio was not monitored or rebalanced to the target asset mix, whereas the other portfolio was rebalanced according to the desired mix. (See the chart above.)

Over the 10-year period, the market value of the rebalanced portfolio never fell below the market value of the portfolio in which no rebalancing occurred. At the end of the period, the market value of the rebalanced portfolio was $42,000 higher, or 8.4% of the original capital of the portfolio. Well worth the effort!

Another reason to adjust your portfolio is advancing age. We believe that as you age (and all other things being equal), the relative weighting of fixed income assets in your portfolio should grow. As well, for a variety of reasons some investors become more (or less) aggressive over the years and this change must be reflected in the overall holdings.

Finally, certain economic conditions lend themselves to shifts in the weighting of certain asset categories that may not otherwise be appropriate.

The main point here is that changes made to a balanced portfolio should be the result of a thoughtful set of plans and have little to do with an attempt to time the market, which is more reflective of the bob-and-weave approach.

The Leveraging Strategy

This is an aggressive strategy with great upside potential as well as some significant risk. The goal is to use other people's money—usually a bank loan—adding it to yours and investing the entire amount. What you owe remains constant, or may be reduced by monthly payments, while the overall investment grows in value.

Let's assume you take $20,000 of your own money and borrow another $80,000 to make a $100,000 investment. Let's assume your investment grows by 20% to $120,000. You still owe $80,000, so you "own" $40,000 of the investment. Although the value of the portfolio grew by only 20%, your "stake" actually doubled from $20,000 to $40,000—a 100% increase!

It can get even better. Assuming you borrowed the money to invest outside your RRSP, the interest you pay the bank to finance the loan will be tax deductible. (Interest on RRSP loans is no longer deductible.) And assuming that you selected investments that generate tax-advantaged dividends or capital gains, your after-tax returns will be better still. (Even though the $100,000 capital gains exemption has been abolished, capital gains are still taxed at only 75% of the amount charged on, say, interest income.)

So far, we've seen only the rosy side of leveraging. But there's another side that must be considered. Let's assume our $100,000 declines in value by 20% to $80,000. That represents the entire amount of your contribution to the total investment. So your original $20,000 will have been wiped out for a pretty frightening loss of 100%!

Given the potential dangers inherent in leveraging strategies, we suggest that you adhere to the following guidelines:

- Borrow only to a maximum of one-third of the total investment.
- Be sure that your cash flow will allow ongoing loan payments; don't expect to pay the loan back from profits.
- Try to avoid securing the loan with other assets, especially your home; unsecured loans are widely available at slightly higher rates.

The Income Splitting Strategy

For those who want to reduce their income tax burden, income splitting is very effective.

Save Taxes Through Income Splitting

The Usual Situation		
	Spouse 1	Spouse 2
Annual retirement income	$100,000	$0
Marginal tax rate*	53.2%	0.0%
Tax liability	$40,509	$0
The Income-Splitting Strategy		
	Spouse 1	Spouse 2
Annual retirement income	$60,000	$40,000
Marginal tax rate*	50.1%	42.7%
Tax liability	$19,377	$10,688
Total tax liability	$30,065	
Tax savings: $10,443 after-tax saving per year		

* Basic personal exemption only

This simple strategy attempts to take a portion of the earnings attributed to a high-income earner, and place it in the hands of the lower-income spouse. By doing so, many thousands of tax dollars can be saved annually. Take a look at the table above.

In most cases, as shown in the first example above, retirement income is concentrated (if not placed exclusively) in the hands of the higher-income earner. By creating and contributing to a spousal RRSP over a number of years, Spouse 1 has achieved the same level of retirement income, but it is more evenly split between Spouse 1 and Spouse 2, as the second example shows.

Notice that in the first example, the tax bill is over $40,000, but in the income-splitting example, the combined tax bill is just over $30,000. This result has been achieved by moving Spouse 1 to a lower tax bracket to pay only about $20,000 in tax instead of $40,000. Spouse 2 now pays tax too, but at a lower rate.

That's an after-tax savings of over $10,000 per year! By repeating the scene over and over again, Spouse 1 and Spouse 2 can likely save well over $100,000 in taxes over 10 years.

surfing

the web

A quality site from "Canada's National Newspaper." The graphics and page setup have been revised, making it more reader-friendly and easier to navigate. There is a daily fund commentary, in addition to articles written by well-regarded Canadian mutual fund analysts. Investors can track their own portfolios, monitor fund prices, and keep up on the latest fund news. The Weekly Fund Feature is an in-depth fund review, complete with performance, cost, and risk ratings. There are also links to *Globe and Mail* articles, as well as Report on Mutual Funds supplements.

www.globefund.com

The Tax-Efficient Portfolio Strategy

Examine the tax-inefficient portfolio below. Notice that the bonds are held outside the RRSP and are therefore fully taxed. The stocks held in an equity fund are inside the RRSP and are therefore tax-free. Because the bonds are taxed, the after-tax return is 11.25%.

Now look at the tax-efficient portfolio and notice that the bonds are held inside the RRSP and are therefore tax-free. The equities are held outside the RRSP, and even though they are subject to tax, capital gains or dividends are taxed more favourably than interest generated by fixed-income vehicles. The after-tax return in this situation is 12.2%, and while that

Tax-Inefficient Portfolio

Asset Class	RRSP	Non-RRSP	Total
Bonds ($100,000 @ 15%)	0	$15,000	$15,000
Stocks ($100,000 @ 15%)	$15,000	0	$15,000
Taxes payable (@ 50%)	0	−$7,500	−$7,500
Total	$15,000	−$7,500	$22,500
After-tax return: $22,500/$200,000 = 11.25%			

Tax-Efficient Portfolio

Asset Class	RRSP	Non-RRSP	Total
Bonds ($100,000 @ 15%)	$15,000	0	$15,000
Stocks ($100,000 @ 15%)	0	$15,000	$15,000
Taxes payable (@ 50%)	0	−$5,625	−$5,625
Total	$15,000	$9,375	$24,375
After-tax return: $24,375/$200,000 = 12.20%			

1% may not sound like a lot, it becomes very significant as it compounds over the years.

The message is that, where possible, hold assets that are fully taxed (fixed income) inside the RRSP and keep more favourably taxed assets (equities) outside the RRSP.

Find Your Own Personal Financial Advisor

You are forced to play the "money game" from the time you begin to earn a living until you die, and many of us will play it for 40, 50, 60 years, or more. Don't you agree that when you're going to play a game for that length of time, it makes sense to be able to play it as well as possible? There are rules to the game and there are strategies you can use to play more effectively and successfully.

In this game, it's important to know who your teammates are and who's the "opposition." The Canada Customs and Revenue Agency makes the rules, interprets the rules, and enforces the rules of the game: CCRA is not on your team.

To learn the rules and the strategies of the money game, you need a financial advisor to work with you over the long term, and more and more people are coming to this conclusion. If, like many others, you are too busy to take the time to learn all the rules and strategies, or if you don't have the interest, the ability, or the inclination to learn them, then you need to find expert advice.

It's true that books like this one can provide some useful assistance, but your personal situation is unlikely to be covered in any book. You really need an individual to coach you, over the long term, in all aspects of your financial life. It's our heartfelt belief that an experienced professional advisor can help you save thousands of dollars in taxes over time and can increase the value of your portfolio by many thousands of dollars over what you can do yourself.

Why would you not use the expertise of someone who can help you achieve those results? Well, more and more people are recognizing the advantages of seeking a financial advisor. But where do you look to find one?

Some people use bank managers, but their expertise is generally limited to loans or mortgages. More recently, banks have hired financial advisors who may be able to help, although they sell only bank-approved products. There are also several bank/brokerage connections now, including Royal Bank/Dominion Securities and Bank of Montreal/Nesbitt Burns.

top funds
close up

We Prefer Using Professional Stock Pickers—Here's Why

We are advocates of using professional money managers to oversee Canadian investment portfolios for many reasons. Here's another one.

A U.S. study concludes that stock analysts who work for an investment firm that underwrites a particular stock are more likely to have a favourable bias towards that stock. The problem is that these "recommended" stocks are also more likely to underperform compared with stocks recommended by analysts without this conflict of interest.

This study has particular relevance to Canadian investors. In our relatively small market, it is the case that for many stocks, especially those issued by small hi-tech and resource companies, the only investment dealer issuing buy/sell recommendations and providing analysis about a particular stock is the same one that underwrites it. In fact, there have been a few celebrated cases where analysts have been censured by their firms after issuing negative reviews of stocks that the firm has underwritten.

Although some individual investors provide their own analysis and due diligence before buying a stock, many rely on what they read in the business section of the newspaper and on investment Web sites and chat lines for their "tips." Quite frankly, we prefer to let trained, professional, and unbiased financial analysts make the buy and sell decisions. In our view, that's just common sense.

Roni Michaely and Kent Womack, "Conflict of Interest and the Credibility of Underwriter Analyst Recommendations," *Review of Financial Studies* 12, no. 4 (1999).

Accountants are often thought to be good financial advisors and no doubt many are. We suggest, however, that you look for someone with a broader overview. Tax considerations are significant, but there are many others that need to be taken into account in creating an overall financial strategy. Lawyers are often relied upon for general financial and investment advice, but they are not trained in investment theory and may have no expertise in the area of asset allocation or in personal taxation.

We recommend that you seek out someone whose professional career is completely focused on providing expert, pertinent, and timely financial advice.

What Qualifications Should Your Financial Advisor Hold?

Generally, someone in the field will have at least completed the Investment Funds course, which, along with being registered by the appropriate Securities Commission, allows one to sell mutual funds to the public. The Canadian Securities course, along with the appropriate registration, allows one to sell a full range of securities (including stocks and bonds as well as mutual funds). All stockbrokers have completed the Canadian Securities course.

But those are minimum qualifications; both are prerequisites for anyone registered to sell securities. You should also look for an advisor who has completed (or is enrolled in) the Certified Financial Planner (CFP) program. It's offered by the Financial Planners Standards Council of Canada (FPSCC) as part of their ongoing educational programs and covers many pertinent topics such as taxation, personal financial planning, asset management, and estate planning.

Some people take advanced programs offered by the Canadian Securities Institute, including the FCSI designation (Fellow of the Canadian Securities Institute) or the new Certified Investment Manager (CIM) designation.

If your advisor has taken, or is taking, any of these programs, it reflects a commitment to ongoing professional development, which will likely be beneficial to you.

As well, you should probably expect your advisor to be a member of the Canadian Association of Financial Planners and adhere to its Code of Ethics.

How Do You Find the Right Advisor?

Many advisors provide an ongoing series of educational seminars, which are intended to provide up-to-the-moment information on trends in the economy, which funds are "hot," methods of tax reduction, and so on. You may find it worthwhile to attend some of these sessions to get a sense of whether you could work with that individual.

Glossary

Active management. An approach to money management whereby managers are active in selecting and discarding stocks in an effort to outperform certain market indices or benchmarks.

Asset allocation. The relative proportions of equities, bonds, cash, real estate, and other asset types held in a portfolio at a given time. In a mutual fund, the portfolio manager often varies these proportions in order to maximize returns when economic conditions change.

Automatic reinvestment. An option available to investors in a mutual fund or other investment whereby income (dividends, interest, or capital gains) distributions are used to purchase additional units of the fund.

Balanced portfolio. The distribution of investments into several asset categories to help increase returns and reduce risk. The basic components of a balanced portfolio are cash, bonds, Canadian and international equities, real estate, oil, gas, and gold. The weighting of the different components varies depending on one's age and aggressiveness as an investor.

Bear market. A stock market whose index of representative stocks, such as the Toronto Stock Exchange 300 Composite Index, is declining in value. A "bearish" investor believes share prices will fall.

Blue-chip stocks. Stocks with good investment qualities. They are usually common shares of well-established companies with good earning records and regular dividend payments that are known nationally for the quality and wide acceptance of their products and services.

Bond. A debt instrument issued by governments and corporations. A bond is a promise by the issuer to pay the full amount of the debt on maturity, plus interest payments at regular intervals.

Bottom-up. A style of investing that places a priority on examining companies that may be appropriate for investment. Less emphasis is placed on macroeconomic considerations. See also "top-down."

Bull market. A stock market whose index has been rising in value. A "bullish" investor believes share prices will rise.

Canada Deposit Insurance Corporation (CDIC). This agency of the Government of Canada insures the deposits of Canadians in banks and trust companies up to $60,000.

Capital cost allowance (CCA). A tax deduction available to reflect the depreciation of various types of assets. Applied to buildings (either commercial or residential), CCA can be used to shelter rental income from real estate investment trusts (REITs).

Capital gain (loss). A profit (or loss) made on the sale of an asset—usually real estate, stocks, bonds, or other capital assets—when the market price rises above or falls below the purchase price.

Closed-end fund. A mutual fund in which the total number of units is limited. If units are not purchased when the fund is initially offered, they can only be purchased from another owner. They often trade on stock exchanges.

Common share. A class of stock that represents ownership, or equity, in a company. Common shares entitle the holder to a share in the company's profits, usually as a dividend. They may also carry a voting privilege.

Consumer price index (CPI). A statistical measure of the cost of living for consumers. Often used to demonstrate general increases in the level of inflation over a period of time.

Correction. When a market index declines from its previous high by 20%, a market correction is said to have taken place.

Creditor proofing. If a person is successfully sued, various assets may be claimed or valued as part of the required compensation. Assets that are creditor proof may not be included as part of the compensation. Insurance products, particularly segregated mutual funds, may be creditor proof and therefore "safe" assets.

Current yield. As applied to money market funds, it refers to the actual rate of return over the past seven days, annualized.

Cyclical stock. A stock within a specific industry sector that is particularly sensitive to changes in economic conditions. The natural resources sector tends to be cyclical, as do particular stocks in the sector.

Deferred sales charge (DSC). An increasingly popular alternative to mutual funds that charge front-end acquisition fees. Here, a fee is paid when the investor sells units in the fund. This usually begins at 4.5% of the unit's value in the first year and declines by 0.5% to 1% per year, eventually reaching 0% several years into the future. Sometimes called an exit fee.

Defined portfolio (unit trust). A defined portfolio consists of an established number of stocks, usually 20 or 25, and these stocks remain constant for the period of the defined portfolio's existence. By contrast, a mutual fund manager buys and sells stocks over a period of time so that the composition of the portfolio could change significantly.

Distribution fees. Fees levied by some mutual fund companies on the value of units purchased with a back-end load or deferred sales charge. While most funds have stopped charging these fees, a few hold-outs remain.

Distributions. The payments made by a mutual fund to its unitholders of the interest, dividends, and/or capital gains earned during the year. Shareholders may either take distributions in cash or reinvest them in additional shares of the fund.

Diversification. Spreading investment risk by investing in a variety of asset categories (stocks, bonds, gold) in different industries and/or countries.

Dividend. A portion of a company's profit paid out to common and preferred shareholders, the amount having been decided by the company's board of directors. A dividend may be in the form of cash or additional stock. A preferred dividend is usually a fixed amount, while a common dividend may fluctuate with the earnings of the company.

Dividend tax credit. A special tax credit applied to reduce the effective rate of tax paid on Canadian dividend income.

Dollar cost averaging. An investment program in which contributions are made at regular intervals with specific and equal dollar amounts. This often results in a lower average cost per unit because more units are purchased when the prices are depressed than when they are high.

Downside risk. The possibility of a fund's performing poorly at any given time, below a given minimum rate of return. Alternately, it describes a fund's average loss.

Equity funds. Mutual funds that invest in common and preferred shares.

Ex-dividend. The date on which distributions that have been declared by a mutual fund are deducted from total net assets. The price of the fund's shares or units will be reduced by the amount of the distribution.

Fixed asset mix. For balanced funds, an approach that fixes the asset mix to be maintained in the fund: often 50% to 60% equity and 40% to 50% fixed income. Compare to an asset allocation fund, where there is no pre-set fixed asset mix.

Fixed income funds. Mutual funds that invest in mortgages, bonds, or a combination of both. Mortgages and bonds are issued at a fixed rate of interest and are known as fixed-income securities.

Front-end commission charge. An acquisition fee based on the total value of mutual fund units purchased. The fees can range from 2% to 9%, but average 4% to 5% on most purchases.

GIC (guaranteed investment certificate). A deposit certificate usually issued by a bank or trust company. An interest-bearing investment that matures after a specified term, usually anywhere from 30 days to five years. The interest remains fixed during this period.

Growth at a reasonable price (GARP). An investment philosophy that directs a manager to seek out growth securities that are not overvalued.

Growth investing. An approach to investing that places greater emphasis on a stock's future growth potential than on its current price. A growth manager may therefore be prepared to pay a higher price for a stock than a value manager would, if he or she believes it has attractive future growth potential. It is seen as a more aggressive style of management than value investing.

Growth stock. Shares of a company whose earnings are expected to grow faster than average.

Hedging. The strategy of taking positions in more than one commodity, security, or asset category in an attempt to reduce investment risk. An investment in gold or oil/natural gas, for example, is often seen as a hedge or protection against inflation.

Income splitting. The process of diverting taxable income from an individual in a high tax bracket to one in a lower tax bracket.

Index. For stocks, an indicator of broad market performance. The Dow Jones industrial average includes the shares of 30 large companies; the Toronto Stock Exchange's composite index includes 300 companies; the Standard & Poor index contains 500 companies. Developed from statistics that measure the state of the economy, based on the performance of stocks or other key indicators such as the consumer price index.

Index fund. A mutual fund designed to match the performance of a recognized group of publicly traded stocks, such as those represented by the TSE 300 Index or the Standard & Poor 500 Index in the U.S.

Interest rate anticipation. An investment style in which a fixed income manager uses macroeconomic analysis to predict changes in interest rates. If the manager expects rates to rise, he or she will by short-term bonds, as they can be turned over quickly and are least sensitive to changes in interest rates. If he or she expects rates to fall, long-term bonds will be purchased, as they offer the best profit opportunities in that circumstance.

Investment fund. See "mutual fund."

Investment policy statement (IPS). A formal written document recommending a specific asset allocation in a portfolio based on an individual investor's circumstances.

Leverage. Using borrowed funds to maximize the rate of return on investment. A potentially dangerous strategy if the investment declines in value.

Liquidity. The ease with which an asset can be sold and converted into cash at its full value.

Management expense ratio (MER). The total of all management and other fees charged to the fund, shown as a percentage of the fund's total assets, or as a dollar amount per $100 of assets.

Management fee. The amount paid annually by a mutual fund to its managers. The average annual fee in Canada is between 1% and 2% of the value of the fund's assets.

Marginal tax rate. The rate at which tax is calculated on the next dollar of income earned. This rate increases at progressively higher income brackets.

Market timing. The process of shifting from one type of investment to another with the intention of maximizing the return as market conditions change.

MBS (mortgage-backed securities). These provide higher yields than many other savings options by investing in first mortgages on residential properties.

Money market fund. Fixed-income mutual funds that invest in short-term securities (maturing within one year).

Morningstar ratings. A popular mutual fund rating system that allocates from one star (low) to five stars (high). Well established in the U.S., Morningstar now operates in Canada as well.

Mortgage. A legal instrument given by a borrower to a lender, entitling the lender to take over pledged property if conditions of the loan are not met.

Multi-Period Composite (MPC). The mathematical model used in this book to compare the returns of similar types of funds over one-year calendar time frames. This model eliminates end-date bias associated with the more traditional use of average annual compound rates of return.

Mutual fund. A professionally managed pool of assets. It represents the contributions of many investors, which are used to purchase a portfolio of securities that meets specific investment objectives. See "open-end fund" and "closed-end fund."

Net asset value (NAV). The value of a fund's assets, less its liabilities. The NAV is used to calculate the buying or selling price of shares or units in a fund, usually expressed as the net asset value per share (NAVPS).

Net asset value per share (NAVPS). The total market value of all securities owned by a mutual fund, less its liabilities, divided by the number of units outstanding.

New economy. A media-generated phrase that refers to the technology, telecommunications, and health care sectors of the economy.

No-load fund. A mutual fund that does not charge a fee for buying or selling its units.

Old economy. A media-generated phrase that refers to the tradition financial services, manufacturing, and natural resources sectors of the economy.

Open-end fund. A mutual fund whose units are offered for sale on a continuous basis; the fund will also buy back units at their current price (net asset value per share). Sometimes called an investment fund, this is the most common type of mutual fund.

Passive management. An approach to money management whereby managers purchase stocks that are part of a market index (for example, the TSE 30 or the S&P 500). Changes are made to the portfolio only as changes are made to the membership within the index.

Portfolio. A group of securities held or owned for investment purposes by an individual or institution. An investor's portfolio may contain common and preferred shares, bonds, options, and other types of securities.

Prospectus. A legal document describing a new issue of securities or a mutual fund that is to be sold to the public. The prospectus must be prepared in accordance with provincial securities commission regulations. It must contain information on any material facts that can have an impact on the value of the investment, such as the fund's investment objectives and policies, services offered, or fees charged. It must also identify any investment restrictions as well as the officers of the company.

Real estate investment trust (REIT). A form of real estate mutual fund that trades on a stock exchange. As a result, it provides greater liquidity than is usually available through a traditional real estate mutual fund. The units generally trade at a discount from net asset value.

Real rate of return. The stated rate of return, less inflation and taxes.

Rebalancing. The practice of adjusting the asset mix in a portfolio on an ongoing basis in order to stay on target with the mix recommended in an investment policy statement (IPS). Research has shown that regular rebalancing improves returns over time.

Registered investment. A security held in a tax-sheltered plan—most often an RRSP or RRIF—that has been approved by the Canada Customs and Revenue Agency.

RESP (Registered Education Savings Plan). A government plan that encourages saving for a child's education by offering a grant of up to $400 per year to supplement contributions made by Canadian families. Assets in the RESP also grow tax free.

Risk. The possibility that some or all of the money put into an investment will be lost.

Risk-free return. The return available from securities that have no risk of loss. Short-term securities issued by the government (such as Treasury bills) normally provide a risk-free return.

Risk tolerance. The ability of a person to tolerate risk. Risk tolerance is a function of the individual's personality and other factors, and is an important element in determining investment strategy.

RRIF (Registered Retirement Income Fund). A non-annuity investment vehicle for maturing RRSPs. It is one of the options available to RRSP holders upon cashing in their retirement funds at age 69 or sooner. RRIFs generally provide a series of payments that increase each year.

RRSP (Registered Retirement Savings Plan). A savings program approved by the Canada Customs and Revenue Agency that permits tax-deferred saving for retirement purposes. Contributions to an RRSP are tax deductible. Earnings on contributions are sheltered from tax while they remain in the plan.

Rule of 72. The calculation to determine how long it will take for a portfolio to double in value. At a 12% return, it will take six years for a portfolio to double ($72 \div 12 = 6$); at a 6% return, it will take twelve years to double ($72 \div 6 = 12$).

Sector rotation. A style of investing that identifies prospective investments (or the weighting of an investment portfolio) according to which sectors of the economy are poised to do well. Often associated with the "top down" approach to investing.

Segregated funds. Funds sold and administered by life insurance companies.

Self-directed RRSP. An RRSP whose investments are controlled by the plan holder. A self-directed RRSP may include stocks, bonds, residential mortgages, or other types of investments approved by the Canada Customs and Revenue Agency.

Sharpe Ratio. Invented by Nobel prize winner Dr. William Sharpe, this ratio is a means of measuring risk-adjusted returns. It is calculated by taking the annual compounded returns of a fund minus the annual compounded return of T-bills (a "risk free" investment) divided by the annualized standard deviation. The higher the Sharpe Ratio the better.

Socially responsible investments (SRI). Managers of these funds are very selective about the companies into which they invest. To make the shortlist for a socially responsible fund, a company must treat its employees well, adhere to pollution and other environmental laws, and refrain from producing and/or selling products deemed socially unacceptable. As a result, SRI funds tend to hold positions in industries like financial services and technology.

Spread trading. A conservative fixed income style of investing where a manager tries to profit from small changes in the yields of bond and debt instruments.

Standard deviation. A traditional method used to quantify risk within a portfolio. It measures the difference (or deviation) between expected return and actual return and identifies that deviation as "risk."

Systematic withdrawal plan (SWP). A plan for withdrawing money from a mutual fund on a regular basis: monthly, quarterly, semi-annually, or annually. Used mostly by investors who require a steady stream of income from their investments.

Taxable income. The amount of annual income that is used to calculate how much income tax must be paid: total earnings for the year, minus deductions.

Tax shelter. An investment that, by government regulation, can be made with untaxed or partly taxed dollars. The creation of tax losses in order to offset an individual's taxable income from other sources thereby reduces tax liability.

Term deposit. Similar to a guaranteed investment certificate. An interest-bearing investment to which an investor commits funds for a specified term and rate of interest.

Top-down. A style of investing that considers the economic big picture to identify sectors of the economy that are expected to outperform. Less importance is attached to identifying individual companies that may do well. See also "bottom-up."

Total return. The amount of income earned from an investment, together with its capital appreciation, expressed as a percentage of the original amount invested. It indicates an investment's performance over a stated period.

Treasury bills. Short-term debt securities sold by governments, usually with maturities of three months to one year. They carry no stated interest rate, but trade at a discount to their face value. The discount represents the market's valuation of the future return at maturity.

Unit. In mutual funds, a unit represents a portion, or share, of the total value of the fund. Units are purchased by investors, and rise or fall proportionately with the net asset value of the fund.

Value investing. An approach to investing that attempts, through the use of various analytical models, to identify companies that are fundamentally strong but may be out of favour in the marketplace and trading at prices that represent a good buy. This conservative approach is often associated with Sir John Templeton and is one that many investment managers claim to use.

Volatility. A measure of a mutual fund's tendency to fluctuate in value. More volatile funds are traditionally considered to have a greater degree of risk, although the fluctuation in value may, in fact, be either up or down.

Index